MESSAGE OF THE FATHERS OF THE CHURCH
General Editor: Thomas Halton

Volume 3

MESSAGE OF THE FATHERS OF THE CHURCH

THE HOLY SPIRIT

by
J. Patout Burns, S.J.
and
Gerald M. Fagin, S.J.

 Michael Glazier, Inc.
Wilmington, Delaware

ABOUT THE AUTHORS

J. Patout Burns, S.J., received his doctorate from Yale University. He has taught at Yale University, the Catholic Theological Union, Lutheran School of Theology in Chicago and the Divinity School of the University of Chicago. He has written widely on patristics and theological topics, and is currently Chairman of the Department of Theology at Loyola University in Chicago.

Gerald M. Fagin, S.J., received his doctorate in theology from the University of St. Michael's College. He is Chairperson of the Religious Studies Department at Loyola University in New Orleans. He is also Editor of *Vatican II: Open Questions and New Horizons.*

First published in 1984 by Michael Glazier, Inc.
1723 Delaware Avenue, Wilmington, Delaware 19806

©1984 by Michael Glazier, Inc. All rights reserved.

Library of Congress Catalog Card Number: 83-81842
International Standard Book Number:
   Message of the Fathers of the Church series:
     (0-89453-312-6, Paper; 0-89453-340-1, Cloth)
   THE HOLY SPIRIT
     (0-89453-315-0, Paper)
     (0-89453-343-6, Cloth)

Cover design: Lillian Brulc

Typography by Susan Pickett

Printed in the United States of America

CONTENTS

Chapter Three
Adored and Honored: The Fourth Century

Chapter Five
The Course of Development

•

Abbreviations

ACW   Ancient Christian Writers
AF   Apostolic Fathers
ANF   Ante-Nicene Fathers
CCL   Corpus Christianorum, series latina
CSEL Corpus Scriptorum Ecclesiasticorum Latinorum
DS   Denzinger-Schoenmetzer: Enchiridion Symbolorum
FC   Fathers of the Church
GCS   Griechischen Christlichen Schriftstellern
LCC   Library of Christian Classics
LQF   Liturgiewissenshaftliche Quellen und Forschungen
NPNF Nicene and Post-Nicene Fathers
PG   Patrologia Graeca
PL   Patrologia Latina
PO   Patrologia Orientalis
SC   Les sources chrétiennes
TCT   The Church Teaches

EDITOR'S INTRODUCTION

The *Message of the Fathers of the Church* is a companion series to The *Old Testament Message* and The *New Testament Message*. It was conceived and planned in the belief that Scripture and Tradition worked hand in hand in the formation of the thought, life and worship of the primitive Church. Such a series, it was felt, would be a most effective way of opening up what has become virtually a closed book to present-day readers, and might serve to stimulate a revival in interest in Patristic studies in step with the recent, gratifying resurgence in Scriptural studies.

The term "Fathers" is usually reserved for Christian writers marked by orthodoxy of doctrine, holiness of life, ecclesiastical approval and antiquity. "Antiquity" is generally understood to include writers down to Gregory the Great (+604) or Isidore of Seville (+636) in the West, and John Damascene (+749) in the East. In the present series, however, greater elasticity has been encouraged, and quotations from writers not noted for orthodoxy will sometimes be included in order to illustrate the evolution of the Message on particular doctrinal matters. Likewise, writers later than the mid-eighth century will sometimes be used to illustrate the continuity of tradition on matters like sacramental theology or liturgical practice.

An earnest attempt was made to select collaborators on a broad inter-disciplinary and inter-confessional basis, the chief consideration being to match scholars who could handle the Fathers in their original languages with subjects in which they had already demonstrated a special interest and competence. About the only editorial directive given to the selected contributors was that the Fathers, for the most part, should be allowed to speak for themselves and that they should speak in readable, reliable modern English. Volumes on individual themes were considered more suitable than volumes devoted to individual Fathers, each theme, hopefully, contributing an important segment to the total mosaic of the Early Church, one, holy, catholic and apostolic. Each volume has an introductory essay outlining the historical and theological development of the theme, with the body of the work mainly occupied with liberal citations from the Fathers in modern English translation and a minimum of linking commentary. Short lists of Suggested Further Readings are included; but dense, scholarly footnotes were actively discouraged on the pragmatic grounds that such scholarly shorthand has other outlets and tends to lose all but the most relentlessly esoteric reader in a semipopular series.

At the outset of his *Against Heresies* Irenaeus of Lyons warns his readers "not to expect from me any display of rhetoric, which I have never learned, or any excellence of composition, which I have never practised, or any beauty or persuasiveness of style, to which I make no pretensions." Similarly, modest disclaimers can be found in many of the Greek and Latin Fathers and all too often, unfortunately, they have been taken at their word by an uninterested world. In fact, however, they were often highly educated products of the best rhetorical schools of their day in the Roman Empire, and what they have to say is often as much a lesson in literary and cultural, as well as in spiritual, edification.

St. Augustine, in *The City of God* (19.7), has interesting reflections on the need for a common language in an expanding world community; without a common language a man is more at home with his dog than with a foreigner as far as intercommunication goes, even in the Roman Empire, which imposes on the nations it conquers the yoke of both law and language with a resultant abundance of interpreters. It is hoped that in the present world of continuing language barriers the contributors to this series will prove opportune interpreters of the perennial Christian message.

Thomas Halton

INTRODUCTION

Contemporary interest in the Spirit has highlighted again the oft-bemoaned neglect of the Spirit in the reflection of the Christian community, especially in the Western tradition. Most Christians profess little knowledge of the Spirit or the workings of the Spirit in the Christian community. The Spirit remains a presence and a force that seems mysterious and little understood. Even Christians who speak easily of Jesus and the Father become strangely reticent when asked to speak about the Spirit. Thus aside from the somewhat mechanical memorization in the past of the gifts and fruits of the Spirit, most Christians have little reflective awareness or understanding of the role of the Spirit in Christian life. Similarly no systematic theology of the Spirit has emerged in the Christian tradition to complement the theology of Christ. Reflection on the Spirit has been done in the context of the theology of the Trinity and the theology of grace, but no separate treatise on the Spirit was developed as part of classical theology. The Spirit is portrayed as transparent, hard to grasp, or, in the words of John's Gospel, as the wind that blows where it will.

Some reasons can be brought forth to explain this neglect, both on the level of experience and on the level of understanding. In the first place, the role of the Spirit is to lead us to Jesus and to the Father, not to center attention on himself. There is an understandable emphasis and focus on the Father and the Son. The Spirit reveals the Son and the Son reveals the Father, but the Spirit is revealed in the inner life of Christians. The Spirit empowers us to pray to the Father through Jesus, but prayer directly to the Spirit is much less frequent in Christian tradition than prayer to the Father for the gift of the Spirit. Second, in the Scriptures, the Father and Son are each manifest as persons: they dialogue with human persons, speaking and listening. The Spirit, however, is not so portrayed; he inspires human speaking but does not himself speak apart from them. Third, the Western theological tradition that followed Augustine stressed the unity of God and the unity of his activity. The proper mission of the Spirit was de-emphasized and the invisible work of grace in the hearts of Christians was appropriated to the Spirit. Finally, the institutional church, with some justification, has been distrustful of the Spirit, for the Spirit has been associated with freedom, risk, breaking away from structures. The Spirit has been falsely identified with rejection of institutions and tied to a false subjectivism dramatized in the not-too-glorious history of enthusiastic sects in the church. Unfortunately this distrust of the Spirit was reinforced in the Catholic tradition at the time of the Reformation.

All these factors have contributed to the neglect of the Spirit in Christian theology. Still the Spirit refuses to be stifled by misconceptions and aberrations. The Spirit breaks the limitations and boundaries of the roles and labels. One evidence of this is the renewed interest in the Spirit in the contemporary church. The Second Vatican Council portrayed the church as a community united in the Spirit, a community in which the Spirit is active in the hearts of all Christians and not just official leaders. This has complemented the desires and needs of contemporary culture for an emphasis on freedom and personal conscience and responsibility. At the same time, the breakdown of the secularism popular after the Council has generated a renewed interest in prayer and discernment as the work of the Spirit, and has focused attention on the inner life of grace as a process of growth and development in the Spirit. Finally, the charismatic renewal has been the occasion for a new experience of the gifts of the Spirit in the Christian community. This experience has been heralded as a sign of the "new Pentecost" called for by Pope John XXIII.

In the context of this renewed interest in the Spirit, this study attempts to make available some of the rich resources of the early tradition of the church on the Spirit. A number of books and articles have described the growth of the tradition of the Spirit in the scripture. This present anthology of texts from the Church Fathers attempts to establish contact with the theological literature of the first five centuries of Christianity. These texts reveal an ongoing concern and a mature reflection on the Spirit that challenge the accusation of a neglect of the Spirit in the Christian tradition. In fact, the early Christian writings provide a profound and extensive reflection on the person and work of the Spirit. The texts in this anthology document the struggle of the early church to come to grips with its experience of the Spirit in the church and in the lives of individual Christians.

The texts also provide a concrete example of the development of a doctrine in the church. Doctrinal formulations that have grown from experience and are the fruit of long and painful struggles tend to become frozen as statements dissociated from those experiences and struggles. Primary sources can revive a sense of that struggle and foster a better understanding of how a doctrine or theology develops. In particular, the texts reveal how from the very beginning, the Christian community was confronted with two distinct but closely related questions about the Spirit: "Who is the Spirit?" and "What is the function of the Spirit in the life of the individual Christian and the Christian community?" The answer to the first question is part of the complex history of the development of the doctrine of the Trinity. The answer to the second question is in some ways less complex; it provides a wealth of material for reflection on the Spirit as the source of sanctification, inspiration, and teaching.

Who is the Spirit?

Most of the theological discussion in the first three and one-half centuries of Christianity centered on the divinity of the Son. Until that question was tentatively resolved at the Council of Nicea in 325, there was little debate over the Spirit. Nicea restricted itself to a simple statement of faith in the Spirit: "We believe in the Holy Spirit." The second half of the fourth century was filled with controversy over the Spirit, but even toward the end of the century, Gregory of Nazianzus could remark somewhat wryly, "To be only a little in error about the Holy Spirit is to be orthodox." Still the fourth century did end with a clear affirmation of the divinity of the Spirit and the lengthy controversy led to a sufficiently sophisticated theology of the Spirit to set the stage for Augustine's classic discussion of the Spirit as the bond of love between the Father and the Son.

As will be clear from the readings in this volume, there were many arguments proposed for the divinity of the Spirit. Some referred to the titles given to the Holy Spirit. Others argued that he performed the divine functions of renewing, creating, sanctifying and deifying. Still others argued from his relation to the Son. One recurring argument was soteriological: if the Spirit is not divine, then he cannot sanctify or divinize the Christian. These arguments were similar to those which had been used earlier to establish the divinity of the Son.

But if the Spirit is divine, what is his relation to the Father and the Son? This more complex question was resolved step by step in the discussions of the fourth and fifth centuries. First, the Spirit was affirmed as divine and as a distinct person. Then he was characterized by his relation to the Father and the Son, and the basis of that relation was specified as the procession of the Spirit from the Father and the Son. This procession was then understood in terms of the love proceeding from the Father and the Son. Thus the Spirit was proclaimed as the love and gift of God. This development from the affirmation of the divinity of the Spirit to the affirmation of the Spirit as gift and love was part of the early church's struggle to answer the question: "Who is the Spirit?" This resulted in a rich theology of the inner life of the Trinity that was the basis for a further theology of the mission of the Spirit.

What is the role of the Spirit?

The second broad question facing the early church was the role of the Spirit in the life of the individual and in the life of the community. The Spirit was first considered as the one who inspired the prophets and writers of the scripture and who spoke through the prophetic utterances of members of the Christian community. Then in response to heretical proclamation of a new prophecy and secret knowledge, the discussion shifted to the operation of the Spirit in the church. The Spirit was seen as active in the church's teaching, in the succession of its bishops, and in its work of sanctification. The work of sanctification, above all, was the work of the Spirit. He is the giver of gifts in baptism; he dwells in the Christian and makes the human share in the divine nature. This idea of deification or divinization was a rich theme in the early church, especially in the East. It is the ultimate vocation of the Christian, a super-human mode of existence characterized by incorruptibility of the body and by illumination of the mind so that the Christian understands as God understands. It is the gift of God's eternal life offered to the Christian. It is the fullness of salvation given through the Spirit.

The Writings

The purpose of this book is to provide representative selections from the writings of the early church on the Holy Spirit. Passages have been chosen that illustrate the development of the doctrine and that articulate the major themes in the reflection of the early Christian community on the Spirit. Some passages have been translated for this book, but for the most part available translations have been used. In most cases, translations have been modified to make them read more smoothly, to eliminate exclusive language, and to standardize capitalization and punctuation. The selections presented are of substantial length so that the reader can enter into the mind and argument of the individual author. Introductions and commentaries are kept to a minimum. They are intended to facilitate reading of the texts themselves.

References in brackets follow each citation of the Scripture. In using these, one must recall that the Eastern Fathers generally used the Septuagint Greek translation of the Hebrew Scriptures, and the Western Fathers used various Latin translations of the Septuagint and the Greek New Testament. The wording of their quotations from Scripture occasionally differs significantly from a modern translation based on a critical edition of the original language. In this volume, the wording used in the patristic text has normally been preserved, particularly when the exegesis or argument depends upon that version.

Chapter One

INSPIRATION AND PROPHECY: THE SECOND CENTURY

Introduction

The writers of the second century can be divided into three groups, both chronologically and according to their concerns and audiences: i) the Apostolic Fathers, ii) the Apologists, and iii) the Defenders of the Orthodox Faith.

i) THE APOSTOLIC FATHERS

The Apostolic Fathers followed immediately on the writers of the New Testament period, about the turn of the first century. Their audience and purpose closely resembled those of the pastoral epistles of the canonical scriptures and some of their works were once considered part of the New Testament. They addressed established Christian communities and dealt in exhortations to individual and communal Christian living. As in the pastorals, doctrinal matters appear only incidentally in their writings.

References to the Holy Spirit were rare and limited to his gift of inspiration. The Old Testament was the Christian Bible at this time, and the inspiration of its prophets and writers was attributed to the Holy Spirit. Subsequently, of course, his inspiration of the New Testament would also be recognized, but at this point the prophetic spirit was recognized in the inspired utterance of the community.

The Apostolic Fathers did not reflect on the person and function of the Holy Spirit. Hence they did not clarify his personal existence and distinguish him from the divine power which comes upon the prophet or the disposition of soul of the pious Christian.

ii) THE APOLOGISTS

As the Christian communities became more visible in society, certain writers began to address themselves to problems raised by the educated classes and civil rulers. In the second half of the second century, the apologists undertook to ·establish the reasonableness and truth of Christian faith and to defend the Christian communities against charges of immorality. Against the objections of Jew and pagan philosopher alike they attempted to show that the worship of Christ was not contrary to belief in the one God. Besides disproving charges that the Christian liturgies involved immoral practices and subverted the civil order, the apologists had to show that Christianity was not a recent invention which could not claim ancient authority. The church claimed the ancient Scriptures and spiritual gifts of Israel as its own.

The apologists distinguished the Son of God from the Father by considering him the agent of creation and the revealer of the invisible deity. They associated the Holy Spirit with the work of the Son, but did not identify functions which were peculiar to him. Their confessions of faith were explicitly triadic and they recognized the Spirit as a personal being, having a position similar to that of the Son as an agent of the One God.

iii) DEFENDERS OF THE ORTHODOX FAITH

A third form of second-century literature was directed

against deviant forms of Christianity. The intended audience was orthodox, however, as the authors sought to discredit heretical movements and protect the congregations from their teaching. Three different opponents can be distinguished.

Gnosticism integrated Christian teaching into an elaborate theory of the universe in which the material world is the final stage of a deteriorating emanation of beings from God. The One God did not himself create the material world. It actually resulted from an aberration in the realm of spiritual beings which derive from the One God. The God of Israel was identified as a lower being, himself outside the realm of the spiritual. Christ was characterized as a spiritual being who appeared in the world to lead the nobler element of humanity beyond its debased material existence into a higher life of communion with the spiritual beings of the divine realm. The true teaching of Jesus had not been given in public, claimed the gnostics, but was privately explained to the disciples and transmitted by them through a secret succession to contemporary theorists. This hidden knowledge was the means of liberation from the material universe and of entrance into the realm of true life.

Marcion was a native of Pontus, on the south shore of the Black Sea, who worked in Rome about 140-160. He found the Christian gospel of love incompatible with the legalistic revelation and sacrificial religion of Israel and rejected any connection between Christ and the Creator God of the Old Testament. Only Paul perceived the radical dichotomy of Jesus' teaching and the religion of the law. On the basis of Paul's epistles, Marcion attempted to reconstruct the true teaching of Jesus by eliminating from the Gospel of Luke all elements which seemed to be derived from the Old Testament.

Montanus was another native of Asia Minor whose influence centered in Phrygia (modern Turkey) toward the end of the second century. He claimed that the Paraclete had now begun a third age demanding a life of rigorous asceticism in preparation for the imminent coming of the Lord. The Montanists claimed exclusive possession of the Spirit and of the full revelation about Jesus. The charismatic gifts of the Spirit in their community were their claim to the power and authority to interpret scripture.

Very little of the Catholic attempt to deal with these deviations has survived. The apologists' assertion that the Son is the divine Logos, the agent in creation and revelation, contradicted the separation of the Son from the Father in the doctrine of the gnostics. Athenagoras wrote a philosophical treatise defending the material condition of humanity and the resurrection of the flesh. Only Irenaeus' work, however, undertook a full examination of the various gnostic systems, a detailing of their inconsistencies, and a development of the corresponding Catholic teaching. The treatises directed against Marcion by Justin Martyr and Theophilus of Antioch have been lost. Though Irenaeus dealt with him in an occasional way, Tertullian's work in the third century is the earliest extant refutation of Marcion's doctrine. Irenaeus also provided evidence of the trouble which Montanism was causing in the Christian communities and attempted to defend against the new movement. Thus, of the attempts to deal with these three deviant forms of Christianity in the second century, only Irenaeus' has survived. In his defense of Christianity, Irenaeus developed the first theory of the operation of the Holy Spirit in creating, in guiding the teaching of the church, and in sanctifying Christians.

The Writings

i) THE APOSTOLIC FATHERS

Clement of Rome (fl. c. 96)

Clement, the bishop of Rome, wrote in the name of his community to the Christian community of Corinth about the year 96, urging them to heal a division caused by revolt against the leaders. He asserted that the scriptures had been inspired by the Holy Spirit who acted as an agent of Christ.

These writings refer to the life and action of Christ and may be used to regulate the life of the Christian communities. His *Epistle to the Corinthians* is also known as *First Clement*, though *Second Clement* is not his work.

First Clement
Chapter 16.[1] It is to the humble that Christ belongs, not to those who exalt themselves above his flock. The scepter of God's majesty, the Lord Jesus Christ, did not come with the pomp of pride or arrogance, though he could have done so. But he came in humility just as the Holy Spirit said of him. For Scripture reads, "Lord, who has believed what we heard? And to who has the arm of the Lord been revealed? Before him we announced that he was like a child, like a root in thirsty ground he has no comeliness or glory. We saw him, and he had neither comeliness nor beauty. But his appearance was ignominious, deficient when compared to man's stature. He was a man marred by stripes and toil, and experienced in enduring weakness. Because his face was turned away, he was dishonored and disregarded. He it is who bears our sins and suffers pain for us." [Is 53:1-4]

Chapter 22.[2] . . . For this is how Christ addresses us through his Holy Spirit; "Come, my children, listen to me. I will teach you the fear of the Lord. Who is there that desires life, and loves to see good days? Keep your tongue from evil and your lips from uttering deceit. Refrain from evil and do good. Seek peace and follow after it." [Ps 34:11-14]

Chapter 45.[3] . . . You have studied Holy Scripture, which contains the truth and is inspired by the Holy Spirit. You realize that there is nothing wrong or misleading written in it. You will not find that upright people have ever been disowned by holy persons. The righteous, to be sure, have been imprisoned, but by the godless. They have been stoned by transgressors, slain by people prompted by abominable

[1]LCC 1,50-51; SC 167,124-126.
[2]LCC 1,54; SC 167,138-140.
[3]LCC 1,64-65; SC 167,174-176.

and wicked rivalry. Yet in such sufferings they bore up nobly. What shall we say, brothers? Was Daniel cast into a den of lions by those who revered God? [Dan 6:16-17] Or was Ananias, Azarias, or Mishael shut up in the fiery furnace by people devoted to the magnificent and glorious worship of the Most High?

Chapter 46. Let us, then, follow the innocent and the upright. They, it is, who are God's elect. Why is it that you harbor strife, bad temper, dissension, schism, and quarreling? Do we not have one God, one Christ, one Spirit of Grace which was poured out on us? And is there not one calling in Christ? Why do we rend and tear asunder Christ's members and raise a revolt against our own body? Why do we reach such a pitch of insanity that we are oblivious of the fact that we are members of each other?

Ignatius of Antioch (d. c. 107)

Ignatius, the Bishop of Antioch, was taken to Rome for martyrdom about 107. During stopovers on this journey he was visited by Christians and later wrote letters to their various communities. The letters were collected and went through revisions at the hands of later editors. A section of one of these letters, to the Church of Philadelphia, claims that the Holy Spirit spoke in Ignatius' prophetic utterance and in his exhortations to unity with the bishop.

Letter to the Philadelphians
Chapter 7.[4] Some there may be who wanted in a human way to mislead me, but the Spirit is not misled, seeing it comes from God. For "it knows whence it comes and whither it goes," [Jn 3:8] and exposes what is secret. When I was with you I cried out, raising my voice — it was God's voice —"Pay heed to the bishop, the presbytery, and the deacons." Some, it is true, suspected that I spoke thus because I had been told in advance that some of you were schismatics. But I swear by him for whose cause I am a prisoner, that

---

[4]LCC 1,109-110; SC 10,146-148.

from no human channels did I learn this. It was the Spirit that kept on preaching in these words, "Do nothing apart from the bishop; keep your bodies as if they were God's temple; value unity; flee schism; imitate Jesus Christ as he imitated his Father."

Hermas (fl. c. 150)

Hermas was a Roman layman who probably wrote his *Shepherd* about the middle of the second century, though some evidence exists for an earlier dating. His work, a collection of visions, mandates and elaborate parables, sets forth an understanding of the church and exhorts Christians to repent of sins which they have committed after baptism. His book was considered part of Scripture in part of the Greek-speaking Church in the third century, but was less widely known and esteemed in the Latin West.

The Shepherd

> Commentary: In this passage Hermas interpreted the command not to grieve the Holy Spirit. He linked the Holy Spirit to the dispositions which afflict the human spirit when it fails to conceive and carry through a good purpose of working or praying.

Mandate 10.2.[5] "Hear then, foolish person," he said, "how grief wears out the Holy Spirit and saves again. Whenever the double-minded person undertakes any enterprise and fails in it because of his double-mindedness, this grief enters into the person and it grieves the Holy Spirit and wears it out. Then again, when ill temper clings to a person concerning some matter and he becomes very bitter, again grief enters into the heart of the person who is ill-tempered, and he is grieved about what he has done and repents, because he has done evil. So this grief seems to possess salvation because he repented his evil deed. So both things grieve the Spirit: double-mindedness, because he did not succeed in his

[5]AF 6,84-85; SC 53[2],188-190.

action, and ill temper grieves the Spirit because he did evil. So both double-mindedness and ill temper are a grief to the Holy Spirit. So cast off grief from yourself and do not distress the Holy Spirit [Eph 4:30] which dwells in you, lest it make petition to God against you and depart from you. For the Spirit of God given for this flesh submits to neither grief nor distress."

3. "So put on cheerfulness, which always finds favor with God and is pleasant to him, and delight in it. For every cheerful person does good things and thinks good things and despises grief. But the sorrowful person always does evil; first he does evil because he grieves the Holy Spirit that was cheerful when given to humans; second, after he has grieved the Holy Spirit, he does wrong by not praying or confessing to God. For the prayer of a grieving person never has the power to go up to the altar of God." "Why," I said, "does not the prayer of one who is grieving go up to the altar of God.?" "Because," he said, "grief sits in his heart, so when mixed with prayer, grief does not allow the prayer to go up in purity to the altar. For just as vinegar and wine mixed together do not have the same pleasant taste, so also grief mixed with the Holy Spirit does not have the same appeal. So cleanse yourself of evil grief and you will live to God, and all will live to God who cast off from themselves grief and put on only cheerfulness."

> Commentary: Prophecy is another work of the Holy Spirit in the Christian. The true prophet cannot manipulate the divine Spirit and does not seek to gratify base desires.

Mandate 11.[6] The one who asks a false prophet about any concern is an idolater and is void of truth and is foolish. For no spirit given by God need be asked, but it has the power of deity in itself to say all things, because it is from above [Jas 3:15], from the power of the divine Spirit. But the spirit that needs to be asked and speaks according to human desire is

[6]AF 6,87-88; SC 53²,194.

earthly and fickle and has no power; and it does not speak at all unless asked. "Sir," I said, "how then will a person know which of them is a prophet and which is a false prophet?" "Hear," he said, "about both prophets, and in the manner that I am going to tell you, you can test the prophet and the false prophet. By his life you test the person that has the divine Spirit. First, then, the one who has the spirit from above is gentle and quiet and humble, and refrains from all evil and worthless desires of this age, and makes himself more needy than all others, and when asked, gives no answer to anyone. Neither does he speak by himself, nor does the Holy Spirit speak whenever a person wishes to speak, but he speaks when God wishes him to speak. So whenever the person who has the divine Spirit comes into an assembly of the righteous who have faith in the divine Spirit, and a prayer is made to God by this assembly, then the angel of the prophetic spirit which is assigned to him fills the person, and that person, having been filled by the Holy Spirit, speaks to the group as the Lord wills. So in this way the divine Spirit is known. So whatever power pertains to the Spirit of deity is of the Lord.

> Commentary: Hermas seems to have identified the Holy Spirit as the divine power which worked in and adopted Jesus Christ as Son of God. This Christology seems to be patterned on the presence of the same Spirit in the prophets.

Parable 5. 6.[7] "Listen," he said, "the Son of God does not appear in the guise of a slave, but appears with great power and authority." "How, sir?" I said, "I do not understand." "Because God planted the vineyard," he said, "that is, created the people, and he turned it over to his Son. And the Son appointed the angels to protect every one of them, and having worked much and endured many labors, he himself cleansed their sins. For no one is able to cultivate a vineyard

[7]AF 6,106-109; SC 53², 236-240.

without labor and hardship. So when he had cleansed the sins of the people, he showed them the paths of life [Ps 16:11] and gave them the law which he received from his Father. You see, then," said he, "that, since he received all power from his Father, he is Lord of the People. But hear why the Lord took, as a counselor concerning the inheritance of the slave, his Son, and the glorious angels. The preexistent Holy Spirit, which created all creation, God caused to dwell in that flesh which he wished. So this flesh, in which the Holy Spirit dwelled, served the Spirit well, living in reverence and purity, and did not defile the Spirit in any way. So because it conducted itself appropriately and purely and worked with the Spirit and collaborated in every deed, acting with strength and courage, he chose it as partner with the Holy Spirit, for the conduct of this flesh pleased God because it was not defiled while it possessed the Holy Spirit on earth. So he took the Son as a counselor, and the glorious angels, that this flesh also, after it served the Spirit blamelessly, would have some place to dwell and not seem to have lost the reward of its servitude. For all flesh in which the Holy Spirit has dwelled, when found undefiled and spotless, will receive a reward."

ii) THE APOLOGISTS

Justin Martyr (c. 100-165)

Justin Martyr was born of pagan parents in Palestine about 100. He was trained as philosopher and his search for truth brought him finally to Christianity. He came to Rome and there composed two apologies, one to the Emperor and one to the Roman Senate. He also published a version of a dialogue in which he had earlier engaged with a Jew named Trypho, in which he spells out the position of Israel in the history of salvation. He was martyred in Rome about 165. Justin based the Christian claims to truth and universality on the divinity of Christ, the Logos of God. Thus, he had to deal with an objection to the unique role of Christ. Justin's answer does not draw a clear distinction between the divine

Word dwelling in Christ and the Spirit which had been given to the prophets of Israel.

Dialogue with Trypho

87.[8] When I had finished, Trypho said, "Now, when I ask the following question I want you to know that I do so, not for the purpose of contradicting you, but only for the sake of gaining information on the subject. Explain to me the following words of Isaiah: 'There shall come forth a rod out of the root of Jesse, and a flower shall rise up out of his root. And the spirit of God shall rest upon him, the spirit of wisdom and understanding, the spirit of counsel and fortitude, the spirit of knowledge and piety; and he shall be filled with the spirit of the fear of the Lord.' [Is 11:1-3] Now you have admitted, he said, that these words were spoken of Christ, who, you claim, already existed as God, and, becoming incarnate by the will of God, was born of a virgin. This, then, is my question: How can you prove that Christ already existed, since he is endowed with those gifts of the Holy Spirit which the above-quoted passages of Isaiah attribute to him as though he had lacked them?"

"You proposed a very sensible and intelligent question," I remarked, "which appears to raise a real difficulty. But, if you really wish a solution to this difficulty, please listen to me. The scriptures state that these gifts of the Holy Spirit were bestowed upon him, not as though he were in need of them, but as though they were about to rest upon him, that is, to come to an end with him, so that there would be no more prophets among your people as of old, as is plainly evident to you, for after him there has not been a prophet among you. Furthermore, please give my words your careful attention, so you may understand that each of your prophets, by receiving one or two powers from God, did and said those things which we have learned from the scriptures. Solomon had the spirit of wisdom, Daniel that of understanding and counsel, Moses that of strength and piety, Elias that of fear, Isaiah that of knowledge, and the others

[8]FC 1,286-288; PG 6,681-685.

likewise had one or two gifts, as had Jeremiah, and the twelve Prophets, and David, and, in short, all your other prophets. The Spirit therefore rested, that is, ceased, when Christ came. For, after humanity's redemption was accomplished by him, these gifts were to cease among you, and, having come to an end in him, should again be given, as was foretold, by him, from the grace of his Spirit's powers, to all his believers according to their merits. I have already affirmed, and I repeat, that it had been predicted that he would do this after his ascension into heaven. It was said, therefore, 'He ascended on high; he led captivity captive; he gave gifts to the sons of men.' [Ps 68:18] And in another prophecy it is said, 'And it shall come to pass after this, that I will pour out my Spirit upon all flesh, and upon my servants, and upon my handmaids, and they shall prophesy.'" [Jl 2:28,29]

Athenagoras (fl. c. 177)

Athenagoras addressed his *Plea Regarding Christians* to Marcus Aurelius from Athens about 177. He was a clear and forceful thinker, the first to offer a philosophical argument for the Three in One God. Although he identified the Son and Spirit as personal beings, agents of the Father God's work in the world, he did not recognize their existence as eternally distinct from the Father's. The Spirit seems to regress into the Father when he is not working in the world. Although the Son was assigned a major role as the chief of God's ministers in governing the world, the Spirit was identified only as inspirer of prophecy.

Plea
10.[9] I have sufficiently shown that we are not atheists since we acknowledge one God, who is uncreated, eternal, invisible, impassible, incomprehensible, illimitable. He is grasped only by mind and intelligence, and surrounded by light, beauty, spirit, and indescribable power. By him the universe was created through his Word, was set in order, and is held

[9]LCC 1,308-309; Schoedel, 20.

together. I say "his Word," for we also think that God has a Son.

Let no one think it stupid of me to say that God has a Son. For we do not think of God the Father or of the Son in the way of the poets, who weave their myths by showing that gods are no better than humans. But the Son of God is his Word in idea and in actuality; for by him and through him all things were made, the Father and the Son being one. And since the Son is in the Father and the Father in the Son by the unity and power of the Spirit, the Son of God is the mind and Word of the Father.

* * *

Indeed we say that the Holy Spirit himself, who inspires those who utter prophecies, is an effluence from God, flowing from him and returning like a ray of sun. Who, then, would not be astonished to hear those called atheists who admit God the Father, God the Son, and the Holy Spirit, and who teach their unity in power and their distinction in rank? Nor is our theology confined to these points. We affirm, too, a crowd of angels and ministers, whom God, the maker and creator of the world, appointed to their several tasks through his Word. He gave them charge over the good order of the universe, over the elements, the heavens, the world, and all it contains.

Theophilus (fl. c. 180)

Theophilus, bishop of Antioch, wrote his apology *To Autolycus* shortly after 180. He was the first to use the term "triad" of God. He distinguished the Son and Spirit by naming one as the Word of God, Logos, and the other as the divine Wisdom, Sophia. Wisdom is described as knowing the future and inspiring the scriptures in ways which would counteract future deviations and heresies.

To Autolycus
Book 2. 10.[10] ... In the first place, in complete harmony they taught us that he made everything out of the non-

[10]Grant, 38-41.

existent. For there was nothing coeval with God; he was his own locus; he lacked nothing; he existed before the ages. He wished to make humans so that he might be known by them; for them, then, he prepared the world. For those who are created have needs, but he who is uncreated lacks nothing.

Therefore, God, having his own Logos innate in his own bowels, generated him together with his own Sophia, vomiting him forth [Ps 45:1] before everything else. He used this Logos as his servant in the things created by him, and through him he made all things. He is called Beginning because he leads and dominates everything fashioned through him. It was he, Spirit of God [Gen 1:2] and Beginning [Gen 1:1] and Sophia [Prov 8:12] and Power of the Most High, [Lk 1:35] who came down into the prophets and spoke through them about the creation of the world and all the rest. For the prophets did not exist when the world came into existence; there were the Sophia of God which is in him and his holy Logos who is always present with him. For this reason he speaks thus through Solomon the prophet, "When he prepared the heaven I was with him, and when he made strong the foundations of the earth I was with him, binding them fast." [Prov 8:27-29] And Moses, who lived many years before Solomon — or rather, the Logos of God speaking through him as an instrument — says, "In the Beginning God made heaven and earth." [Gen 1:1] First he mentioned Beginning and creation, and only then did he introduce God, for it is not right to mention God idly and in vain. [cf. Exod 20:7] For the divine Sophia knew in advance that some persons were going to speak nonsense and make mention of a multitude of non-existent gods. Therefore, in order for the real God to be known through his works, and to show that by his Logos God made heaven and earth and what is in them, he said, "In the Beginning God made heaven and earth." Then after mentioning their creation he gives us an explanation, "And the earth was invisible and formless, and darkness was above the abyss, and the Spirit of God was borne above the water." [Gen 1:2]

These are the first teachings which the divine scripture gives. It indicates that the matter from which God made and fashioned the world was in a way created, having been made by God.

iii) DEFENDERS OF THE ORTHODOX FAITH

Irenaeus (c. 130-200)

Irenaeus was a native of Asia Minor and claimed contact with the apostolic age through having listened to Polycarp speak about the Apostle John. He was a priest in Lyons and became bishop in 180. Using gnostic documents and some of the works of the apologists, he undertook to describe and refute the gnostic system of Valentinus in his five-part *Against the Heresies.* A subsequent *Demonstration of the Apostolic Preaching* presents a concise, non-polemical exposition of Christian faith. He dealt at some length with the role of the Holy Spirit in creation and revelation, in the teaching of the church, and in the salvation of the individual Christian.

Irenaeus used a sequential model of the operation of the Trinity. Creation and revelation begin in the Father, are carried through by the Son and completed by the Holy Spirit. The Spirit forms the human person in the image of Christ who then leads him to the Father. The Spirit was given to the apostles so that they would teach and write the Gospels with full understanding of the mission of Christ. The same Spirit remains in the church after the apostles and insures the true interpretation of the scriptures. The Spirit makes truly spiritual persons; he works in them to subdue the passions of the flesh and bring the body to immortal life.

Against the Heresies

> Commentary: Irenaeus argued that the Holy Spirit gave the apostles perfect knowledge of the gospel they preached and wrote.

Book 3, Chapter 1. 1.[11] We have learned the plan of our

[11]Trans. J.P. Burns; SC 211,20-24.

salvation from none other than those through whom the gospel has come down to us. First they proclaimed it publicly and subsequently, by the will of God, handed it down to us in the Scriptures to be the foundation and support of our faith. It is wrong to assert that the apostles preached before their own knowledge was perfect, as some persons boast that they improve on the apostles. After our Lord rose from the dead, when the Holy Spirit came down upon them, the apostles were invested with power from on high; they were filled with all his gifts; they had perfect knowledge. Then they went out to the ends of the earth; they preached the glad news of the good things which come to us from God; they proclaimed heaven's peace to humanity. Each individually and equally possessed the gospel of God. Matthew also published a written Gospel for the Hebrews in their own language at the same time that Peter and Paul were preaching at Rome and laying the foundation of the church there. Once they were gone, Mark, who had been Peter's disciple and interpreter, handed down his preaching in writing to us. Similarly, Luke recorded in a book the gospel preached by Paul, whose companion he had been. Afterwards, John, the disciple of the Lord who had leaned on his breast, himself published the gospel while he was living at Ephesus in Asia.

> Commentary: The Holy Spirit continues to inspire understanding in those who hear the preaching so that they can distinguish truth from error. Irenaeus gave a short summary of the church's teaching, the Rule of Faith.

Chapter 4. 1.[12] Since we have such evidence, we can easily obtain the truth from the church and need not seek it from others. As a rich man deposits his money in a bank, so the apostles placed the whole truth in the church's hands. Thus anyone who wishes can draw the water of life from her. [Rev 22:17] She is the entrance way to life; all others are thieves and robbers. [Jn 10:8,9] Because of this, we must

[12]SC 211,44-50.

avoid them; with great zeal, we should love what belongs to the church and grasp the tradition of truth. Consider these situations. Suppose that a dispute about some issue of no particular importance were to arise among us. Should we not have recourse to the oldest churches, the ones in which the apostles lived, in order to reach precision on the disputed matter? What would we do if the apostles had left no scriptures? In that instance, would it not be necessary to follow the tradition which they handed down to those to whom they gave charge of the churches?

2. Many barbarian peoples who have come to believe in Christ assent to this tradition. They have salvation written by the Spirit in their hearts, without paper or ink. [2 Cor 3:3] They carefully preserve the ancient tradition and believe in one God, the Creator of heaven and earth and everything in them, in Christ Jesus, the Son of God, who, because of his surpassing love for the work formed through him, consented to be born of the virgin in order to unite humanity to God through his very self, who suffered under Pontius Pilate and rose again, and was taken up in splendor, who shall come in glory, the Savior of those to be saved and the Judge of those to be judged, who will send into eternal fire those who distort the truth and despise his Father and his own coming. People who have embraced this faith without relying on written documents are barbarians as far as our language is concerned. In doctrine, custom and way of life, because of this faith, they are most wise. They live in righteousness, chastity and wisdom and are pleasing to God. If anyone were to preach the inventions of the heretics to these people in their own language, they would immediately shut their ears and flee as far as possible. They would not bear even to hear this blasphemous speech. Relying on the ancient apostolic tradition, they refuse to consider the doctrines suggested in these pretentious presentations. Neither church nor doctrine has even been established among these preachers.

Commentary: Irenaeus explained that the Spirit first descended upon Jesus and was then shared with his followers. The Spirit is compared to moisture which brings compact unity and fruitfulness to the church and the Christian.

Chapter 17. 1.[13] They [the apostles] recorded what actually happened: that the Spirit of God descended upon him as a dove. As I have noted, Isaiah speaks of this Spirit, "The Spirit of God shall rest upon him," [Is 11:2] and, "The Spirit of the Lord is upon me, because he has anointed me." [Is 61:1] The Lord declares of this Spirit, "It is not you who will speak, but the Spirit of your Father who will speak in you." [Mt 10:20] Similarly, in giving the disciples the power of rebirth into God, he said to them, "Go and teach all nations, baptizing them in the name of the Father and of the Son and of the Holy Spirit." [Mt 28:19] God promised through the prophets that in the last days he would pour out this Spirit on his servants and handmaids, so that they would prophesy. [Jl 2:28,29] For this reason, he also descended upon the Son of God, made Son of Man, and thus in union with him became accustomed to dwell in the human race, to rest with human beings and to dwell in the works formed by God. He accomplished the Father's will in them and renewed them from their old habits into the newness of Christ.

2. David asked this Spirit for the human race, "Establish me with your all-governing Spirit." [Ps 51:12] As Luke says, he descended upon the disciples on the day of Pentecost after the Lord's ascension. He had power over all nations to lead them into the way of life and to open the new Covenant to all. By his power, the disciples were of one accord and sang praises to God in all different languages. The Spirit joined distant tribes into unity and offered to the Father the first-fruits of all the nations. [Acts 2] Thus the Lord promised to send the Comforter, who would join us to God. Just as dry wheat cannot be shaped into a cohesive lump of dough or a loaf held together without moisture, so in the same way, we many could not become one in Christ Jesus

[13]SC 211,328-336.

without the water which comes from heaven. As dry earth bears no fruit unless it receives moisture, so we also were originally dry wood and could never have borne the fruit of life without the rain freely given from above. Our bodies have been joined into the unity which leads to incorruption through the washing; our souls have received it through the Spirit. Both are necessary, since both contribute to the divine life. Our Lord had compassion on that erring Samaritan woman who committed fornication by contracting many marriages rather than remaining with one husband. He pointed out and promised living water to her so that by having living water springing up to eternal life within her, she would no longer thirst or have to seek out and work to acquire refreshing water. [Jn 4:7-26] The Lord received this living water as a gift from his Father and himself confers it on those who share in him by sending the Holy Spirit over all the earth.

3. God chose Gideon to save Israel from the power of the foreign nations. Gideon foresaw this gracious gift and changed his request. At first the dew was only on the fleece of wool which represented the people. By his request, he prophesied that it would be dry, indicating that they would no longer have the Holy Spirit of God. [Jg 6:36-40] As Isaiah says, "I will also command the clouds not to rain upon it." [Is 5:6] The dew, which represented the Spirit of God who descended upon the Lord, would be spread throughout all the earth, "the spirit of wisdom and understanding, the spirit of counsel and might, the spirit of knowledge and piety, the spirit of the fear of God." [Is 11:2] Further, he conferred this Spirit upon the church and sent the Comforter from heaven throughout all the world. The Lord tells us that the devil was cast down from the heavens like lightning. [Lk 10:18] We need the dew of God, therefore, so that we are not consumed by fire or rendered fruitless, so that we may have an Advocate where we have an accuser. To the Holy Spirit, the Lord entrusted his own man, who had fallen among thieves. He had compassion on humanity, bandaged its wounds, and gave two royal denarii, so that we who received the image and signature of the

Father and Son by the Spirit might make the denarius entrusted to us bear fruit and repay it with interest to the Lord.

> Commentary: The Spirit is the moving and life-giving force in the church. Outside the Spirit-filled church one finds only error and death.

Chapter 24. 1.[14] ... The preaching of the church has been shown consistent; it continues on an even course. We have proved that it receives the testimony of the prophets, the apostles and all the disciples — a witness which includes the beginning, the middle and the end, the entire divine economy and the operation which is directed to humanity's salvation and provides the foundation of our faith. We have received this faith from the church and carefully preserve it. By the Spirit of God, it continually renews its youth. Like a precious treasure in an excellent container, it causes the containing vessel to renew its youth as well. This gift of God has been entrusted to the church just as breath was given to the work God formed so that all the members may be vivified by receiving it. The Holy Spirit has been distributed through the church as the means of communion with Christ and of confirming our faith, as the pledge of incorruption, and the ladder of ascent to God. "For in the church," it is said, "God has established apostles, prophets, teachers," [1 Cor 12:28] and all the other ways in which the Spirit works. Those who do not join themselves to the church do not share in him. Instead they deprive themselves of life by their perverse opinions and scandalous behavior. Where the church is, there is the Spirit of God; where the Spirit of God is, there is the church and every grace. The Spirit is truth. Therefore those who do not share in the Spirit are neither nourished to life from the mother's breast nor do they enjoy that most clear fountain which springs from the body of Christ. Instead they dig themselves broken cisterns, made from ditches of dirt, and drink putrid water from the mud. They

[14]SC 211,470-474.

flee the faith of the church to avoid being proven wrong and reject the Spirit so that they will not be taught.

> Commentary: In this extended passage Irenaeus set forth his understanding of the role of the Son and Spirit as the agents of the Father in creation, revelation and glorification. He denied the gnostic assertion of discontinuity between creation and salvation, showing that the gradual revelation of the Father through the work of the Son and Spirit gives life to the world and humanity.

Book 4, Chapter 20. 1.[15] The angels neither made nor formed us, for only the Word of God has the power to make an image of God, not angels or anyone else, no power far removed from the Father of all things. God had no need of such beings to accomplish the plans which he had himself determined in advance. As though he had not his own hands. The Word and Wisdom, the Son and Spirit, are always present with him. By them and in them, he freely and independently made all things. To them, he speaks when he says, "Let us make humans after our own image and likeness." [Gen 1:26] He took from himself the substance of the creatures, the pattern of the things made and the plan for all the furnishings in the world.

> Commentary: The process of salvation was described by Irenaeus as a gradual revelation of the Father. The divine light confers life on humanity in three stages. When the splendor of the Father's own glory finally shines upon him, a person receives immortal life.

6. Humans, therefore, shall see God so that they may live. They will be made immortal by the seeing and attain to God. As I have already said, the prophets figuratively foretold precisely this: that God would be seen by human beings who bore his Spirit and always waited patiently for his coming. Thus Moses says in Deuteronomy, "In that day we shall see

[15]SC 100,624-626,642-652.

that God will speak to a person and he shall live." [Deut 5:24] Certain ones of these people saw the prophetic Spirit and his works which were poured out for all sorts of gifts. Others saw the coming of the Lord and his ministry from the beginning, through which he fulfilled the will of the Father both in heaven and on earth. Still others saw the glories of the Father, adapted in each age to the persons who saw and heard them then and to those who would hear them later. This, then, was the way God revealed himself. Through all of this, the Father God made himself known. The Spirit worked; the Son ministered; the Father approved; and humanity was perfected for its salvation.

> Commentary: Irenaeus summarized the work of the Word with the assertion that his revelation of the Father gives life to all things living in the world. The glory or masterpiece of the divine Light is humanity whose life consists in the vision of God.

7. Thus, from the beginning the Son is the revealer of the Father, since he was with the Father from the beginning. At chosen times and for their benefit, he shows humanity prophetic visions, diversities of gifts, his own ministries, and the Father's glory — all like a well composed and harmonious melody. Where there is composition, there is melody; where melody, chosen time; where chosen time, there is profit. For this reason, the Word became the dispenser of the Father's grace for the benefit of humanity. For the sake of human beings, he has executed so great a plan. He revealed God to humans and presented humans to God. All the while, he preserved the invisibility of the Father, so that humans would neither despise God nor lack goals for future development. At the same time he made God visible to humans through the various economies lest humanity perish from its very being by total deprivation of God. The glory of God is living humanity and human life consists in the vision of God. If the revelation of God through the creation itself has given life to all things which live on the earth, how much

more does the revelation of the Father through the Word give life to those who see God!

> Commentary: The Holy Spirit prepared humanity for the perception of God Incarnate by instruction, symbolic action and visions of the future events. Through the Wisdom of God humanity is enabled to receive the revelation of the Word.

8. Since, therefore, the Spirit of God indicated the future through the prophets in order to form and dispose us in advance for submission to God, and since that future would consist in humanity seeing God through the good pleasure of the Father, then it was fitting that those who prophesied the future should themselves see the God whom they declared humans would see. Thus he would not only be prophetically announced as God and Child of God, as Son and Father, but he would be seen by all his members who were sanctified and instructed in the things of God. In this way, humanity would be formed and trained in advance to draw near to the glory which was destined to be revealed subsequently to those who love God. [Rom 8:18,28] The prophets prophesied not only in word but by their visions, their way of life and the works they performed according to the guidance of the Holy Spirit. This was the way they saw the invisible God. Isaiah says, "I have seen with my eyes the King, the Lord of Hosts," [Is 6:5] to indicate that humans would see God with their eyes and hear his voice. This was the way they saw the Son of God living as a human among humans. They prophesied what would happen; they spoke of him as present even before he was actually there; they announced the suffering of the one incapable of suffering; they said that the one then in heaven had come down into the dust of death. [Ps 22:15] The same is true of all the other operations of his recapitulation. Some they saw by visions; others they signified in a figurative way by action. They saw the things which would be seen in a visible way; they proclaimed in words the things which would be heard; they

performed in action the things which would be accomplished. All these things they announced prophetically.

> Commentary: In defending the resurrection and glorification of the flesh against gnostic rejections of everything material, Irenaeus had to explain how the flesh could inherit the Kingdom of God. He distinguished flesh, soul and spirit within the human being and showed how the divine Spirit purifies the human spirit and enables a person to master the weakness of the flesh.

Book 5, Chapter 9. 1.[16] Among the other truths proclaimed by the Apostle is, "Flesh and blood cannot inherit the kingdom of God."[1 Cor 15:50] In their folly, all the heretics adduce this text; from it, they attempt to prove that the divine handiwork cannot be saved. They do not understand that a complete human being is composed of three things: flesh, soul and Spirit. One of these, the Spirit, forms and saves. Another, flesh, is formed and saved. The third, the soul, comes between these two: sometimes it follows the Spirit and is raised up by it; sometimes it gives in to the flesh and falls into earthly desires. Those, then, who lack the part which saves and fashions into life, these are and reasonably will be designated as "flesh and blood," since they do not have the Spirit of God in them. This is why the Savior elsewhere referred to them as the dead, "Let the dead bury their dead." [Lk 9:60] They do not have the Spirit which gives a human person life.

2. Others fear God, trust in the coming of his Son, and establish the Spirit of God in their hearts through faith. These are appropriately referred to as pure, spiritual and living unto God because they have the Spirit of the Father who purifies a person and lifts him up to the life of God. According to the Lord's teaching, as the flesh is weak so the Spirit is willing, that is, capable of accomplishing whatever he urges. [Mt 26:41] If, then, anyone will allow the readiness of the Spirit to be joined, as a stimulus, to the weakness of the flesh, then the strong will necessarily prevail over the

[16]SC 153,106-116.

weak. The weakness of the flesh will be absorbed by the strength of the Spirit and the person will be no longer carnal; he will be spiritual because of the communion of the Spirit. In this way the martyrs bear witness and despise death, following the readiness of the Spirit rather than the weakness of the flesh. The flesh whose weakness has been so absorbed manifests the power of the Spirit. In absorbing its weakness, the Spirit receives the flesh as its own inheritance. A living human person is formed of these two: he lives by sharing in the Spirit; he is human by the substance of the flesh.

3. Without the Spirit of God, the flesh is dead, deprived of life, and incapable of inheriting the kingdom of God. In the same way, the blood is irrational, like water poured out on the ground. [Ps 79:3] Therefore he says, "As was the earthly, so are those who are earthly." [1 Cor 15:48] But where the Spirit of the Father is found, there is a living person. The blood animated by reason is preserved by God for vengeance. [Rev 6:10, 19:2] The flesh taken as an inheritance by the Spirit forgets what it is and takes on the character of the Spirit and is conformed to the Word of God. Thus the Apostle says, "As we have borne the image of the earthly, so also shall we bear the image of the heavenly." [1 Cor 15:49] What is the earthly? What was fashioned. What is the heavenly? The Spirit. He asserts that when we were deprived of the heavenly Spirit, we lived according to the oldness of the flesh in disobedience to God. So, now that we have received the Spirit, "let us walk in the newness of life," in obedience to God. [Rom 6:4] Since, therefore, we cannot be saved without the Spirit of God, the Apostle urges us to guard the Spirit of God by faith and a pure life. For if we do not share in this divine Spirit, we will lose the Kingdom of Heaven. This is the reason why he proclaims that flesh and blood alone cannot inherit the kingdom of God.

The Demonstration of the Apostolic Preaching

Commentary: This short, non-polemical exposition of the faith summarizes much of Irenaeus' teaching on the Holy Spirit which was given in *Against the Heresies*.

Chapter 5.[17] Thus then there is shown forth One God, the Father, not made, invisible, Creator of all things; above whom there is no other God, and after whom there is no other God. And, since God is rational, therefore by the Word he created the things that were made; and God is Spirit, and by the Spirit he adorned all things: as also the prophet says, "By the word of the Lord were the heavens established, and by his Spirit all their power." [Ps 33:6] Since then the Word establishes, that is to say, gives body and grants the reality of being, and the Spirit gives order and form to the diversity of the powers; rightly and fittingly is the Word called the Son, and the Spirit the Wisdom of God. Well also does Paul his apostle say, "One God, the Father, who is over all and through all and in us all." [Eph 4:6] For over all is the Father; and through all is the Son, for through him all things were made by the Father; and in us all is the Spirit, who cries Abba Father, [Gal 4:6] and fashions humans into the likeness of God. Now the Spirit shows forth the Word, and therefore the prophets announced the Son of God; and the Word utters the Spirit, and therefore is himself the announcer of the prophets, and leads and draws humanity to the Father.

Concluding Reflections

The scanty literary evidence of Christian appreciation of the person and work of the Holy Spirit in the second century makes an assessment of its evolution difficult. The Apostolic Fathers and apologists attributed only the inspiration of prophecy in the Old Testament and the church to the operation of the Spirit. Prophetic utterance, however, was understood in two different ways. The prophet might be under the influence of an impersonal divine power through which he, a human person, is moved to speak. The true

[17]ACW 16,73-74; PO 12,663-664.

prophet is recognized by his personal morality and his refraining from self-serving commands and predictions. Alternately, the prophet might be viewed as the medium or instrument of the speaking of a divine person. Thus Ignatius of Antioch disclaimed personal knowledge of the schism against which the Spirit preached through him. Hermas assigned control over the human instrument to the divine Spirit and warned against saddening him.

Even when the personal existence of the Spirit was recognized, he was not clearly distinguished from the Word of God. According to Clement, Christ speaks through the Spirit which inspired the Old Testament prophets. Hermas found the difference between the Spirit and the divine element in Christ hard to conceive and maintain. Justin Martyr, however, indicated the distinction by explaining that the Spirit ceased to function and rested while the Word was working in the world.

By integrating the prophetic function into the history of salvation as a gradual revelation of the divine, Irenaeus both expanded the scope of the Spirit's operation and manifested his personal existence. The Holy Spirit prepared humanity for the reception of the Word of God and thus for being led to the fullness of life in the knowledge of the Father. Through prophetic word and action, the Spirit previewed the activity of the Word on earth and his manifestation of the divine in human form. The fashioning of the flesh of Christ was attributed to the Word himself, but the Spirit descended upon Christ at his baptism and through him was accustomed to dwell among humans. After the resurrection, the Spirit descended upon the church to guide and maintain it in truth. The Spirit accompanies the preacher and writes the gospel in the hearts of his converts. All of these operations are adapted to the stages of humanity's growth toward full life in God.

In addition, Irenaeus expanded the Spirit's work into the sanctification of the Christian. The Spirit strengthens the soul against the influence of the fleshly appetites.

All these operations indicate the intelligence, planning and willing of the Spirit, thus delineating his personality.

Although Irenaeus did not consistently maintain the distinct characterizations of the Son and Spirit as Word and Wisdom, his description and coordination of their individual operation established separate personal identities for each.

The defenders of orthodoxy in the early third century, Hippolytus and Tertullian, as well as subsequent writers such as Cyprian, Novatian and Origen, built upon the foundation laid by Irenaeus. They emphasized the Spirit's role as the source of sanctifying power in the church and as its guide to the proper understanding of the teaching of Jesus.

Chapter Two

FROM CHARISM TO OFFICE: THE THIRD CENTURY

Introduction

The literature dealing with the Holy Spirit in the third century was primarily in the Western Church and was concerned with the operation of the Spirit within the church. Irenaeus' emphasis on the presence of the Spirit in a succession of teachers was echoed early in the century by Tertullian and Hippolytus. The focus soon shifted, however, from questions of true doctrine to the maintenance of proper discipline. The Spirit figured prominently in discussions of the readmission of sinners to communion, the disciplinary powers of bishops, and the power of schismatic communities to administer the sacraments.

The mark of the true church in the second century was authentic teaching. In the third century, as the church expanded and began to settle into the world, schismatic communities asserted that by abusing the power to forgive sins and failing to maintain primitive discipline, the church had lost the Holy Spirit and the power to sanctify. Tertullian offered an apology for the Montanist sect which based its claim to exclusive possession of the Spirit on obedience to

the new disciplinary and ascetical injunctions of the Paraclete. Hippolytus accused the Catholic bishop of Rome,
Callistus, of pandering to human weakness and perversity in
his policy of reconciling Christians who sinned after baptism. Novatian's schismatic community refused to communicate with those who had denied the faith in time of
persecution, those whom his rival, Cornelius, had readmitted to the church's communion. In each case, the issue was
primarily disciplinary. The underlying doctrinal assumption, however, was a close link between the Holy Spirit and
the sanctifying power of the church.

The Catholic response had the same foundation but a
different logic. Because the Spirit had been given to the
church in the person of Peter and the apostles, those bishops
in legitimate succession from them hold in common the
power to forgive sins and to sanctify by the Holy Spirit.
Bishops who separate themselves from the unity of the
church can neither receive nor retain the Holy Spirit. Consequently they lose the power to forgive sins by baptism or to
transmit the Spirit by imposing hands.

By the middle of the century, the discussion centered on
the status of converts who came to the Catholic communion
after having first been baptized in an heretical or schismatic
communion. Novatian, the Roman schismatic, and
Cyprian, the African Catholic, both insisted that the Holy
Spirit was operative only in the true church: baptism outside
it was empty and must be repeated for the convert to receive
the forgiveness of sins and the grace of the Holy Spirit. The
bishop of Rome, Stephen, asserted the tradition of his
church which recognized any baptism in the divine name
and only imposed hands on repentant heretics and schismatics to admit them to Catholic communion. The anonymous *Treatise on Rebaptism* defended the Roman
position, but recognized that outside the church one
receives neither forgiveness nor the Spirit.

Third-century authors also stressed the Spirit's charismatic gifts and strengthening of Christians in virtuous life.
The operation of the Spirit was particularly evident in the
combat and triumph of the martyrs.

This discussion in the earlier half of the third century tended to obscure rather than clarify the personality of the Holy Spirit. Hippolytus' detailing of the various spirits received by different orders of the clergy and Cyprian's arguments that only certain churchmen retain and transmit the Spirit give the impression that the Holy Spirit is a divine quality or power bestowed upon humans. Reflection on the personality of the Spirit and his relation to the Father and Son continued in the work of Tertullian and Novatian in the West. In the East, Origen developed the Logos theology begun by the second-century apologists to include the Holy Spirit. In his being, the Spirit is subordinate to both the Father and the Son; he works as their agent among the saints to illumine and sanctify. The unity of the Trinity is maintained through monarchy: the doctrine that the Father is the one source of the Son and Spirit, and through them of all the beings which comprise the universe.

The Writings

Tertullian (c. 160-220)

Tertullian was a Carthaginian converted to Christianity near the end of the second century. He began his literary career (about 195) as an apologist, arguing against pagans and Jews. His attention soon turned to the heretics and he undertook a series of expositions and defenses of the truths of the Christian faith. About 207 he began to fall under Montanist influence and became a member of the sect about six years later. He is thought to have died about 220.

Tertullian's are among the earliest extant Christian works in Latin and he determined much of the vocabulary of subsequent Western theology. He spoke of the Holy Spirit in a variety of contexts. The Spirit strengthens the martyrs, whose power to extend the peace of the church to those who had denied the faith Tertullian recognized early in his career. The Spirit is called Vicar of Christ because of his office of preserving the church in the teaching of Christ and the apostles. The same Spirit comes down on the water of baptism and bestows its sanctifying power.

In the works which evidence Montanist influence and conviction, Tertullian presented a different understanding of the operation of the Spirit. Montanus had stressed the presence of the charismatic gifts in his community, but Tertullian's emphasis fell on the content of the new prophecy — the call for an ascetic life and rigorous church discipline. The Paraclete who spoke through Montanus confirmed and clarified the teaching of Christ, but demanded a more rigorous moral practice. Christ forbade the divorce which Moses had allowed, but the Spirit now prohibits even the second marriage after a spouse's death which Christ and the apostles had permitted. Tertullian contrasted the "psychics" — sensate or passionate Catholics — who reject the demands of the Paraclete with the "spirituals" who follow Montanist prophecy. He asserted that neither bishop nor martyr could forgive serious sin committed after baptism. The "spiritual" person, who has such power, was prohibited by the Spirit from exercising it lest Christians grow lax.

In his work against Praxeas, Tertullian refuted the Modalist interpretation of the unity of God as one individual who assumes three successive roles. The Son and Spirit are distinct persons who derive from the Father but remain inseparably united to him in will and action.

To the Martyrs

> Commentary: This letter was addressed as an exhortation to imprisoned Christians. It asserts that the Spirit strengthens them in the confession of the faith and maintains them in peace and unity so that they may even extend it to others who have been excluded from the community.

1.[1] . . . In the first place, then, O blessed, "do not grieve the Holy Spirit" (Eph 4:30) who has entered prison with you.

[1]FC 40, 17-19; CCL 1, 3.

For, if he had not accompanied you there in your present trial, you would not be there today. See to it, therefore, that he remain with you there and so lead you out of that place to the Lord. Indeed, the prison is the devil's house, too, where he keeps his household. But you have come to the prison for the very purpose of trampling upon him right in his own house. For you have engaged him in battle already outside the prison and trampled him underfoot. Let him, therefore, not say, "Now that they are in my domain, I will tempt them with base hatreds, with defections or dissensions among themselves." Let him flee from your presence, and let him, coiled and numb, like a snake that is driven out by charms or smoke, hide away in the depths of his den. Do not allow him the good fortune in his own kingdom of setting you against one another, but let him find you fortified by the arms of peace among yourselves, because peace among yourselves means war with him. Some, not able to find peace in the church, are accustomed to seek it from the martyrs in prison. For this reason, too, then, you ought to possess, cherish and preserve it among yourselves that you may perhaps be able to bestow it upon others also.

On Prescription against Heretics

> Commentary: Continuing Irenaeus' debate with the gnostics over the interpretation of scripture, Tertullian argued that the Holy Spirit was given to the apostles to guarantee their understanding of the truth Jesus taught.

Chapter 22.[2] ... They usually tell us that the apostles did not know all things, but even in this they are impelled by the same madness: they end up at the opposite extreme and assert that the apostles certainly knew all things, but did not deliver all things to everyone. In either case they expose Christ to blame for having sent out apostles who had either too much ignorance or too little simplicity. Who that has a

---

[2]ANF 3,253; CCL 1, 203-204.

sound mind can possibly suppose that the apostles were ignorant of anything, whom the Lord ordained to be teachers, keeping them, as he did, inseparable from himself in their attendance, in their discipleship, in their companionship, to whom, "when they were alone, he used to explain" [Mk 4:34] all things which were obscure, telling them that "to them it was given to know those mysteries," [Mt 13:11] which it was not permitted the people to understand?...No doubt he had once said, "I have yet many things to say to you, but you cannot hear them now;" but even then he added, "when he, the Spirit of Truth, shall come, he will lead you into all truth." [Jn 16:12,13] He thus shows that there was nothing of which they were ignorant, to whom he had promised the future attainment of all truth by the help of the Spirit of Truth. And assuredly he fulfilled his promise, since it is proved in the Acts of the Apostles that the Holy Spirit did come down. Now they who reject that scripture can neither belong to the Holy Spirit, seeing that they cannot acknowledge that the Holy Spirit has been sent even yet to the disciples, nor can they presume to claim to be a church themselves who positively have no means of proving when, and with what swaddling-clothes this body was established.

> Commentary: In passing to his second argument, Tertullian spoke of the Holy Spirit as the Steward of God and Vicar of Christ whose mission is to maintain the church in truth.

Chapter 28.[3] Grant, then, that all have erred; that the Apostle was mistaken in giving his testimony; that the Holy Spirit had not such respect for any one church as to lead it into truth, although sent with this view by Christ, and for this purpose asked from the Father that he might be the teacher of truth; grant, also, that he, the Steward of God, the Vicar of Christ, neglected his office, permitting the churches for a time to understand differently, and to believe differently,

[3]ANF 3, 256; CCL 1, 209.

what he himself was preaching through the apostles. Is it likely that so many churches, and they so great, should have gone astray into one and the same faith? No accidental occurrence distributed among many people produces one and the same effect. Error of doctrine in the churches must necessarily have resulted in a variety of consequences. When, however, that which is deposited among many is found to be one and the same, it is not the result of error, but of tradition. Can any one, then, be reckless enough to say that those who handed on the tradition were in error?

On Baptism

> Commentary: In this treatise Tertullian explained the ritual of Christian initiation. The Spirit rests upon the waters of baptism and cleanses from sin. He indicated that the church is explicitly mentioned in the baptismal creed.

Chapter 6.[4] Not that the Holy Spirit is given to us in the water, but that in the water we are made clean by the action of the angel, and made ready for the Holy Spirit. Here also a type had come first. As John was our Lord's forerunner, preparing his ways, so also the angel, the mediator of baptism, makes the ways straight for the Holy Spirit who is to come next. He does so by that cancelling of sins which is granted in response to faith signed and sealed in the Father and the Son and the Holy Spirit. For if in three witnesses every word shall be established, how much more shall the gift of God? By the benediction we have the same mediators of faith as we have sureties of salvation. That number of the divine names of itself suffices for the confidence of our hope. Yet because it is under the charge of three that profession of faith and promise of salvation are in pledge, there is a necessary addition, the mention of the church: because where there are the three, the Father and the Son and the Holy Spirit, there is the church, which is a body of three.

[4]Evans, 15-17; CCL 1, 282.

> Commentary: After explaining the post-baptismal anointing, Tertullian moved to the imposition of hands which confers the Holy Spirit upon the newly baptized.

Chapter 8.[5] Next follows the imposition of the hand in benediction, inviting and welcoming the Holy Spirit. Human ingenuity has been permitted to summon spirit to combine with water, and by application of a man's hands over the result of their union to animate it with another spirit of excellent clarity: and shall not God be permitted, in an organ of his own, by the use of holy hands to play a tune of spiritual sublimity? At this point that most Holy Spirit willingly comes down from the Father upon bodies cleansed and blessed, and comes to rest upon the waters of baptism as though revisiting his primal dwelling-place. He came down upon our Lord in the form of a dove, and thus the nature of the Holy Spirit was clearly revealed in a creature of simplicity and innocence, since even physically the dove is without gall: which is why he says, "Be simple, like doves." [Mt 10:16] And this too has the support of a type which had preceded: for as, after those waters of the Flood, by which the ancient iniquity was cleansed away, after the baptism (so to express it) of the world, a dove as herald announced to the earth peace from the wrath of heaven, having been sent forth of the ark and having returned with an olive-leaf [Gen 8:10,11] and towards the heathen too this is held out as a sign of peace — by the same divine ordinance of spiritual effectiveness the dove who is the Holy Spirit is sent forth from heaven, where the church is which is the type of the ark, and flies down bringing God's peace to the earth which is our flesh, as it comes up from the washing after the removal of its ancient sins. "But," you object, "the world sinned once more, so that this equating of baptism with the flood is not valid." The world sinned, and so is appointed for the fire, as also a person is when he renews his sins after baptism: so that this also needs to be accepted as a sign and a warning to us.

[5]Evans, 17-19; CCL 1, 283.

On the Veiling of Virgins

> Commentary: While rejecting any development or change of the doctrine expressed in the Rule of Faith, Tertullian asserted that the Holy Spirit was sent as the Vicar of Christ to advance discipline. As a guide to practice, the Spirit completes the work of Christ.

Chapter 1.[6] . . . The rule of faith, indeed, is altogether one, alone unchangeable and irreformable: the rule of believing in only one God omnipotent, the Creator of the universe, and his Son Jesus Christ, born of the Virgin Mary, crucified under Pontius Pilate, raised again the third day from the dead, received in the heavens, sitting now at the right hand of the Father, destined to come to judge the living and the dead through the resurrection of the flesh. This law of faith being constant, the other points of discipline and way of life may be changed and corrected when the grace of God intervenes and accomplishes this purpose. For what kind of assumption is it, that, while the devil is always operating and adding daily to the ingenuities of iniquity, the work of God should either have ceased, or else stopped advancing? Actually the reason why the Lord sent the Paraclete was, that, since human mediocrity was unable to take in all things at once, discipline should, little by little, be directed, ordained, and brought to perfection by that Vicar of the Lord, the Holy Spirit. "Still," he said, "I have many things to say to you, but you are not yet able to bear them: when that Spirit of Truth shall have come, he will lead you into all truth, and will report to you the things to come." [Jn 16:12-13] Thus, he declared the work of the Spirit. This, then, is the Paraclete's guiding office: the direction of discipline, the revelation of the Scriptures, the reformation of the intellect, the advance toward the "better things.". . . They who have received him set truth before custom. They who have heard him prophesying even to the present time, not of old, bid virgins be wholly covered.

[6]ANF 4, 27-28; CCL 2, 1209-1210.

On Monogamy

> Commentary: Tertullian here argued for the Montanist
> practice of monogamy which forbade marriage after the
> death of a spouse. He defended the novelty and rigor of
> the Paraclete's disciplinary revelations. A spirit opposed
> to Christ, he argued, would first corrupt the faith and
> then introduce a new discipline. By confirming the teach-
> ing of Christ, the Paraclete validates the disciplinary
> development.

Chapter 2.[7] And so they [Catholics] attack the law of
monogamy as though it were a heresy; nor have they a
cogent reason for rejecting the Paraclete apart from their
assumption that he has revealed a completely new way of
life, and one indeed which they find difficult to follow.
Therefore, the first point we must take up in our consideration of the subject at hand is whether or not it is possible that
the Paraclete has revealed anything at all which is an inno-
vation opposed to Catholic tradition, or which imposes
moral obligations upon us inconsistent with the light
burden referred to by the Lord. The Lord himself has
spoken pertinently on both these subjects. For he says, "I
have yet many things to speak to you, but you cannot bear
them now; when the Holy Spirit is come, he will introduce
you to all truth." [Jn 16:12-13] Thus, of course, he sufficiently indicates that the Holy Spirit will reveal such things
as may be considered innovations, since they were not
revealed before, and burdensome, since it was for this reason that they were not revealed.

But, you object, on the basis of this argument any novelty
at all, any oppressive obligation can be called a revelation of
the Paraclete, even though it be from the evil spirit. No,
certainly not. For the evil spirit would betray himself by the
very heterodoxy of his teaching. First of all, he perverts the
faith and thus, too, he perverts good morals, because what is
first in order must needs be first destroyed; and this means

---

[7]ACW 13, 71-72; CCL 2, 1229-1230.

faith, for it is ever the precursor of right conduct. A person's view of God must be heretical before he develops heretical views about his law.

The Paraclete has many things to teach which the Lord deferred until such time as he should come. It is by a predetermined plan that this is done. First he will bear witness to the selfsame Christ in whom we place our faith, and to the whole design of God's creation; and he will glorify him and bring to mind the things that he has said. [Jn 16:14] And when thus he is recognized according to the plan which was determined from the beginning, then will he make known the many things which have to do with the way of life we are to follow. These things will be authenticated by the integrity of his teaching. They may be new because they are revealed only now, and they may be burdensome because up to now they were not required of us. Nevertheless, their author is the very same Christ who said that he had yet many other things which the Paraclete should teach, things which would be found no less a burden by people of our own day than by those who in his day could not bear them.

On Modesty

> Commentary: The rigors of Montanist discipline included a refusal to readmit Christians who sinned after baptism to the communion of the church. Tertullian recognized that Christ, the apostles and prophets had the power to forgive major sins: a power they proved by miracles and balanced by severity. The officers of the church, having no such power, can act only as ministers of the Spirit, who forbids the forgiving of post-baptismal sin. Tertullian's adversary here seems to have been a bishop of Carthage.

Chapter 21.[8] But I will descend even to this point of the argument now, making a separation between the doctrine of apostles and their power. Discipline governs a person,

[8]ANF 4, 98-100; CCL 2, 1326-1328.

power sets a seal upon him; apart from the fact that power is the Spirit, but the Spirit is God. What, moreover, used the Spirit to teach? That there must be no communicating with the works of darkness. Obey what he commands. Who, moreover, was able to forgive sins? This is his prerogative alone: for "who remits sins except God alone?"[Mk 2:7], so much the more for mortal sins, which have been committed against himself and against his temple. For, as far as you are concerned, you are commanded, in the person of Peter, to forgive even seventy times sevenfold those who are guilty of offense against you personally. And so, even if it were conceded that the blessed apostles had granted forgiveness for a crime which only God can forgive, they would have had the right to do so, not in the exercise of discipline, but of power. For they both raised the dead, which God alone can do, and restored the handicapped to their integrity, which none but Christ can do. They even inflicted plagues, which Christ would not do since severity was not proper for the one who had come to suffer. Both Ananias and Elymas were stricken — Ananias with death, Elymas with blindness — in order that by this very fact it might be proved that Christ had had the power of doing even such miracles. [Acts 5:5, 13:11] So, too, the prophets of old had granted to the repentant the pardon of murder and adultery, while at the same time they gave manifest proofs of severity. Therefore show even now, apostolic sir, prophetic evidences, so that I may recognize your divine virtue, and thereby vindicate for yourself the power of remitting such sins! If, however, you have had the functions of discipline alone assigned to you, and the duty of presiding not as a ruler but as a servant, then who or how great are you, that you should grant forgiveness? By exhibiting neither the prophetic nor the apostolic character, you lack that power to pardon.

"But," you say, "the church has the power of forgiving sins." This I acknowledge and affirm more than you. I have the Paraclete himself in the persons of the new prophets, saying, "The church has the power to forgive sins; but I will not do it, lest they commit others because of it." "What if a spirit of false prophecy had made that declaration?" you object. It would have been more like a subverter on the one hand to commend himself on the score of clemency, and on the other to influence all others to sin. Or if the spirit of false prophecy has attempted to promote this viewpoint which is in accordance with "the Spirit of Truth," it follows that "the Spirit of Truth" does indeed have the power of indulgently granting pardon to fornicators, but wills not to do it if it will involve harm for the majority.

> Commentary: Turning to the bishop's justification of his action, Tertullian argued that the power of binding and loosing was given to Peter personally, for specific tasks. It was not for pardoning capital sins committed after baptism.

Because the Lord has said to Peter, "Upon this rock will I build my church," "to you I have given the keys of the kingdom of heaven;" or "Whatever you bind or loose on earth, shall be bound or loosed in heaven," [Mt 16:18,19] you presume that the power of binding and loosing has carried down to you, that is, to every church akin to Peter. What sort of person are you, subverting and wholly changing the manifest intention of the Lord, who conferred this gift personally upon Peter? "On you," he says, "I will build my church;" and "I will give to you the keys," not to the church; and "whatever you loose or bind," not what they loose or bind. The result makes this clear. On Peter himself the church was built; that is, through him. Peter himself used the key — you see what key: "Men of Israel, let what I say sink into your ears: Jesus the Nazarene, a man destined by God for you," and so forth. [Acts 2:22] Peter himself, therefore, was the first to unlock, in Christ's baptism, the entrance to the heavenly kingdom, in which both these sins that had been bound are loosed and those which have not been loosed are bound in accordance with true salvation. He bound Ananias with the bond of death, and the paralyzed man he loosed from his lack of health. Moreover, in that dispute about the observance or non-observance of the law, Peter was the first of all to be endowed with the Spirit, and, after reflecting on the calling of the nations, he said, "And now why are you tempting the Lord, imposing upon the brethren a yoke which neither we nor our fathers were able to support? But however, through the grace of Jesus we believe that we shall be saved in the same way as they."[Acts 15:7-11] This judgment loosed those parts of the law which were abandoned, and bound those which were retained. Hence the power of loosing and of binding committed to Peter had nothing to do with the capital sins of believers. Since the Lord had given him a precept that he must grant pardon to a brother sinning against him even "seventy times sevenfold," he would then have commanded him to bind —that is, to retain — only such sins as may have been committed against the Lord, not against a brother. For forgiving sins committed against a human being constitutes a prior judgment against also remitting sins against God.

What, then, has this to do with the church, and especially your church, sensualist? For, in accordance with the person of Peter, it is to spiritual persons that this power will belong, either to an apostle or to a prophet. For the very church itself is, properly and principally, the Spirit himself, in whom is the Trinity of the one Divinity — Father, Son and Holy Spirit. The Spirit unites that church which the Lord has made to consist in "three." And thus, from that time forward, every number of persons who may have joined together in this faith is accounted "a church," from the Author and Consecrator of the church. And accordingly "the church," it is true, will forgive sins: but it will be the church of the Spirit, by means of a spiritual person; not the church which consists of a number of bishops. For right and judgment is the Lord's, not the servant's; God's himself, not the priest's.

Against Praxeas

> Commentary: In this late work, Tertullian defended the distinction of the three divine persons and developed an understanding of their unity. The deity is one principle (*monarchia*) of reality, but its operations (economy) manifest distinct elements. The Son and Spirit are here

united to the Father through their derivation from him. Tertullian did not here suppose that the three divine persons are coequal or coeternal.

Chapter 8.[9]... For God brought forth the Word, as also the Paraclete teaches, as a root brings forth the ground shoot, and a spring the river, and the sun its beam: for these manifestations also are projections of those substances from which they proceed. You need not hesitate to say that the shoot is son of the root and the river son of the spring and the beam son of the sun, for every source is a parent and everything that is brought forth from a source is its offspring — especially the Word of God, who also in an exact sense has received the name of Son. Yet the shoot is not shut off from the root nor the river from the spring nor the beam from the sun, any more than the Word is shut off from God. Therefore according to the precedent of these examples I profess that I say that God and his Word, the Father and his Son, are two: for the root and the shoot are two things, but conjoined; and the spring and the river are two manifestations, but undivided; and the sun and its beam are two aspects, but they cohere. Everything that proceeds from something must of necessity be another beside that from which it proceeds, but it is not for that reason separated from it. But where there is a second one there are two, and where there is a third there are three. For the Spirit is third with God and his Son, as the fruit out of the shoot is third from the root, and the irrigation canal out of the river third from the spring, and the illumination point out of the beam third from the sun: yet in no respect is he alienated from that origin from which he derives his proper attributes. In this way the Trinity, proceeding by intermingled and connected degrees from the Father, in no respect challenges the monarchy, while it conserves the quality of the economy.

Commentary: Tertullian proposed the person-substance language which Latin theology later adopted for trinitarian doctrine.

[9]Evans, 139-141; CCL 2, 1167-1168.

Chapter 25.[10] After Philip and the whole context of that question, [Jn 14:8] the things which follow down to the end of the Gospel continue in the same kind of discourse, in which the Father and the Son are distinguished as being each himself. He promises that when he has ascended to the Father he will also request of the Father the Paraclete, and will send him specifying "another." [Jn 14:16] But we have already explained in what sense he means "another." Moreover he says, "He will take of mine," [Jn 16:14] as I myself have taken of the Father's. So the close series of the Father in the Son and the Son in the Paraclete makes three who cohere, the one attached to the other. And these three are one thing, not one person, in the sense in which it was said, "I and the Father are one," [Jn 10:30] in respect of unity of substance, not of singularity of number.

Hippolytus (c. 170-235)

Hippolytus, probably Greek by birth and education, was an influential presbyter of the Roman Church in the first part of the third century. First he disagreed with Bishop Zephyrinus. When Zephyrinus' successor, Callistus, relaxed the church's penitential discipline to readmit adulterers and those involved in irregular marriages to communion, Hippolytus formed a schismatic community which upheld the earlier discipline. He may have been reconciled during the exile he shared with his Catholic counterpart, Pontianus, prior to their deaths about 235. He was honorably buried and regarded as a martyr of the Roman Church.

Hippolytus' *Refutation of All Heresies* details the errors of gnostic teachers and other forms of deviant Christianity, including that of Zephyrinus and Callistus. His *Apostolic Tradition* provides an early witness to the liturgy of the Roman Church, including the rites of baptism, eucharist

[10]Evans, 169; CCL 2, 1195.

and various ordinations. The Spirit is called down upon the church as guide and sanctifier in the prayers of these ceremonies. An identification of the divine Spirit as a person like the Father and Son is less evident than in the writings of Tertullian.

The Refutation of All Heresies

> Commentary: Hippolytus repeated the assertion that the Holy Spirit was given to the apostles and added that he was passed along by succession of office from them.

Preface, 5.[11] Now it seems expedient, even at the expense of a more protracted investigation, not to shrink from labor; for we shall leave behind us no small help to human life against the recurrence of error, when all are made to view, in a clear light, the clandestine rites of these people [gnostics], and the secret orgies which, keeping under their own control, they transmit to the initiated only. None will refute these, save the Holy Spirit who is given to the church. The apostles first received the Spirit and then transmitted it to those who have rightly believed. But we, as being their successors, and as participators in this grace, high-priesthood, and office of teaching, as well as being designated guardians of the church, must be found neither deficient in vigilance nor disposed to suppress correct doctrine. Laboring with every energy of body and soul we do not tire in our attempt to make a fitting return to our divine Benefactor. Yet we do not repay him in a becoming manner unless we are diligent in discharging the trust committed to us, careful to fulfill the measure of our particular opportunity, and to impart to all without grudging whatever the Holy Spirit supplies.

The Apostolic Tradition

> Commentary: This earliest ritual of ordination interprets the imposition of hands as a transmission of the Holy

[11]ANF 5, 10; GCS 26, 2.

Spirit and the bestowal of the spiritual gifts necessary for church office..Particularly important are the powers of ruling, of offering prayer and gifts, and of forgiving sins.

1.[12] We have duly completed what needed to be said about "Gifts," describing those gifts which God by his own counsel has bestowed on humans in offering to himself his own image which had gone astray. But now, moved by his love to all his saints, we pass on to our most important theme, "The Tradition," our teacher. And we address the churches, so that they who have been well trained, may by our instruction hold fast that tradition which has continued up to now and, knowing it well, may be strengthened. This is needful, because of that lapse or error which recently occurred through ignorance and because of ignorant persons. The Holy Spirit will supply perfect grace to those who believe rightly, that they may know how all things should be transmitted and kept by those who rule the church.

2. Let the bishop be ordained after he has been chosen by all the people. When he has been named and shall please all, let him, with the presbytery and such bishops as may be present, assemble with the people on a Sunday. While all give their consent, the bishops shall lay their hands upon him, and the presbytery shall stand by in silence. All indeed shall keep silent, praying in their heart for the descent of the Spirit. Then one of the bishops who are present shall, at the request of all, lay his hand on him who is ordained bishop, and shall pray as follows, saying:

3. God and Father of our Lord Jesus Christ, Father of mercies and God of all comfort, who dwells on high yet has respect for the lowly, who knows all things before they come to pass. You have appointed the borders of your church by the word of your grace, predestinating from the beginning the righteous race of Abraham. And making them princes and priests, and not leaving your sanctuary without a ministry, from the beginning of the world you have been well pleased to be glorified among those whom you have chosen.

[12]Easton, 33-35; LQF 39, 2-10.

Pour forth now that power, which is yours, of your royal Spirit [Ps 51:12], which you gave to your beloved servant Jesus Christ, which he bestowed on his holy apostles, who established the church in every place, the church which you have sanctified to unceasing glory and praise of your name. You who know the hearts of all, grant to this your servant, whom you have chosen to be bishop, to feed your holy flock and to serve as your high priest without blame, ministering night and day, to propitiate your countenance without ceasing and to offer to you the gifts of your holy church. And by the Spirit of high-priesthood to have authority to remit sins according to your precept, to loose every bond according to the authority which you gave to your apostles, and to please you in meekness and purity of heart, offering to you an odor of sweet savor. Through your Servant Jesus Christ our Lord, through whom be glory, might, honor to you with the Holy Spirit in the holy church, both now and always and world without end. Amen.

> Commentary: Hippolytus then described the eucharistic service. The Spirit is here associated with the birth of Christ from Mary. He is also called down upon the gifts that those who share them may participate in the Spirit.

4.[13] The bishop shall proceed:
We give thanks, O God, through your beloved Servant Jesus Christ, whom at the end of time you sent to us a Savior and Redeemer and the Messenger of your counsel. Who is your Word, inseparable from you; through whom you made all things and in whom you are well pleased. Whom you sent from heaven into the womb of the Virgin, and who, dwelling within her, was made flesh, and was manifested as your Son, being born of the Holy Spirit and the Virgin. Who, fulfilling your will, and winning for himself a holy people, spread out his hands when he came to suffer, that by his death he might set free those who believe in you. Who, when he was betrayed to his willing death, that he might bring death to

---

[13]Easton, 35-36; LQF 39, 12-16.

nought, and break the bonds of the devil, and tread hell under foot, and give light to the righteous, and set up a boundary post, and manifest his resurrection, taking bread and giving thanks to you said: Take, eat; this is my body, which is broken for you. And likewise also the cup, saying: This is my blood, which is shed for you. As often as you perform this, perform my memorial.

Having in memory, therefore, his death and resurrection, we offer to you the bread and the cup, giving you thanks, because you have counted us worthy to stand before you and to minister to you.

And we pray that you would send your Holy Spirit upon the offerings of your holy church; that, gathering them into one, you would grant to all your saints who partake to be filled with the Holy Spirit, that their faith may be confirmed in truth, that we may praise and glorify you. Through your Servant Jesus Christ, through whom be glory and honor to you, with the Holy Spirit in the holy church, both now and always and world without end. Amen.

> Commentary: In the ordination of a presbyter, the Spirit is invoked under the title of counsel for the church. The presbyter does not receive the power to forgive sins.

8.[14] But when a presbyter is ordained, the bishop shall lay his hand upon his head, while the presbyters touch him, and he shall say according to those things that were said above, as we have prescribed concerning the bishop, praying and saying:
God and Father of our Lord Jesus Christ, look upon this your servant, and grant him the Spirit of grace and counsel of a presbyter, that he may sustain and govern your people with a pure heart; as you looked upon your chosen people and commanded Moses to choose presbyters, whom you filled with your Spirit, which you gave to your servant. [Num 11:24-26] And now, O Lord, grant that the Spirit of your grace may be unfailingly preserved among us, and make us

---

[14]Easton, 37-38; LQF 39, 20-22.

worthy that, believing, we may minister to you in simplicity of heart, praising you. Through your Servant Jesus Christ, through whom be glory and honor to you with the Holy Spirit in the holy church, both now and always and world without end. Amen.

> Commentary: The bishop and presbyter are clearly distinguished by the former's power to ordain. The deacon receives the gift of service from the Spirit by the imposition of the bishop's hands.

9.[15] When the deacon is ordained, this is the reason why the bishop alone shall lay his hands upon him: he is not ordained to the priesthood but to serve the bishop and to carry out the bishop's commands. He does not take part in the council of the clergy; he is to attend to his own duties and to make known to the bishop such things as are needful. He does not receive that Spirit that is possessed by the presbytery, in which the presbyters share; he receives only what is confided in him under the bishop's authority.

For this cause the bishop alone shall make a deacon. But on a presbyter, however, the presbyters shall lay their hands because of the common and like Spirit of the clergy. Yet the presbyter has only the power to receive; but he has no power to give. For this reason a presbyter does not ordain the clergy; but at the ordination of a presbyter he seals while the bishop ordains.

Over a deacon, then, he shall say as follows:
O God, who has created all things and has ordered them by your Word, the Father of our Lord Jesus Christ, whom you sent to serve your will and to manifest to us your desire; grant the Holy Spirit of grace and care and diligence to this your servant, whom you have chosen to serve the church and to offer in your holy sanctuary the gifts that are offered to you by your appointed high priests, so that serving without blame and with a pure heart he may be counted worthy of this exalted office, by your goodwill, praising you continu-

---

[15]Easton, 38-39; LQF 39, 22-26.

ally. Through your Servant Jesus Christ, through whom be glory and honor to you, with the Holy Spirit, in the holy church, both now and always and world without end. Amen.

> Commentary: Hippolytus also described the ritual of initiation. In the baptismal creed, the Spirit is associated with the birth of Christ, the holiness of the church and the resurrection of the flesh.

21.[16] And when he who is being baptized goes down into the water, he who baptizes him, putting his hand on him, shall say thus:
Do you believe in God, the Father Almighty?
And he who is being baptized shall say:
I believe.
Then holding his hand placed on his head, he shall baptize him once. And then he shall say:
Do you believe in Christ Jesus, the Son of God, who was born of the Holy Spirit of the Virgin Mary, and was crucified under Pontius Pilate, and was dead and buried, and rose again the third day, alive from the dead, and ascended into heaven, and sat at the right hand of the Father, and will come to judge the living and the dead?
And when he says:
I believe,
he is baptized again. And again he shall say:
Do you believe in the Holy Spirit, and the holy church, and the resurrection of the flesh?
He who is being baptized shall say accordingly:
I believe,
and so he is baptized a third time.
And afterward, when he has come up out of the water, he is anointed by the presbyter with the oil of thanksgiving, the presbyter saying:
I anoint you with the holy oil in the name of Jesus Christ.
And so each one, after drying himself, is immediately clothed, and then is brought into the church.

[16]Easton, 46-48; LQF 39, 48-54.

Commentary: The baptized person is then formally received into the community by the imposition of hands. The bishop's prayer attributes the remission of sins to the operation of the Holy Spirit in baptism.

22. Then the bishop, laying his hand upon them, shall pray, saying: O Lord God, who made them worthy to obtain remission of sins through the laver of regeneration of the Holy Spirit, send into them your grace, that they may serve you according to your will; for yours is the glory, to the Father and the Son, with the Holy Spirit in the holy church, both now and world without end. Amen.
Then pouring the oil of thanksgiving from his hand and putting it on his forehead, he shall say:
I anoint you with holy oil in the Lord, the Father Almighty and Christ Jesus and the Holy Spirit.
And signing them on the forehead he shall say:
The Lord be with you;
and he who is signed shall say:
And with your spirit.
And so he shall do to each one.
And immediately thereafter they shall join in prayer with all the people, but they shall not pray with the faithful until all these things are completed. And at the close of their prayer they shall give the kiss of peace.

Teaching of the Apostles

The Teaching of the Apostles was written as an instruction in church order under the name of the twelve apostles in Syria during the first half of the third century. The author explained the discipline of the excommunication of sinners and the readmission of penitents by the imposition of hands. This conferral of the Spirit follows the remission of sins by baptism or by the works of repentance and admits a person to eucharistic fellowship.

Chapter 10: ii.39. [17] "As a heathen, then, and as a publican let

[17]Connolly, 103-104.

him be accounted by you" [Mt 18:17] who has been convicted of evil deeds and falsehood; and afterwards, if he
promise to repent — even as when the heathens desire and
promise to repent, and say "We believe," we receive them
into the congregation that they may hear the word, but do
not communicate with them until they receive the seal and
are fully initiated: so neither do we communicate with these
until they show the fruits of repentance. But let them by all
means come in, if they desire to hear the word, that they may
not wholly perish; but let them not communicate in prayer,
but go forth without. For they also, when they have seen
that they do not communicate with the church, will submit
themselves, and repent of their former works, and strive to
be received into the church for prayer; and they likewise
who see and hear them go forth like the heathen and publicans, will fear and take warning to themselves not to sin, lest
it so happen to them also, and being convicted of sin or
falsehood they be put forth from the church.

ii.41. And afterwards, as each one of them repents and
shows the fruits of repentance, receive him to prayer after
the manner of a heathen. And as you baptize a heathen and
then receive him, so also lay hands upon this person, while
all pray for him, and then bring him in and let him communicate with the church. For the imposition of hands shall be
to him in the place of baptism: for whether by the imposition
of hands, or by baptism, they receive the communication of
the Holy Spirit.

Origen (c. 185-254)

Origen was born of Christian parents in Alexandria
about 185. His father died a martyr in 202 and his mother is
said to have prevented Origen himself from following his
lead only by hiding his clothes so that he could not go out of
the house. On a journey to Rome in 212, he heard Hippolytus preach. Origen excelled as a student of both scripture
and philosophy. In the period from 218 through 230 he
engaged in teaching and writing in Alexandria. Difficulties
with his bishop arose out of an irregularity in his ordination

as presbyter and he settled at Caesarea in Palestine where he continued his work. He was tortured during the persecution of Decius in 250 and died later without regaining his health.

Little of Origen's immense literary output has survived because of his posthumous condemnation as a heretic at the Second Council of Constantinople in 553. Of the works used here, a part of the *Commentary on the Gospel of John* exists in Greek; except for fragments, *On First Principles* remains only in the adapted Latin version of Rufinus of Aquilea who tried to establish Origen's orthodoxy at the end of the fourth century by omitting or modifying offensive sections of his work.

In order to maintain the unity of God, Origen continued the earlier practice of subordinating the Son to the Father and the Spirit to the Son. Only the Father is fully God: the Son and Spirit are lesser divine beings. The Son is characterized as the Word of God who gives reason and truth to rational beings. The Spirit is the source of holiness in the saints and leads the believer to the right sense of scripture; as Paraclete he gives joy and comfort. Origen reflects both the basic orientation of the Logos theology and the growing awareness of the role of the Spirit in the church.

On First Principles

> Commentary: The three divine persons are distinguished by the realms over which they exercise dominion. The Father gives being; the Son supplies reason and knowledge; the Spirit sanctifies. The work of the divine persons prepares for the reception of Christ. Through this participation in Christ, a person actually advances in holiness. Although Origen links the work of the Spirit and the mission of Christ, he does not assert that Christ sends the Spirit.

Book 1, Chapter 3. 5.[18] . . . The God and Father who holds the universe together is superior to every being that exists,

---

[18]Butterworth, 33-34; SC 252, 152.

for he imparts to each one from his own existence that which each one is; the Son, being less than the Father, is superior to rational creatures alone (for he is second to the Father); the Holy Spirit is still less and dwells within the saints alone. So that in this way the power of the Father is greater than that of the Son and of the Holy Spirit, and that of the Son is more than that of the Holy Spirit, and in turn the power of the Holy Spirit exceeds that of every other holy being.

8.[19] ... God the Father bestows the gift of existence on all; and a participation in Christ, in virtue of his being the Word or Reason, makes them rational. From this it follows that they are worthy of praise or blame, because they are capable alike of virtue and of wickedness. Accordingly there is also available the grace of the Holy Spirit, that those beings who are not holy in essence may be made holy by participating in this grace. When therefore they obtain first of all their existence from God the Father, and secondly their rational nature from the Word, and thirdly their holiness from the Holy Spirit, they become capable of receiving Christ afresh in his character of the righteousness of God, those, that is, who have been previously sanctified through the Holy Spirit. And such as have been deemed worthy of advancing to this degree through the sanctification of the Holy Spirit obtain in addition the gift of wisdom by the power of the working of God's Spirit. This is what I think Paul means when he says that "to some is given the word of wisdom, to others the word of knowledge, by the same Spirit." [1 Cor 12:8] And while pointing out the distinction of each separate gift he refers them all to the fount of the universe when he says, "There are diversities of workings, but one God, who works all things in all." [1 Cor 12:6]

Thus the working of the Father, which endows all with existence, is found to be more glorious and splendid, when each one, through participation in Christ in his character of wisdom and knowledge and sanctification, advances and comes to higher degrees of perfection. And when a person, by being sanctified through participation in the Holy Spirit,

[19]Butterworth, 38-39; SC 252, 162-164.

is made purer and holier, he becomes more worthy to
receive the grace of wisdom and knowledge, in order that all
stains of pollution and ignorance may be purged and
removed and that he may make so great an advance in
holiness and purity that the life which he received from God
shall be such as is worthy of God, who gave it to be pure and
perfect, and that that which exists shall be as worthy as he
who caused it to exist. Thus, too, the person who is such as
God who made him wished him to be, shall receive from
God the power to exist forever and to endure for eternity.
That this may come to pass, and that those who were made
by God may be unceasingly and inseparably present with
him who really exists, it is the work of Wisdom to instruct
and train them, and lead them on to perfection, by the
strengthening and unceasing sanctification of the Holy
Spirit, through which alone they can receive God.

> Commentary: Irenaeus, Tertullian and Hippolytus relied
> on the Spirit for an accurate interpretation of the histori-
> cal meaning of scripture against the allegorical interpre-
> tations of the gnostics. Origen assigned to the Spirit the
> revelation of the true allegorical significance of the scrip-
> tural text which gnostics failed to find. By explaining the
> way God governs the world, the Spirit consoles the
> faithful.

Book 2, Chapter 7. 2.[20] . . . Through the grace of the Holy
Spirit, then, along with the many other results, this most
splendid fact is revealed, that whereas the truths written in
the Prophets and the Law of Moses were formerly understood by very few, namely by the prophets alone, and there
was scarcely anywhere one out of the whole people who
could get beyond the literal meaning and perceive something greater, that is, could detect a spiritual sense in the
Law and Prophets, now there are innumerable multitudes
of believers, almost all of whom, although unable to explain
logically and clearly the process of their spiritual percep-

[20]Butterworth, 119; SC 252, 328-330.

tion, have the firm conviction that circumcision ought not to be understood literally, nor the Sabbath rest, nor the pouring out of an animal's blood, nor the fact that oracles were given by God to Moses on these points; and there is no doubt that this discernment is suggested to them all by the power of the Holy Spirit.

4. But the Paraclete, who is called the Holy Spirit, is so called from his work of "consolation"; for anyone who has been deemed worthy to partake of the Holy Spirit, when he has learned his unspeakable mysteries, undoubtedly obtains consolation and gladness of heart. Since by the Spirit's guidance he has come to know the reasons for all things that happen, and why and how they happen, his soul can never be in any way disquieted, or admit any feeling of sadness; nor is it in anything affrighted, for it clings to God's Word and Wisdom and "in the Holy Spirit calls Jesus Lord." [1 Cor 12:3]

Commentary on John

> Commentary: The analysis of the origin of the Holy Spirit proceeded through a listing of alternatives: that all the divine persons are equal, that they are not distinct, that the Spirit is made through the Word. Origen chose the last hypothesis, giving the Father alone the privilege of being the source. The Spirit derives from the Father through the Son. He applies the gifts of God to the saints.

Book 2, Chapter 10.[21] . . . Now if, as we have seen, all things were made through him [the Word], we have to enquire if the Holy Spirit also was made through him. It appears to me that those who hold the Holy Spirit to be created, and who also admit that "all things were made through him," must necessarily assume that the Holy Spirit was made through the Logos, the Logos accordingly being older than he. And he who refuses to admit that the Holy Spirit was made through Christ must, if he admits the truth of the statements

---

[21]ANF 9, 328-329; SC 120, 252-256.

of this Gospel, assume the Spirit to be uncreated. There is a third resource besides these two (that of allowing the Spirit to have been made by the Word, and that of regarding it as uncreated), namely, to assert that the Holy Spirit has no essence of his own beyond the Father and the Son. But on further thought one may perhaps see a reason to consider that the Son is second beside the Father, being the same as the Father. Yet a distinction is manifestly drawn between the Spirit and the Son in the passage, "Whoever shall speak a word against the Son of Man, it shall be forgiven him, but whoever shall blaspheme against the Holy Spirit, he shall not have forgiveness, either in this world or in the world to come." [Mt 12:32] We consider, therefore, that there are three hypostases: the Father and the Son and the Holy Spirit. At the same time we believe nothing to be uncreated but the Father. We therefore, as the more pious and the truer course, admit that all things were made by the Logos, and that the Holy Spirit is the most excellent and the first in order of all that was made by the Father through Christ. And this, perhaps, is the reason why the Spirit is not said to be God's own Son. The Only-begotten alone is by nature, and from the beginning, a Son, and the Holy Spirit seems to have need of the Son, to provide him with his essence, so as to enable him not only to exist, but to be wise and reasonable and just, and all that we must think of him as being. All this he has by participation of the character of Christ, of which we have spoken above. And I consider that the Holy Spirit supplies the material of the gifts which come from God to those who, through him and through participation in him, are called saints. Thus this material of the gifts is made powerful by God, is ministered by Christ, and owes its actual existence in humans to the Holy Spirit. I am led to this view of the charisms by the words of Paul which he writes somewhere, "There are diversities of gifts but the same Spirit, and diversities of ministries but the same Lord. And there are diversities of operations, but it is the same God that works all in all." [1 Cor 12:4-6]

> Commentary: To explain why the Spirit sent the Son into the world, Origen asserted that the Spirit was himself unequal to the task of effecting salvation. The Spirit joined the Son in his work by descending on Christ and remaining with him.

Book 2, Chapter 11.[22] When we find the Lord saying, as he does in Isaiah, [cf., Is 48:16] that he is sent by the Father and by his Spirit, we have to point out here also that the Spirit is not originally superior to the Savior. The Savior takes a lower place in order to carry out the plan which had been made that the Son of God should become human. Should any one balk at our saying that the Savior in becoming human was made lower than the Holy Spirit, we ask him to consider the words used in the Epistle to the Hebrews, where Jesus is shown by Paul to have been made less than the angels on account of the suffering of death. "We behold him," he says, "who has been made a little lower than the angels, Jesus, because of the suffering of death, crowned with glory and honor." [Heb 2:9] And this must certainly be added, in order to be delivered from the bondage of corruption, the creation and especially the human race, required the introduction into human nature of a blessed and divine power, which should set right what was wrong upon the earth. This action fell to the part, as it were, of the Holy Spirit. But the Spirit, unable to accomplish such a task, puts forward the Savior as the only one able to endure such a conflict. The Father, therefore, the principal, sends the Son, but the Holy Spirit also sends him and directs him to go before, promising to descend, when the time comes, upon the Son of God, and to work with him for the salvation of humanity. This he did, when, in a bodily shape like a dove, he flew to him after the baptism. He remained on him, and did not pass him by, as he might have done with humans unable to bear his glory continuously. Thus John, when explaining how he knew who Christ was, spoke not only of the descent of the Spirit on Jesus, but also of its remaining upon him. For it is written that John said, "He who sent me to baptize said, 'He

[22]ANF 9,329; SC 120, 258-262.

on whom you shall see the Spirit descending and remaining, that is he who baptizes with the Holy Spirit and with fire.'" [Jn 1:32,33] It is not said only, "He on whom you shall see the Spirit descending," since the Spirit no doubt descended on others too, but "descending and remaining." Our examination of this point has been somewhat extended, since we were anxious to make it clear that if all things were made by him, then the Spirit also was made through the Word, and is seen to be one of the "all things" which are inferior to their maker. This view is too firmly settled to be disturbed by a few words which may be adduced to the opposite effect.

Novatian (d. 258)

Novatian was a Roman presbyter who served as spokesman of the presbyters who governed that church after Bishop Fabian had been martyred in the Decian persecution in 249. When Cornelius was elected bishop after the persecution, Novatian joined a splinter party and was consecrated its bishop. This group refused to accept the policy which was agreed upon by the Catholic bishops of allowing those who failed during the persecution to be readmitted to communion after performing penance. Novatian insisted on rebaptizing those who came over to him from Cornelius' communion, thus implying that this church had lost the Holy Spirit by its lax discipline. Novatian himself died a martyr in 258.

In his *Treatise on the Trinity*, written before these events, Novatian described the roles of the Spirit who strengthened and enlightened the apostles and perfects the church by the gifts he bestows. Further, he listed the works of the Spirit in individual Christians and attributed to him the triumph of both martyrs and virgins.

Treatise Concerning the Trinity
Chapter 29.[23] Next, well-ordered reason and the authority of our faith bid us (in the words and the writings of our Lord set down in orderly fashion) to believe, after these things,

[23]FC 67, 99-104; CCL 4, 69-72.

also in the Holy Spirit, who was in times past promised to the church, and duly bestowed at the appointed, favorable moment. He was indeed promised by the Prophet Joel but bestowed through Christ. "In the last days," says the prophet, "I will pour out from my spirit upon my servants and handmaids." [Jl 2:28] And the Lord said, "Receive the Holy Spirit; whose sins you shall forgive, they are forgiven; and whose sins you shall retain, they are retained." [Jn 20:22-23] Now Christ the Lord sometimes calls the Holy Spirit the Paraclete and at other times proclaims him to be the Spirit of Truth. [Jn 14:16-17, 15:26] He is not new in the gospel, nor has he been given in a novel way. For it was he who in the prophets reproved the people and in the apostles gave an invitation to the gentiles. The former deserved to be reproved because they disregarded the law, and those of the gentiles who believe deserve to be assisted by the patronage of the Spirit, because they ardently desire to attain to the law of the gospel. There are, undoubtedly, different kinds of functions in him, since different times have different kinds of needs; yet he who acts thus is not different on that account. Nor is he someone else because he acts so; rather he is the selfsame one, distributing his functions according to the times, conditions, and circumstances of human events. Accordingly the Apostle Paul says, "Since we have the same Spirit, as shown in that which is written, 'I believed, and so I spoke,' we also believe and so we speak." [2 Cor 4:13]

> Commentary: Novatian used a catalogue of scriptural references to the Spirit in expanding the explanation of his operations in the church and the individual Christian.

Therefore, it is one and the same Spirit who is in the prophets and in the apostles. He was, however, in the former only for awhile; whereas he abides in the latter forever. In other words, he is in the prophets but not to remain always in them, in the apostles that he might abide in them forever. He has been apportioned to the former in moderation, to the latter, he has been wholly poured out; he was sparingly given to the one, upon the other, lavishly bestowed. He was not, however, manifested before the Lord's resurrection but conferred by Christ's resurrection. In fact, Christ said, "I will ask the Father and he will give you another Advocate that he may be with you forever, the Spirit of Truth;" [Jn 14:16-17] and, "When the Advocate has come whom I will send you from my Father, the Spirit of Truth, who proceeds from my Father;" [Jn 15:26] and, "If I do not go, the Advocate will not come to you; but if I go, I will send him to you;" [Jn 16:7] and, "when the Spirit of Truth has come, he will guide you to all truth." [Jn 16:13] Since the Lord was about to go to heaven, he had to give the Paraclete to his disciples, that he might not leave them as orphans, [Jn 14:18] as it were, and abandon them without a defender or some sort of guardian. That would not have been proper at all.

It is he who strengthened their hearts and minds, who clearly brought out for them the mysteries of the gospel, who was within them the enlightener of divine things; through strength given by him they feared neither bonds nor imprisonment for the sake of the Lord's name. Yes, they even trampled underfoot the very powers and torments of the world, because they were already armed and fortified through him and possessed within themselves the gifts which the same Spirit distributes and consigns, as if they were ornaments, to the church, the Bride of Christ. In fact, it is he who places prophets in the church, instructs teachers, bestows the gift of tongues, effects cures and miracles, does wondrous deeds, grants the power of discerning spirits, confers the power of administration, suggests what decisions should be made, and sets in order and arranges whatever charismatic gifts there are. Thus, he makes the church of the Lord perfect and complete in every respect and in every detail.

He it is who came upon the Lord as a dove after he had been baptized, and abode in him. [Mt 3:16] In Christ alone he dwells fully and entirely, not lacking in any measure or part, but in all his overflowing abundance dispensed and sent forth, so that other humans might receive from Christ a first outpouring, as it were, of his graces. For the fountain-head of the entire Holy Spirit abides in Christ, that from him might be drawn streams of grace and wondrous deeds because the Holy Spirit dwells affluently in Christ. In fact, Isaiah prophesied this when he said, "And the Spirit of wisdom and of understanding rests upon him, the Spirit of counsel and might, the Spirit of knowledge and piety, and the Spirit of the fear of the Lord has filled him." [Is 11:2] He reiterated the very same thing in another passage in the person of the Lord himself, "The Spirit of the Lord is upon me, because he has anointed me; to bring good news to the poor he has sent me." [Is 61:1] Likewise David says, "Therefore God, your God, has anointed you with oil of gladness above your fellow kings." [Ps 45:8] The Apostle Paul says of him, "For he who does not have the Spirit of Christ, he does not belong to Christ;" [Rom 8:9] and, "where the Spirit of the Lord is, there is freedom." [2 Cor 3:17]

He it is who effects from water a second birth, the seed, as it were, of a divine generation. He is also the consecrator of a heavenly birth, "the pledge" of a promised "inheritance," [Eph 1:14] a kind of written bond, so to speak, of eternal salvation. He it is who makes us the temple of God and makes us his dwelling place. He importunes the divine ears "on our behalf with ineffable groanings," thereby discharging his duties as Advocate and rendering his services in our defense. He has been given to dwell in our bodies and to bring about our sanctification. He brings our bodies, by this operation of his in us, to eternity and to the resurrection of immortality, inasmuch as he accustoms them to be mingled in himself with celestial power and to be associated with the divine eternity of his Holy Spirit. For in him and through him, our bodies are trained to advance to immortality, learning to bridle themselves with moderation according to his commands. For it is he who lusts against the flesh, because the flesh is contrary to him. [Gal 5:17] It is he who checks insatiable desires, breaks unbridled lust, quenches illicit passions, overcomes fiery assaults, averts drunkenness, resists avarice, drives away wanton revelries, binds together noble loves, strengthens good affections, does away with factions, explains the Rule of Truth, refutes heretics, banishes the impious and guards the Gospels.

Of him the Apostle likewise writes, "Now we have received not the spirit of the world, but the Spirit that is from God." [1 Cor 2:12] Of him he exults when he says, "But I think that I also have the Spirit of God." [1 Cor 7:40] Of him he says, "And the Spirit of the prophets is under the control of the prophets." [1 Cor 14:32] Of him he states, "Now the Spirit expressly says that in later times some will depart from the faith, giving heed to deceitful spirits and doctrines of devils, speaking lies hypocritically, and having their conscience seared." [1 Tim 4:1-2] Grounded in this Spirit "no one" ever "says 'Anathema' to Jesus;" [1 Cor 12:3] no one has denied that Christ is the Son of God, nor has rejected God the Creator; no one utters any words against the scriptures; no one lays down alien and sacrilegious ordinances; no one makes contradictory laws. Whoever "shall have blasphemed" against him, "does not have forgiveness, either in this world or in the world to come." [Mt 12:32] It is he who in the apostles renders testimony to Christ, in the martyrs manifests the unwavering faith of religion, in virgins encloses the admirable continence of sealed chastity. In the other people, he keeps the laws of the Lord's teaching uncorrupted and untainted. He destroys heretics, corrects those in error, reproves unbelievers, reveals impostors, and also corrects the wicked. He keeps the church uncorrupted and inviolate in the holiness of perpetual virginity and truth.

Cyprian (d. 258)

Cyprian was a rhetorician converted to Christianity in Carthage in 246. Nourished on a diet of scripture and the writings of Tertullian, he quickly became prominent in his community and was chosen its bishop only two years later. When the Decian persecution broke out, he went into hiding and directed his church through letters. He was an energetic leader and asserted the right of the bishop to judge the cases of those who denied the faith, opposing some of the martyrs and confessors who claimed for themselves the power to grant readmission to the peace of the church without requiring penance of the lapsed. After the persecution, he joined in the moderate policy of the Roman bishop, Cornelius, which was opposed both by these laxists and by Novatian's rigorist party which refused to readmit any lapsed. Cyprian was at odds with Cornelius' successor, Stephen, on the question of the validity of a baptism administered by schismatics, in this case, Novatian. He and Stephen engaged in a bitter exchange which was terminated only by their martyrdoms, Stephen's in 257 and Cyprian's the following year.

In dealing with the Novatian's rigorous schism, Cyprian argued that only bishops who were legitimately ordained in succession from the apostles and remain in the one church had the Holy Spirit. The members of this world-wide communion of bishops have the power to forgive sins, to confer the Holy Spirit by imposing hands, and to sanctify the church. The forgiveness of sins through the one church which has the Holy Spirit was an article of his creed. Cyprian's theology effectively locked the sanctifying power of the Holy Spirit into the one Catholic communion and located it in the person of the bishop. The "church of the Spirit" and the "spirituals" which Tertullian found only in Montanism were identified by Cyprian with a church constituted by the communion of bishops succeeding to the college of apostles and holding the Spirit as a common possession.

Epistle 10: To the Martyrs and Confessors

> Commentary: Cyprian asserted that the Holy Spirit spoke in the martyr when he was questioned and prophesied the victory.

3.[24] He who once conquered death for us always conquers it in us. "But when they deliver you up," he says, "do not be anxious what you are to speak; for what you are to speak will be given you in that hour. For it is not you who are speaking, but the Spirit of your Father who speaks through you." [Mt 10:19-20]

[24]FC 51, 26; CSEL 3.2, 492.

The present conflict has furnished proof of the matter. A voice filled with the Holy Spirit broke forth from the lips of the martyr when the most blessed Mappalicus said to the proconsul in the midst of his torments, "Tomorrow you will see the combat." And what he spoke with the testimony of virtue and faith the Lord fulfilled. A celestial struggle took place and the servant of God was crowned in the contest of the promised combat. This is the struggle which the Prophet Isaiah foretold of old saying, "It is not a weak contest for you with humans, since God assures the combat." [Is 7:13] And that he might show what this struggle would be, he added, saying, "Behold a virgin shall conceive in the womb, and bear a son, and you shall name him Emmanuel." [Is 7:14] This is the struggle of our faith in which we contend, in which we conquer, in which we are crowned.

Epistle 57: To Cornelius, Bishop of Rome

> Commentary: The Holy Spirit warned Cyprian of an approaching struggle. The bishops, who had the gifts of Tertullian's spiritual person, should heed the advice and grant the church's peace to all who are doing penance for their earlier failure.

5.[25] Lest, then, the sheep entrusted to us by the Lord be demanded back from our mouth by which we refuse peace, by which we respond with the severity of human cruelty rather than that of divine and fatherly love, it has seemed best to us, from the suggestion of the Holy Spirit and the warning of the Lord through many and clear visions, because the enemy is announced and shown to be threatening us, to assemble the soldiers of Christ within the camp and, after the case of each has been examined, to give peace to the lapsed, nay rather, to supply arms to those about to fight. We believe that this will please you also in the contemplation of the mercy of the Father.

But if any one of our colleagues remains who thinks that

[25]FC 51, 161-162; CSEL 3.2, 655-656.

peace should not be given to our brothers and sisters when the struggle is imminent, he will render an account in the day of judgment to the Lord either for his distressing censure or for his inhuman harshness. Because it was fitting to faith and love and solicitude, we made known those things which were in our conscience. The day of battle had approached; the violent enemy was pressing upon us quickly; the battle came not such as it was before, but more serious and graver by far. This was shown frequently to us by divine warnings; concerning this we were frequently admonished by the providence and mercy of the Lord. With his help and goodness, we who trust in him can be safe because he who in peace announces that there will be combat for his soldiers will give the victory to those fighting in union. We trust that you, dearly beloved Brother, are always well.

Epistle 73: To Bishop Jubaianus of Mauretania

> Commentary: Cyprian asserted that the Holy Spirit, the power to forgive sins, was given first to Peter and then to the other apostles. Only their successors established within the church can exercise this power.

7.[26] But it is clear when and through whom the remission of sins can be given, which is certainly given in baptism. For the Lord first gave to Peter, upon whom he built the church and whence he instituted and showed the origin of unity, that same power that what he had absolved upon earth might be absolved. And after the resurrection, he also speaks to the apostles, saying, "As the Father has sent me, I also send you." When he had said this, he breathed upon them and said to them, "Receive the Holy Spirit; whose sins you shall forgive, they are forgiven him and whose you shall retain, they are retained." [Jn 20:21-23] Whence we know that only in the church with prelates established by evangelical law and the ordination of the Lord is it lawful to baptize and to give the remission of sins; but, outside, nothing can

[26]FC 51, 272-273; CSEL 3.2, 783-784.

be either bound or absolved where there is no one who can either bind or absolve.

Epistle 74: To Bishop Pompey

> Commentary: Some Catholic bishops objected that the name of Jesus was adequate for baptism even outside the church. Cyprian replied that Christ, the Holy Spirit, the church and baptism could not be separated.

5.[27] Or if they assign the efficacy of baptism to the majesty of the name so that they who are baptized in the name of Jesus Christ, anywhere and in any way it may be, are considered renewed and sanctified, why, in the name of the same Christ, are not hands imposed upon the baptized there for him to receive the Holy Spirit? Why does not the same majesty of the same name which they contend was valid for the sanctification of baptism prevail for the imposition of hands? For, if he who was born outside the church can be made a temple of God, why cannot the Holy Spirit also be infused into the temple; for whoever, after his sins have been made manifest, has been sanctified in baptism and reformed spiritually to the new person has become fit to receive the Holy Spirit since the Apostle says, "As many soever of you as have been baptized into Christ, have put on Christ? [Gal 3:27].

He who, baptized among the heretics, can put on Christ, can much more receive the Holy Spirit whom Christ sent. Otherwise, he who has been sent will be greater than he who sends, that the one baptized outside should, indeed, begin to have put on Christ, but should not have been able to receive the Holy Spirit, as if either Christ could be put on without the Spirit or the Spirit separated from Christ. It is also stupid for them to say that, although the second nativity, by which we are born in Christ through the washing of regeneration, is spiritual, anyone can be born spiritually among the heretics where they say the Spirit is not. For water alone cannot cleanse sins and sanctify a person unless he also has the Holy Spirit. Wherefore, it is necessary either for them to

[27]FC 51, 288-289; CSEL 3.2, 802-803.

concede that the Spirit is there where they say there is baptism or that there is no baptism where the Spirit is not because there can be no baptism without the Spirit.

Treatise on Rebaptism

The *Treatise on Rebaptism* is an anonymous defense of the Roman position on heretical baptism which attacks an unnamed opponent of this policy, who may well have been Cyprian. This purpose and approach offer evidence that the treatise was written in the second half of the third century.

The author distinguished baptism of water, of blood, and of Spirit. He accepted the assertion that the Holy Spirit cannot be found among heretics or schismatics and he taught that neither baptism of water nor of blood is salvific outside the church. Within the Catholic church, the salvific baptism of the Spirit may precede, accompany or follow water baptism and may be given in martyrdom without any water baptism or imposition of episcopal hands.

Chapter 10.[28] . . . Our salvation is accomplished in baptism of the Spirit which is usually joined to the baptism of water. Hence when the baptism is given by one of us [bishops], let it be done fully and solemnly, with all that is prescribed and the omission of nothing. If through urgency it is given by a minor cleric, let us attend to the consequences, that it may be completed by us, or reserved for the Lord himself to complete. If, as can happen, it is given by someone outside the church, let it be corrected so that the person can be admitted. The Holy Spirit is not present outside the church. Nor is faith sound among either heretics or those in schism. Hence those who do penance, and are corrected through the teaching of truth and through their faith once it is restored by the purification of their hearts, should be strengthened only by spiritual baptism — the imposition of the bishop's hand and the conferral of the Holy Spirit. The church customarily confers the sign of true faith in this way lest we seem to despise the invocation of the name of Jesus which

[28]Trans. J.P. Burns; CSEL 3.3, 82.

itself cannot be removed. Although this invocation will accomplish salvation only if it is followed by the further action we have specified, still it must not be despised. The one baptism which the Apostle asserts is efficacious through the persevering invocation of the name of Jesus which no one can take away once it is invoked. Thus we would act against the decree of the apostles in daring to repeat this invocation out of an excessive care to supply, even to repeat, baptism. If someone who returned to the church refused to be baptized again, we would actually deprive him of spiritual baptism by our concern to prevent his being deprived of water baptism.

> Commentary: Three forms of baptism, each of which may confer the Spirit, are distinguished. The Holy Spirit has shown that he cannot be bound and limited, as Cyprian had asserted, but moves as he wills. The Spirit can even come upon a person without any water baptism.

Chapter 15.[29] We have distinguished three types of spiritual baptism, let us offer evidence for the explanation we have given, lest we seem to propose only a private and unfounded opinion. John instructs us when he says of our Lord in his Epistle, "This is he who came by water and blood, Jesus Christ, not with the water only but with the water and the blood. And the Spirit is the witness, because the Spirit is the truth. There are three witnesses, the Spirit, the water, and the blood; and these three agree. [1 Jn 5:6-8] From this we infer that water usually gives the Spirit and a person's own blood gives the Spirit and the Spirit himself gives the Spirit. As water or blood is poured out, so the Spirit is poured by the Lord over all who believe. Hence people can be baptized by water, and also by their own blood, and finally by the Holy Spirit. Thus Peter says, "but this is what was spoken by the prophet, 'And in the last days it shall be, God declares, that I will pour out my Spirit upon all flesh, and your sons and your daughters shall prophesy,

[29]CSEL 3.3, 87-89.

and your young men shall see visions, and your old men shall dream dreams; yes, and on my men servants and my maid-servants in those days I will pour out my Spirit.'" [Acts 2:16-18] In the Old Testament we see that this Spirit was imparted not generally or abundantly, but to some. Either he was communicated to some, or he came down upon certain individuals, or invested them, or was upon them. Thus we notice that the Lord said to Moses about the seventy elders, "I will take some of the Spirit which is upon you and put it upon them." [Num 11:17] Thus according to this promise, God put upon them some of the Spirit which was upon Moses and they prophesied in the camp. As a spiritual person, Moses rejoiced in this development. But he was persuaded by Joshua, the son of Nun, to forbid it, although he was himself unwilling. Thus it stopped. Further, in the Book of Judges and similarly in the Book of Kings, we see that the Spirit of the Lord was upon, or came upon, many: Othniel, Gideon, Jephthah, Samson, Saul, David and others. The Lord teaches us that the Spirit comes upon them freely and by his own decision, "the Spirit blows where he will. You hear its sound but do not know whence it comes or whither it goes." [Jn 3:8] Thus the Spirit is found occasionally even upon those who are unworthy of him, not without cause or intent, but for some necessary purpose. Thus he came upon Saul and he prophesied. Later, however, after the Spirit of the Lord had departed from him and an evil spirit from the Lord tortured him, Saul sent messengers to find David and then himself followed in order to kill him. At that point they all came upon a group of prophets, began to prophesy, and were thus prevented from accomplishing their plan. We believe that the Spirit who was upon them caused this, according to God's marvellous purpose and intention. [1 Sam 19:20-24] This Spirit filled John the Baptist even from his mother's womb [Lk 1:41] and rested on those who were with the centurion Cornelius even before they were baptized with water. [Acts 10:44-48]

The Spirit is joined to human baptism, either preceding or following it, or when the water baptism is supplemented he reposes on those who believe. Thus he directs us either to give baptism with the full ritual, or to supplement it when it has been given in the name of Jesus Christ by someone else. We should do this, as we have argued, by preserving the most holy invocation of the name of Jesus Christ and observing as well the custom and authority of so many ages and persons which claim our reverence.

Concluding Reflections

Christian writers of the third century continued to utilize a subordinationist viewpoint in discussing the divine persons. The Father was regarded as the source of all reality, the principle whence all being derives. The Son and Spirit are first in a procession or emanation which subsequently brings forth angels, humans and the whole material world. Unlike all else, however, the Son and Spirit belong to the divine realm as the Father's agents in the operations of creation, governance, salvation, and sanctification. They are distinct personifications of the Father's own reality, his Word and Wisdom.

The Son and Spirit are united to the Father and to one another by their derivation and their sharing in the divine operation. Similarly, they are distinguished from one another by their peculiar roles in that economy. In this context, the Spirit was identified through his peculiar effects, all of them associated with the Christian community. The Spirit was credited with teaching, sanctification and discipline in the church.

Tertullian and Hippolytus followed Irenaeus in claiming that the Spirit sent upon the church by Christ maintains the fidelity of its preaching to the gospel of Christ. The Spirit directs a reading of the scriptures according to the clear meaning expressed in the Rule of Faith and rejects the more elaborate interpretation of the gnostics. Origen, on the other hand, claimed the Spirit as guide in searching the scriptures for their deeper meaning, the allegorical readings which transcend the historical narrative.

The Spirit was particularly recognized as the source of the church's power to sanctify. The Spirit forgives sins in baptism. Through the imposition of the bishop's hands, he descends upon the newly baptized and the repentant sinner to join them to the eucharistic fellowship. In the prayers of ordination, the Spirit is called down upon the officers of the church, asked to empower and guide them.

His role as sanctifier gave the Spirit a special authority in the discipline of the church. All recognized that a certain purity must be maintained within the community. Tertullian, Hippolytus and Novatian asserted that the traditional community had failed to meet that standard of purity in one way or another and had thereby lost the sanctifying power of the Spirit. While Hippolytus and Novatian established rival episcopates, Tertullian challenged the validity of church office, of the church of the bishops. He preferred the spiritual ascetic whose authority and sanctifying power rested on obedience to the dictates of the Paraclete rather than on succession from the apostles. Cyprian subsequently met Tertullian's challenge by displaying some of the gifts of prophecy and vision, claiming the guidance of the Spirit in his disciplinary decisions. In theory, however, he insisted on the communion of bishops, the succession to the apostolic college, as the seat of the Holy Spirit within the church.

The more significant challenge to the authority of the bishops and their claim to maintain and transmit the Holy Spirit in the Christian communities came from the confessors and martyrs. Their combat was inspired by the Spirit. By his presence they claimed the right to forgive sins and readmit the fallen to the communion of the church. Cyprian was most successful in both recognizing the work of the Spirit in the martyrs and asserting the bishop's authority over the power of sanctification.

Finally, the *Treatise on Rebaptism* disputed the Cyprianic claims which restricted the Holy Spirit to the church and the sacramental action to her officers. The Spirit moves where he will.

Although the role of the Spirit as sanctifier was central to

the fourth-century discussions of his divinity, the disciplinary issues and his restriction to the bishops in the church
were not fully discussed and settled until the beginning of
the fifth century in Augustine's reply to the Donatists.

Chapter Three

ADORED AND HONORED:
THE FOURTH CENTURY

Introduction

The fourth century was a time of great turmoil and theological debate in the church. The century began with a certain calm, but the deceptive air of unanimity was soon shattered by the Arian controversy and the long and complex struggle to arrive at an articulation of the basic doctrine of the Trinity. The problem was somehow to reconcile the divinity of the Son and of the Spirit with the unity of God. Sabellianism and Arianism offered two clear solutions to the problem, but the church repeatedly rejected them as distortions of the gospel message.

Modalism or Sabellianism affirmed that God revealed himself successively in three different ways or modes that were not distinct. Ultimately, then, it denied any plurality or distinction in God. The more systematic form of this doctrine arose in the third century, but it remained a recurring temptation throughout the fourth century, especially in the Western Church.

Arius was a priest in Alexandria who came into prominence around 318. He affirmed the absolute uniqueness and transcendence of God, whom he recognized as the unoriginate source of all reality. The essence of the Godhead could in no way be shared or communicated, so the pre-existent Word who became flesh was a creature, created out of nothing by the Father. Though the Son was far above all other creatures, he was not of the same substance as the Father and was not co-eternal with him. As a creature, he had a beginning.

Arius was condemned at the Council of Nicea called by Emperor Constantine in 325 in the hope of keeping unity in the Empire. Nicea imposed a creed to be accepted by all. It affirmed that the Son was of the substance of the Father, consubstantial (*homoousios*). Unfortunately, the Council did not immediately resolve the Arian question. The fifty years after the Council were filled with confusion and bitter dispute about the meaning and the orthodoxy of the term *homoousios* that had been applied to the Son.

During those years the question of the Spirit became more central. Nicea had restricted itself to one line on the Spirit: "We believe in the Holy Spirit." Arius and his followers in fact had denied the divinity of the Spirit, but the discussion in the first half of the fourth century centered on the Son, so there was no need to affirm anything explicit about the Spirit. Even as late as 348, Cyril of Jerusalem, though discussing at length the functions of the Spirit, expressed reluctance to raise the question of the divinity and personality of the Spirit. Only in the second half of the century, in response to a recurring denial of the Spirit's divinity, did Athanasius write the first real treatise on the Spirit in which he defended the consubstantiality of the Spirit with the Father and the Son. The subsequent discussion in the East was to help clarify the *homoousion* doctrine in regard to the Son as well as the Spirit and to lead to a doctrine of the Trinity that balanced the unity of the Godhead with the distinction of persons.

The central figures in this further discussion were the Cappadocians — Basil, Gregory of Nazianzus, and Gregory of Nyssa. They struggled against the Pneumatomachians (Spirit-fighters) who denied the full deity of the Spirit. The

Pneumatomachians were also called Macedonians, after the Semi-Arian bishop of Constantinople, but there is no evidence that he had any connection with them. The Cappadocians also attempted to distinguish the Spirit from the Father and the Son in terms of origin and mutual relations. Since the Father was considered to be without origin and the source of the Son and the Spirit, the problem was to differentiate between the mode of origin of the Son and of the Spirit.

Finally, at the Council of Constantinople in 381 and the local Council of Rome in 382, the full divinity of the Spirit and his existence as a distinct hypostasis were asserted. After almost four centuries, the church had formulated an answer to the question of the equality of the Spirit and his distinct existence.

The fourth century Fathers also continued the discussion of the Spirit's role in sanctification. They professed that the Spirit dwells in the soul and makes Christians sharers in the divine nature. The Spirit is the source of rebirth and the giver of life in baptism. The Spirit, then, must be divine: if he is not, he cannot make us sharers in God's nature.

The Writings

Cyril of Jerusalem (c. 315-386)

Cyril became bishop of Jerusalem in about 348. He is best known for his twenty-four catechetical lectures which were probably delivered shortly after he became bishop. These consist of an introductory discourse, eighteen lectures given during Lent to the candidates for baptism at Easter, and five instructions addressed to the newly baptized during Easter week. Cyril spoke more as a pastor than as a theologian. He was reluctant to go beyond Scripture and to engage in metaphysical discussion. For this reason, he cautioned against curious inquiry into the nature of the Spirit. He did speak, however, of the Spirit as sharing in the Father's Godhead and as being glorified with the Father and the Son.

He discoursed at greater length on the work of the Spirit. The Spirit is the sanctifier and deifier who seals the soul at baptism and dwells in its inmost recesses. He is the giver of many, varied gifts and graces, and comes to save, to teach, to strengthen, to enlighten.

Catechetical Lectures

> Commentary: These passages deal primarily with Cyril's ideas on the unity and nature of the Spirit. Cyril was hesitant to say more about the Spirit than is given in the Scriptures.

Lecture 16.2.[1] ... Let us then speak concerning the Holy Spirit only what is written. If something is not written, let us not be concerned about it. The Holy Spirit himself spoke the Scriptures. He has thus spoken concerning himself as much as he pleased, or as much as we could receive. Let us therefore say those things which he said; for whatsoever he has not said, we dare not say.
3. There is only one Holy Spirit, the Comforter. As there is one God the Father, and no second Father; and as there is one Only-begotten Son and Word of God, who has no brother; so is there only one Holy Spirit, and no second spirit equal in honor to him. Now the Holy Spirit is a power most mighty, a being divine and unsearchable. He is living and intelligent, a sanctifying principle of all things made by God through Christ. He illumines the souls of the just; he was in the prophets; he was also in the apostles in the New Testament. Despise those who dare to separate the operation of the Holy Spirit. There is one God, the Father, Lord of the Old and of the New Testament; and one Lord, Jesus Christ, who was foretold in the Old Testament and came in the New; and one Holy Spirit, who through the prophets preached of Christ, and when Christ was come, descended, and manifested him.

[1]NPNF 2.7, 115; PG 33, 919.

> Commentary: Cyril used the image of water to speak of the unity of the Spirit and the diversity of his activity and his gifts.

12.[2] Why did he [Christ] call the grace of the Spirit water? Because by water all things subsist; because water brings forth grass and living things; because the water of the showers comes down from heaven; because it comes down in one form, but works in many forms. For one fountain waters the whole of Paradise, and one and the same rain comes down upon all the world. Yet it becomes white in the lily, red in the rose, purple in violets and hyacinths, different and varied in each species. It is one in the palm tree, another in the vine, and all in all things. Yet it is one in nature, not different from itself. The rain does not change itself to come down first as one thing and then as another. It adapts itself to the constitution of each thing which receives it and becomes what is suitable to each. Thus also the Holy Spirit, being one and of one nature and indivisible, divides his grace to each, "according as he will." [1 Cor 12:11] As the dry tree, after partaking of water, puts forth shoots, so also the soul in sin, when it has been made worthy of the Holy Spirit through repentance, brings forth clusters of righteousness. Though he is one in nature, yet he works many virtues by the will of God and in the name of Christ. He employs the tongue of one person for wisdom; the soul of another he enlightens by prophecy; to another he gives power to drive away devils; to another he gives interpretation of the divine scriptures. He strengthens one person's self-control; he teaches another the way to give alms; another he teaches to fast and discipline himself; another he teaches to despise the things of the body; another he trains for martyrdom; he is diverse in different persons, yet not diverse from himself.

> Commentary: Cyril went on to contrast the work of the devil and the work of the Spirit. He gave an almost lyrical description of how the Spirit comes to enlighten the soul.

[2]NPNF 2.7, 118; PG 33, 932-933.

15.[3] ... For this name of spirit is common to many things; every thing which does not have a solid body is in a general way called spirit. Since, therefore, the devils have no such bodies, they are called spirits; but there is a great difference. The unclean devil, when he comes upon a person's soul (may the Lord deliver from him every soul of those who hear me and of those who are not present), he comes like a wolf upon a sheep, thirsting for blood, and ready to devour. His coming is most fierce; it feels most oppressive; the mind is darkened. His attack is an injustice, as is his usurpation of another's possession.... The devils are truly enemies of humans, treating them in a foul and merciless way.

16. Such is not the Holy Spirit. God forbid! For his doings tend the contrary way, towards what is good and salutary. First, his coming is gentle; the awareness of him is fragrant; his burden is most light; beams of light and knowledge shine forth before his coming. He comes with the kindness of a true guardian. For he comes to save and to heal, to teach, to admonish, to strengthen, to exhort, to enlighten the mind, first of the one who receives him and afterwards of others through him. As a person who has been in darkness and suddenly beholds the sun is enlightened in his bodily sight and plainly sees things which he had not seen, similarly one to whom the Holy Spirit is given is enlightened in his soul and sees things beyond human sight, which he had not known; his body is on earth, yet his soul mirrors the heavens.

Commentary: The following passages deal with the Spirit in baptism.

Lecture 17.13.[4] ... On the day of Pentecost, I say, they [the apostles] were sitting, and the Comforter came down from heaven, the guardian and sanctifier of the church, the ruler of souls, the pilot of the tempest-tossed, who leads the

---

[3]NPNF 2.7, 119; PG 33, 940-941.
[4]NPNF 2.7, 127-128; PG 33, 985.

wanderers to the light, presides over the combatants, and crowns the victors.

14. He came down to clothe the apostles with power and to baptize them, for the Lord says, "You shall be baptized with the Holy Spirit not many days hence." [Acts 1:5] This grace was not partial; his power was in full perfection. For as one who plunges into the waters and is baptized is surrounded on all sides by the waters, so were they baptized completely by the Holy Spirit. The water flows round the outside only, but the Spirit baptizes also the soul within, and that completely. Why do you wonder? Take an example from matter, poor indeed and common, yet useful for the simpler sort. If the fire passing in through the mass of the iron makes the whole of it fire so that what was cold becomes burning and what was black is made bright, if fire which is a body thus penetrates and works without hindrance in iron which is also a body, why are you amazed that the Holy Spirit enters into the very inmost recesses of the soul?

> Commentary: The next passage speaks of the Spirit sealing the soul. Cyril also pointed out the need for faith to receive the Spirit.

35.[5] ... Approach the minister of baptism, but as you approach, think not of the face of him you see, but remember this Holy Spirit of whom we are now speaking. For he is present in readiness to seal your soul, and he shall give you that seal at which evil spirits tremble, a heavenly and sacred seal.

* * *

36. Yet he tests the soul. He does not cast his pearls before swine. If you play the hypocrite, though a human minister may baptize you now, the Holy Spirit will not baptize you. If you approach with faith, however, though humans serve in what is seen, the Holy Spirit bestows what is unseen.

[5]NPNF 2.7, 132; PG 33, 1009.

Commentary: Finally, the Christian in baptism is
anointed with the Holy Spirit as Christ was, so that the
Christian shares in the divine nature. The ointment is a
symbol of the Spirit that sanctifies the soul.

Lecture 21.2.[6] . . . Christ was not anointed by humans with
oil or material ointment. The Father had already appointed
him to be Savior of the whole world, anointed him with the
Holy Spirit. . . . As Christ was in reality crucified, buried,
and raised, and you are in baptism accounted worthy of
being crucified, buried, and raised together with him in a
likeness, so it is with the anointing also. As he was anointed
with an ideal oil of gladness, that is, with the Holy Spirit,
who is called oil of gladness because he is the author of
spiritual gladness, so you were anointed with ointment,
having been made partakers and fellows of Christ.
3. Beware of supposing this to be ordinary ointment. For as
the bread of the eucharist, after the invocation of the Holy
Spirit, is no longer mere bread, but the Body of Christ, so
also after the invocation this holy ointment is no longer
simple or ordinary ointment. It is Christ's gift of grace. By
the advent of the Holy Spirit, it is made fit to impart his
divine nature. This ointment is symbolically applied to your
forehead and your other senses; while your body is anointed
with the visible ointment, your soul is sanctified by the holy
and life-giving Spirit.

Athanasius (c. 295-373)

Athanasius was born about 295 in Alexandria. In 319 he
was ordained a deacon by his bishop Alexander. In 325 he
accompanied Alexander to the Council of Nicea and there
began his struggle with the Arians and his lifelong defense of
the Nicene faith. In 328 he succeeded Alexander as bishop of
Alexandria. He was exiled five times from his episcopal see
because of the Arians who recognized him as their greatest
opponent. Though he is usually associated with the defense

[6]NPNF 2.7, 149-150; PG 33, 1089-1092.

of the consubstantiality of the Son, he also made a significant contribution to the theology of the Spirit.

In his *Letters Concerning the Holy Spirit* in 359, Athanasius, in response to Bishop Serapion, composed the first real
treatise on the Holy Spirit. The purpose of the letters was to
refute the Tropici, probably a local Egyptian group, who
denied the divinity of the Spirit. The Tropici were so named
because they interpreted in a tropical, i.e., metaphorical,
sense those passages from Scripture opposed to their doctrine. Originally Arians, the Tropici now differed from the
Arians in accepting the divinity of the Son. Like the Arians,
however, they continued to deny the divinity of the Spirit,
since it was not part of the Nicene definition. They thought
the Spirit was a creature, or, more precisely, an angel,
superior to other angels but to be classified among the
"ministering spirits." The Spirit was, then, "other in substance" from the Father and the Son.

In the letters, Athanasius argued that the Spirit has
nothing in common with creatures. He belongs to the eternal and indivisible Triad. Since it would not be possible to
include a creature in this Triad, the Spirit must be consubstantial. Further, Athanasius argued from the divinity of the
Son to the divinity of the Spirit, showing how the Spirit
belongs in essence to the Son who is consubstantial with the
Father and showing how the Spirit is the principle of
Christ's life within us. Finally, Athanasius argued that the
Spirit must be divine since through the Spirit we become
sharers in the divine nature.

The following selection from Athanasius is taken from
the first letter to Serapion. The letter is quoted at some
length to show the style and logic of Athanasius' defense of
the Spirit.

To Serapion

> Commentary: In these first two paragraphs, Athanasius
> argued that the position of the Tropici is inconsistent
> because in rejecting the divinity of the Spirit, they in fact
> reject the divinity of the Son. He also sets forth two of his

basic arguments. First, that the Spirit has the same one-ness with the Son as the Son has with the Father. Secondly, God is a Triad that cannot contain creator and creature and thus the Spirit must be of the same nature as the Father and the Son.

1.[7] Your sacred Kindness's letter was delivered to me in the desert. Though the persecution directed against us was indeed bitter, and a great search made by those who sought to slay us, yet "the Father of mercies and God of all com-fort" [2 Cor 1:3] used even this letter to comfort us. As I remembered Your Kindness and all my friends, I imagined that you were with me at that moment. I was indeed very glad to have your letter. But when I read it, I began again to be despondent because of those who once before set them-selves to make war against the truth. You write, beloved and truly longed for, yourself also in distress, that certain per-sons, having forsaken the Arians on account of their blas-phemy against the Son of God, yet oppose the Holy Spirit, saying that he is not only a creature, but actually one of the ministering spirits, and differs from the angels only in degree. In this they pretend to be fighting against the Arians; in reality they are controverting the holy faith...

2. To the Arians indeed this way of thinking is not strange. Having once denied the Word of God, they naturally say the same evil things against his Spirit. Therefore it is not neces-sary to say anything more in reply to them; what has pre-viously been said against them is sufficient. But it is right that, in some way (as they themselves would say!) we should make a careful reply to those who have been deceived about the Spirit. We might well wonder at their folly, inasmuch as they will not have the Son of God to be a creature — indeed, their views on this are quite sound! How then have they endured so much as to hear the Spirit of the Son called a creature? Because of the oneness of the Word with the Father, they will not have the Son belong to things origi-nated, but rightly regard him as Creator of things that are

[7]Shapland, 58-65; PG 26, 529-533.

made. Why then do they say that the Holy Spirit is a creature, who has the same oneness with the Son as the Son with the Father? Why have they not understood that, just as by not dividing the Son from the Father they ensure that God is one, so by dividing the Spirit from the Word they no longer ensure that the Godhead in the Triad is one, for they tear it asunder, and mix with it a nature foreign to it and of a different kind, and put it on a level with the creatures? On this showing, once again the Triad is no longer one but is compounded of two differing natures; for the Spirit, as they have imagined, is essentially different. What doctrine of God is this, which compounds him out of creator and creature? Either he is not a Triad, but a dyad, with the creature left over. Or, if he be Triad — as indeed he is! —then how do they class the Spirit who belongs to the Triad with the creatures which come after the Triad? For this, once more, is to divide and dissolve the Triad. Therefore, while thinking falsely of the Holy Spirit, they do not think truly even of the Son. For if they thought correctly of the Word, they would think soundly of the Spirit also, who proceeds from the Father, and, belonging to the Son, is from him given to the disciples and all who believe in him. Nor, erring thus, do they so much as keep sound their faith in the Father. For those who "resist the Spirit," as the great martyr Stephen said, deny also the Son. [Acts 7:51] But those who deny the Son have not the Father.

> Commentary: In paragraphs 3 through 18, which are not contained here, Athanasius criticized the Tropicist exegesis of several texts of Scripture and then showed the absurdity and the impertinence of their argument that the Spirit, if not a creature, must be a son. He then resumed the basic argument of the letter. In paragraphs 19 through 21, part of which follows, he affirmed the basic unity of the Triad and described how the activity of the Son is accomplished in the Spirit who is the image of the Son.

20.[8] ... As the Son is an only-begotten offspring, so also the Spirit, being given and sent from the Son, is himself one and not many, nor one from among many, but Only Spirit. As the Son, the living Word, is one, so must the vital activity and gift whereby he sanctifies and enlightens be one perfect and complete. This is said to proceed from the Father, because it is from the Word, who is confessed to be from the Father, that it shines forth, and is sent and is given. The Son is sent from the Father; for he says, "God so loved the world that he gave his only begotten Son."[Jn 3:16] The Son sends the Spirit; "If I go away," he says, "I will send the Paraclete." [Jn 16:7] The Son glorifies the Father, saying, "Father, I have glorified you." [Jn 17:4] The Spirit glorifies the Son; for he says, "He shall glorify me." [Jn 16:14] The Son says, "The things I heard from the Father speak I unto the world." [Jn 8:26] The Spirit takes of the Son; "He shall take of mine" he says, "and shall declare it unto you."[Jn 16:14] The Son came in the name of the Father. "The Holy Spirit," says the Son, "whom the Father will send in my name." [Jn 14:26] 21. But if, in regard to order and nature, the Spirit bears the same relation to the Son as the Son to the Father, will not he who calls the Spirit a creature necessarily hold the same to be true also of the Son? For if the Spirit is a creature of the Son, it will be consistent for them to say that the Word is a creature of the Father. By holding such opinions the Arians have fallen into the Judaism of Caiaphas. But if those who say such things about the Spirit claim that they do not hold the opinions of Arius, let them avoid his words and keep from impiety toward the Spirit. For as the Son, who is in the Father and the Father in him, is not a creature but pertains to the essence of the Father (for this you also profess to say); so also it is not lawful to rank with the creatures the Spirit who is in the Son, and the Son in him, nor to divide him from the Word and reduce the Triad to imperfection.

Commentary: Athanasius drew a sharp contrast between the Spirit and creatures. Creatures are sanctified and

[8]Shapland, 116-133; PG 26, 577-593.

anointed and sealed by the Spirit. By contrast, the Spirit is from God. He is the source of holiness and sanctification, the unction and the seal.

22. ... For if, as no one knows the things of God except the Spirit who is in him, would it not be evil speech to call the Spirit who is in God a creature, who searches even the deep things of God? For from this the speaker will learn to say that the human spirit is outside the person himself, and that the Word of God, who is in the Father, is a creature.

Again, the Spirit is, and is called, Spirit of holiness and renewal. For Paul writes, "Declared to be the Son of God with power, according to the Spirit of holiness, by the resurrection of the dead; even Jesus Christ our Lord."[Rom 1:4] Again he says, "But you were sanctified, but you were justified in the name of our Lord Jesus Christ and in the Spirit of our God."[1 Cor 6:11] And when writing to Titus, he said, "But when the kindness of God our Savior and his love toward humanity appeared, not by works done in righteousness which we did ourselves, but according to his mercy he saved us, through the washing of regeneration and renewing of the Holy Spirit which he poured out upon us richly through Jesus Christ our Savior, that being justified by his grace, we might be made heirs, according to the hope of eternal life." [Tit 3:4-7] But the creatures are sanctified and renewed: "You shall send forth your Spirit, and they shall be created, and you shall renew the face of the earth." [Ps 104:30] And Paul says, "It is impossible for those who were once enlightened and tasted of the heavenly gift, and were made partakers of the Holy Spirit,..." [Heb 6:4]

23. He, therefore, who is not sanctified by another, nor a partaker of sanctification, but who is himself partaken, and in whom all the creatures are sanctified, how can he be one from among all things or pertain to those who partake of him? For those who say this must say that the Son, through whom all things came to be, is one from among all things.

He is called a life-giving Spirit. For it says, "He that raised up Christ from the dead shall give life also to your mortal bodies through his Spirit that dwells in you." [Rom 8:11]

The Lord is the very life, [Acts 3:15] and "author of life," as Peter put it. And as the Lord said himself, "The water that I shall give him shall become in him a well of water springing up into eternal life. . . .[Jn 4:14] But this he spoke concerning the Spirit which they that believed in him were to receive." [Jn 7:39] But the creatures, as has been said, are given life through him. He who does not partake of life, but is himself partaken and gives life to the creatures, what kinship can he have with things originated? How can he belong to the creatures which in him are given life from the Word?

The Spirit is called unction and he is seal. For John writes, "As for you, the unction which you received of him abides in you, and you do not need anyone to teach you, but his unction — his Spirit — teaches you concerning all things." [1 Jn 2:27] In the Prophet Isaiah it is written, "The Spirit of the Lord is upon me, because the Lord has anointed me."[Is 61:1] Paul says, "In whom having also believed, you were sealed for the day of redemption." [Eph 4:30] But the creatures are sealed and anointed and instructed in all things by him. If the Spirit is the unction and seal with which the Word anoints and seals all things, what likeness or similarity could the unction and the seal have to the things that are anointed and sealed? Thus by this consideration also he could not belong to the "all things." The seal could not be from among the things that are sealed, nor the unction from among the things that are anointed; it pertains to the Word who anoints and seals. For the unction has the fragrance and odor of him who anoints; and those who are anointed say, when they receive of it, "We are the fragrance of Christ." [2 Cor 2:15] The seal has the form of Christ who seals, and those who are sealed partake of it, being conformed to it, as the Apostle says, "My little children, for whom I am again in travail until Christ be formed in you."[Gal 4:19] Being thus sealed, we are duly made, as Peter put it, "sharers in the divine nature."[2 Pet 1:4] Thus all creation partakes of the Word in the Spirit.

Commentary: Athanasius argued that the Spirit makes us

sharers in the divine nature and thus the Spirit must be divine. Further, as image of the Son, the Spirit cannot be a creature unless the Son is also a creature.

24. Further it is through the Spirit that we are all said to be partakers of God. For it says, "Know you not that you are a temple of God and that the Spirit of God dwells in you? If any one destroys the temple of God, God shall destroy him; for the temple of God is holy, which temple you are." [1 Cor 3:16-17] If the Holy Spirit were a creature, we should have no participation of God in him. If indeed we were joined to a creature, we should be strangers to the divine nature inasmuch as we did not partake therein. But, as it is, the fact of our being called partakers of Christ and partakers of God shows that the unction and seal that is in us belongs, not to the nature of things originate, but to the nature of the Son who, through the Spirit who is in him, joins us to the Father. This John taught us, as is said above, when he wrote, "Hereby we know that we abide in God and he in us, when he has given us of his Spirit." [1 Jn 4:13] But if, by participation in the Spirit, we are made "sharers in the divine nature," we would be mad to say that the Spirit has a created nature and not the nature of God. For it is on this account that those in whom he is are made divine. If he makes humans divine, it is not to be doubted that his nature is of God.

Yet more clearly, for the destruction of this heresy, the Psalmist sings, as we have said before, in the one hundred and third psalm, "You shall take away the Spirit, and they shall die and return to their dust. You shall put forth your Spirit, and they shall be created, and you shall renew the face of the earth." [Ps 104:29-30] And Paul wrote to Titus, "Through the washing of regeneration and renewing of the Holy Spirit, which he poured out upon us richly through Jesus Christ...." [Tit 3:5-6] But if the Father, through the Word, in the Holy Spirit, creates and renews all things, what likeness or kinship is there between the Creator and the creatures? How could he possibly be a creature, in whom all things are created? Such evil speech leads on to blasphemy against the Son; so that those who say the Spirit is a creature say also that the Word is a creature, through whom all things are created.

The Spirit is said to be, and is, the image of the Son. For, "Whom he foreknew, he also foreordained to be conformed to the image of his Son." If then they admit that the Son is not a creature, neither may his image be a creature. For as is the image, so also must he be whose image it is. Hence the Word is justly and fitly confessed not to be a creature, because he is the image of the Father. He therefore who counts the Spirit with the creatures will surely count the Son among them also, and thereby will speak evil of the Father as well, by speaking evil against his image.

> Commentary: In the next paragraph, Athanasius spoke of the relation between the Son and the Spirit and creation. The Spirit bestows divine life and sonship on creation.

25. The Spirit, therefore, is distinct from the creatures, and is shown rather to be proper to the Son and not alien from God. As for that wise question of theirs, "If the Spirit is from God, why is he not himself called son?", already, in what precedes, we have shown it rash and presumptuous, and we show it no less so now. Even though he is not called Son in the scriptures, but Spirit of God, he is said to be in God himself and from God himself, as the Apostle wrote. And if the Son, because he is of the Father, is proper to his essence, it must be that the Spirit, who is said to be from God, is in essence proper to the Son. And so, as the Lord is Son, the Spirit is called Spirit of sonship. Again, as the Son is Wisdom and Truth, the Spirit is described as Spirit of Wisdom and Truth. Again the Son is the Power of God and Lord of Glory, and the Spirit is called Spirit of Power and of Glory. So scripture refers to each of them. Paul wrote to the Corinthians, "Had they known, they would not have crucified the Lord of glory." [1 Cor 2:8] And, elsewhere, "For you received not the spirit of bondage again to fear, but you received the Spirit of adoption." [Rom 8:15] Again, "God sent forth the Spirit of his Son into your hearts crying, Abba

Father." [Gal 4:6] Peter wrote, "If you are reproached for the name of Christ, blessed are you; because the Spirit of glory and of power rests upon you." [1 Pet 4:14] The Lord called the Spirit, "Spirit of truth" and "Paraclete"; whence he shows that the Triad is in him complete. In him the Word makes glorious the creation, and, by bestowing upon it divine life and sonship, draws it to the Father. But that which joins creation to the Word cannot belong to the creatures; and that which bestows sonship upon the creation could not be alien from the Son. For we should have otherwise to seek another spirit, so that by him this Spirit might be joined to the Word. But that would be absurd. The Spirit, therefore, does not belong to things originated; he pertains to the Godhead of the Father, and in him the Word makes things originated divine. But he in whom creation is made divine cannot be outside the Godhead of the Father.

> Commentary: In paragraphs 26 and 27, Athanasius again contrasted the Spirit and creatures. The Spirit is incapable of change and is present in all things. Creatures are changeable and bound to one place. Creatures partake of the Spirit; the Spirit is partaken.

26. That the Spirit is above the creation, distinct in nature from things originated, and proper to the Godhead, can be seen from the following consideration also. The Holy Spirit is incapable of change and alteration. For it says, "The Holy Spirit of discipline will flee deceit and will start away from thoughts that are without understanding." [Wis 1:5] And Peter says, "In the incorruptibility of the meek and quiet Spirit." [1 Pet 3:4] Again, in Wisdom, "Your incorruptible Spirit is in all things." [Wis 12:1] And if "no one knows the things of God save the Spirit of God which is in him," [1 Cor 2:11] and, as James said, in God "there is no variation nor shadow that is cast by turning" [Jas 1:17] — the Holy Spirit, being in God, must be incapable of change, variation, and corruption. But the nature of things originated and of things created is capable of change, inasmuch as it is outside the essence of God, and came into existence from that which is

not. For it says, "Every man is a liar," [Ps 116:11] and, "All have sinned and come short of the glory of God." [Rom 3:23] "And angels which kept not their own principality, but left their proper habitation, he has kept in everlasting bonds under darkness unto the judgement of the great day." [Jude 6] In Job, "If he puts no trust in his holy angels...and against his angels he imputes evil...and the stars are not pure in his sight." [Job 15:15, 4:18, 25:5] Paul writes, "Know you not that we shall judge angels? How much more things that pertain to this life?" [1 Cor 6:3] We have heard too that the devil, who was "between the cherubim" and was "the seal of the likeness," fell "as lightning from heaven." But if, while creatures are by nature capable of change, and such things are written about angels, the Spirit is the same and unalterable; if he shares the immutability of the Son, with him abiding ever unchangeable — what likeness can there be between the unchangeable and the things that change? It will be clear that he is not a creature, nor does he belong in essence to the angels, for they are changeable, but he is the image of the Word and pertains to the Father.

Again, the Spirit of the Lord fills the universe. Thus David sings, "Whither shall I go from your Spirit?" [Ps 139:7] Again, in Wisdom it is written, "Your incorruptible Spirit is in all things." [Wis 12:1] But things originated are all in places apportioned to them: sun, moon, and stars in the firmament, clouds in the air. For humans he has "set the bounds of the peoples." [Dt 32:8] The angels are "sent forth" [Heb 1:14] for ministries. "And the angels came to stand before the face of the Lord," [Job 1:6] as it is written in Job. And Jacob the patriarch dreamed, "And behold! A ladder set up on the earth, and the top of it reached to heaven; and the angels of God ascended and descended upon it." [Gen 28:12] But if the Spirit fills all things, and if the angels, being his inferiors, are circumscribed, and where they are sent forth, there are they present; it is not to be doubted that the Spirit does not belong to things originated, nor is he an angel at all, as you say, but by nature is above the angels. 27. From what follows, also, we may see how the Holy Spirit is partaken and does not partake. (We must not mind repeating ourselves.) For, "It is impossible," it says, "for those who were once enlightened and tasted of the heavenly gift, and were made partakers of the Holy Spirit, and tasted the good Word of God...." " The angels and the other creatures partake of the Spirit himself; hence they can fall away from him whom they partake. But the Spirit is always the same; he does not belong to those who partake, but all things partake of him. But if he is always the same and always partaken; and if the creatures partake of him — the Holy Spirit can neither be an angel nor a creature of any kind, but proper to the Word. And being given by the Word, he is partaken by the creatures. For they would have to say that the Son is a creature, of whom we are all made partakers in the Spirit.

Again, the Holy Spirit is one, but the creatures are many. For the angels are "thousand thousand" and "ten thousand times ten thousand," and there are many lights and thrones and lordships and heavens and cherubim and seraphim and many archangels. In a word, creatures are not one but, taking all together, many and diverse. But if the Holy Spirit is one, and the creatures many and angels many — what likeness can there be between the Spirit and things originate? It is obvious that the Spirit does not belong to the many nor is he an angel. But because he is one, and, still more, because he is proper to the Word who is one, he is proper to God who is one, and one in essence with him.

These sayings concerning the Holy Spirit, by themselves alone, show that in nature and essence he has nothing in common with or proper to creatures, but is distinct from things originate, proper to, and not alien from, the Godhead and essence of the Son; in virtue of which essence and nature he is of the Holy Triad, and puts their stupidity to shame.

Synod of Alexandria, 362

Athanasius wrote his *Letters to Serapion* while in exile from his diocese because of the Arian controversy. When he was allowed to return under the new emperor Julian in 362, he set about reconciling the Arians and the orthodox party. He held a synod at Alexandria in 362. The assembled bishops addressed a letter to the Church of Antioch that is preserved among the works of Athanasius. Among other things, it sets down the conditions on which communion should be granted to those Arians who wished to re-unite: an affirmation of the Nicene faith, a condemnation of Arianism, and a rejection of the doctrine that the Spirit is a creature. The letter provides, then, a statement of a synod on the divinity of the Spirit, almost twenty years before the Council of Constantinople.

Tome or Synodal Letter to the People of Antioch

3.[9] As many then as desire peace with us . . . and those again who are seceding from the Arians, call to yourselves, and receive them as parents their children, and welcome them as tutors and guardians; and unite them to our beloved Paulinus and his people, without requiring more from them than to anathematize the Arian heresy and confess the faith confessed by the holy fathers at Nicea, and to anathematize also those who say that the Holy Spirit is a creature and separate from the essence of Christ. For this is in truth a complete renunciation of the abominable heresy of the Arians, to refuse to divide the Holy Trinity, or to say that any part of it is a creature. For those who, while pretending to cite the faith confessed at Nicea, venture to blaspheme the Holy Spirit, do nothing more than in words deny the Arian heresy while they retain it in thought.

> Commentary: The letter also affirms the orthodoxy of those who say there are three hypostases in God and those who say there is only one, recognizing that it is merely a difference of terminology. With reference to those who speak of three hypostases, the bishops accept as orthodox their trinitarian statement, including an affirmation of the consubstantiality of the Spirit with the Father and the Son.

5. . . . . We asked them, "What then do you mean by it, or why

[9]NPNF 2.4, 483-484; PG 26, 797-801.

do you use such expressions [three hypostases]?" They replied that it was because they believed in a Holy Trinity, not a trinity in name only, but existing and subsisting in truth, "Both a Father truly existing and subsisting, and a Son truly substantial and subsisting, and a Holy Spirit subsisting and really existing do we acknowledge." Neither had they said there were three Gods or three beginnings, nor would they at all tolerate such as said or held this. They acknowledged a Holy Trinity but one Godhead, and one Beginning, and that the Son is coessential with the Father, as the fathers said. The Holy Spirit is not a creature, nor external, but proper to and inseparable from the essence of the Father and the Son.

Hilary of Poitiers (c. 315-367)

Hilary was born about 315 and converted from Neoplatonism as an adult. About 353 he became bishop of Poitiers but was sent into exile in Phrygia (modern Turkey) in 356 because of his outspoken opposition to Arianism. During this four-year exile he composed the twelve books of his *On the Trinity*. Before his death in 367 he had gained a reputation as the leading Latin theologian of his age.

Hilary proved the consubstantiality of the Father and Son by showing that they hold the one divine nature and operation in common. He then distinguished the Holy Spirit from this divine nature which is itself spiritual and holy. The Holy Spirit is characterized as the Gift of God because of his work in the faithful. The divinity of the Spirit is then proven by the independence of his work in creatures, which is subject to no limits, and by his searching the depths of God.

On the Trinity

> Commentary: In paragraph 29, Hilary dismissed those who deny the existence of the Spirit. As is clear from scripture, the Spirit exists and is joined with the Father and the Son. The Spirit is God's gift to the faithful, a gift given and possessed.

Book 2.29.[10] Concerning the Holy Spirit, I should not be silent, and yet I have no need to speak. Still, for the sake of those who are ignorant, I cannot refrain. There is no need to speak, because we are bound to confess him, proceeding as he does from Father and Son. For my own part, I consider it wrong to discuss the question of his existence. He does exist, since he is given, received, retained. He is joined with Father and Son in our confession of the faith, and cannot be excluded from a true confession of Father and Son. Take away a part, and the whole faith is marred. If anyone demands what meaning we attach to this conclusion, he, as well as we, has read the words of the Apostle, "Because you are children of God, God has sent the Spirit of his Son into our hearts, crying Abba, Father," [Gal 4:6] and "Grieve not the Holy Spirit of God, in whom you have been sealed," [Eph 4:30] and again, "But we have received not the spirit of this world, but the Spirit which is of God, that we may know the things given unto us by God," [1 Cor 2:12] and also, "You are not in the flesh but in the Spirit, if the Spirit of God is in you. If anyone has not the Spirit of Christ, he is not his," [Rom 8:9] and further, "If the Spirit of him that raised up Jesus from the dead dwells in you, he that raised up Christ from the dead shall give life to your mortal bodies as well for the sake of his Spirit which dwells in you." [Rom 8:11] Therefore since he is, and is given, and is possessed, and is of God, let those who deny him take refuge in silence. They ask, "Through whom is he? To what end does he exist? Of what nature is he?" We answer that he it is through whom all things exist and from whom are all things, and that he is the Spirit of God, God's gift to the faithful. If our answer displease them, their displeasure must also fall upon the apostles and the prophets, who spoke of him exactly as we have spoken. And furthermore, the Father and Son must incur the same displeasure.

Commentary: Hilary exhorted his reader to seek and

[10]NPNF 2.9, 60; PL 10, 69-70.

> make use of the gift of the Spirit that is offered to all and is
> given according to the measure of the desire to receive it.

35.[11] Let us therefore make use of this great benefit, and seek for personal experience of this most needful Gift. For the Apostle says, in words I have already cited, "We have not received the spirit of this world, but the Spirit which is of God, that we may know the things that are given to us by God." [1 Cor 2:12] We receive him, then, that we may know. Faculties of the human body, if denied their exercise, will lie dormant. The eye without light, natural or artificial, cannot fulfil its task; the ear will be ignorant of its function unless some voice or sound is heard; the nostrils unconscious of their purpose unless some scent is breathed. Not that the faculty will be absent, because it is never called into use, but that there will be no experience of its existence. So, too, the human soul, unless through faith it has appropriated the Gift of the Spirit, will have the innate faculty of apprehending God, but will be destitute of the light of knowledge. That Gift, which is in Christ, is one, yet offered, and offered fully, to all. It is denied to none and given to each according to the measure of his willingness to receive. Its stores are the richer, the more earnest the desire to earn them. This Gift is with us to the end of the world, the solace of our waiting, the assurance, by the favors which he bestows, of the hope that shall be ours, the light of our minds, the sun of our souls. This Holy Spirit we must seek and must earn, and then hold fast by faith and obedience to the commands of God.

> Commentary: Hilary ended his book with a prayer to the Father. In the two paragraphs given here, he professed his belief that the Spirit subsists eternally and dwells in the Father. Though his intellect cannot comprehend it, he believed that the Spirit is from the Father through the Son.

Book 12.55.[12] But for my part, I cannot be content by the

---

[11]NPNF 2.9, 61; PL 74-75.
[12]NPNF 2.9, 233; PL 10, 468-471.

service of my faith and voice, to deny that my Lord and my God, Your Only-begotten, Jesus Christ, is a creature. I must also deny that this name of "creature" belongs to your Holy Spirit, seeing that he proceeds from you and is sent through him, so great is my reverence for everything that is yours. Nor, because I know that you alone are unborn and that the Only-begotten is born of you, will I refuse to say that the Holy Spirit was begotten, or will I assert that he was ever created. I fear the blasphemies which would be insinuated against you by such use of this title "creature," which I share with the other beings brought into being by you. Your Holy Spirit, as the Apostle says, searches and knows your deep things, and as Intercessor for me speaks to you words I could not utter. Shall I express, or rather dishonor, by the title "creature," the power of his nature which subsists eternally, derived from you through your Only-begotten? Nothing, except what belongs to you, penetrates into you; nor can the agency of a power foreign and strange to you measure the depth of your boundless majesty. To you belongs whatever enters into you; nor is anything which dwells in you through its searching power alien to you.

56. But I cannot describe him, whose pleas for me I cannot describe. As in the revelation that your Only-begotten was born of you before times eternal, when we cease to struggle with ambiguities of language and difficulties of thought, the one certainty of his birth remains. So I hold fast in my consciousness the truth that your Holy Spirit is from you and through him, although I cannot comprehend it by my intellect. For in your spiritual things I am dull, as your Only-begotten says, "Do not marvel that I said to you, you must be born anew. The Spirit breathes where it will. You hear the voice of it but do not know whence it comes or whither it goes. So is every one who is born of water and of the Holy Spirit."[Jn 3:7-8 adapted] Though I hold a belief in my regeneration, I hold it in ignorance; I possess the reality, though I do not comprehend it. For my own consciousness had no part in causing this new birth, which is manifest in its effects. Moreover, the Spirit has no limits: he speaks when he will, and what he will, and where he will. Since, then, the

cause of his coming and going is unknown, though the watcher is conscious of the fact, shall I count the nature of the Spirit among created things, and limit him by fixing the time of his origin? Your servant John says, indeed, that all things were made through the Son, who as God the Word was in the beginning, O God, with you. [Jn 1:1-3] Again, Paul recounts all things as created in him, in heaven and on earth, visible and invisible. [Col 1:16] And, while he declared that everything was created in Christ and through Christ, he thought, with respect to the Holy Spirit, that the description was sufficient, when he called him your Spirit. I will think in these matters with these men, peculiarly your elect. Just as, following their example, I will say nothing beyond my comprehension about your Only-begotten, but simply declare that he was born, so also following their example I will not trespass beyond that which human intellect can know about your Holy Spirit, but simply declare that he is your Spirit. May my lot be no useless strife of words, but the unwavering confession of an unhesitating faith!

Didymus the Blind (c. 313-c. 398)

Didymus was head of the catechetical school at Alexandria. Though he lost his sight at an early age, he still became an outstanding scholar and teacher. His treatise *On the Holy Spirit,* written sometime before 381 in Greek, survives only in Jerome's Latin translation. Didymus proved the divinity of the Spirit from his immutability and his role of sanctifier. The Spirit subsists in all the divine gifts and sanctifies all creatures and thus he must be of a different nature than creatures. Didymus also argued that the Spirit is not separate from the Father and the Son. The three Persons of the Trinity have the same operations and thus the same substance. The Spirit is not an operation of God but a subsistent nature. He is sent by the Father and the Son.

On the Holy Spirit

9.[13] Finally, it is impossible for anyone to receive the grace of God if he does not have the Holy Spirit, on whom, as we demonstrated, all the gifts of God depend. For in fact the one who possesses him acquires also the speech of wisdom and the other good things completely. Scriptural language proves clearly that the Holy Spirit is the substance of all the good things of God, as we said a little while ago when we took as our model, "The Father will give the Holy Spirit to those who ask him," [Lk 11:13] and, "The Father will give good things to those who ask him." [Mt 7:11] We ought not think that the Holy Spirit is divided according to their substances because a large number of good things is mentioned; for he is invulnerable and indivisible and unchangeable. Rather according to his different influences and understandings he is referred to by the many names of good things. He adapts to the advantage of each person, so that sharing in him does not bring one and the same power to all. Yet those he chooses to visit are filled with good things.

> Commentary: Didymus argued that only a divine being can be shared by others. As poured out, therefore, the Holy Spirit is uncreated.

11.[14] ... Of course the pouring out of the Spirit [Rom 5:15, Lk 11:13, Jl 2:28] is for the sake of prophesying and seeing the meaning and beauty of truth. Note that the very term "pouring out" indicates that the Holy Spirit is uncreated. When he sends an angel or another creature, God does not say, "I shall pour out my angel or principality or throne or domination." [Jl 2:28] Obviously, this way of speaking belongs only to the case of things which are shared by others. Thus we spoke a little while ago about God's love, which has been poured out in the hearts of those who receive the Holy Spirit, "God's love has been poured out in your hearts by the

[13]Trans. O. V. LeBlanc; PL 23.111
[14]PL 23, 114.

Holy Spirit which was given to you." [Rom 5:5] The Savior too, since he can be shared, is said to have been poured out like ointment, "Your name is oil poured out." [Cant 1:3]

> Commentary: The three divine persons have a single operation. Thus they have a single being. Didymus employed the Nicene formula, consubstantial (*homoousios*), extending it to the Spirit.

17[15] . . . Therefore whoever shares in the Holy Spirit shares immediately in the Father and the Son. And he who has love from the Father has it from the Son and joined with the Holy Spirit. And he who has a share of the grace of Jesus Christ has that grace given by the Father through the Holy Spirit. For in all these things it is proven that the operation of the Father and of the Son and of the Holy Spirit is the same. But those who have the same operation have the same substance, because those things which are *homoousia* in the same substance have the same operations and those which are of different substance and not *homoousia* are different and separate in operation.

> Commentary: Christ and the Spirit share one operation in governing the church.

24.[16] . . . For when the Savior sent his disciples to preach the gospel and to teach the doctrines of truth, it is said that the Father appointed in the church first apostles, next prophets, then teachers. The Apostle makes a similar statement, "Since we have been approved by God to be entrusted with the gospel, we speak to please not humans but God who tested our heart." [1 Th 2:4] The same people whom Christ ordered to be teachers, the Father also tested, and the Holy Spirit is said to have appointed to be stewards and rulers in the church. If indeed when he was at Miletus, Paul had gathered the presbyters from several places and from many

[15]PL 23, 119.
[16]PL 23, 124.

churches [not just those from Ephesus], he [would still have] said, "Take care for yourselves and for all the flock, over whom the Holy Spirit has made you guardians [*episcopos*], to direct the church of the Lord which he won through his own blood." [Acts 20:28] For if the Holy Spirit has placed in charge of the church those persons whom Christ sent to preach the gospel and baptize the nations, and they also being appointed by the judgment of the Father, then there is no doubt that the work and the approval of the Father and the Son and the Holy Spirit are one, and as a result that the substance of the Trinity is the same.

Epiphanius (c. 315-403)

Epiphanius, bishop of Constantia in Cyprus, was a more than ardent defender of the faith of Nicea. Both in his life and in his writings, he relentlessly attacked every heresy he encountered. The *Ancoratus* (the firmly-anchored person) was written in 374 to provide an anchor of faith for those struggling against heresy. In the work, Epiphanius presented a developed doctrine of the Trinity and in particular of the Spirit. He clearly called the Spirit God. The Spirit is ever with the Father and the Son and proceeds from the Father and receives from the Son. Epiphanius also spoke of the role of the Spirit as teacher and sanctifier.

Ancoratus

Commentary: In this first selection, Epiphanius expressed his belief that the Spirit is of the one divine substance. There exists a Trinity, but a Trinity of the same being. The Son and the Spirit are coeternal with the Father. The Father is unbegotten and uncreated. The Son is begotten but not created. The Spirit is not begotten and not created, but is of the same substance as the Father and the Son.

6.4.[17] When "of one substance" is mentioned, it clearly refers

[17]Trans. T. H. Tobin; PG 43, 25.

to one substance; but it also shows that the Father is of this substance, that the Son is of this substance, and that the Holy Spirit is of this substance. Whenever someone says "of the same substance," he is referring to nothing other than that same divinity (that the Son is God from God and the Holy Spirit is God from that same divinity) and not to three gods. Nor, when we speak of the Son and the Father as God, do we speak of two gods. For, our God is one, as the blessed Moses says, "The Lord, your God, is one Lord."[Dt 6:4] We do not call God the Father, God the Son, and God the Holy Spirit "gods." There is then no "multitude of gods" in God. The one divinity of the Father, the Son, and the Holy Spirit is indicated by these three names. And there are not two sons because the only-begotten Son is one while the Holy Spirit is the Spirit of holiness, the Spirit of God who is eternally with the Father and the Son. This Spirit is not something other than God but from God, "proceeding from the Father and receiving from the Son." [Jn 15:26, 16:14] But the only-begotten Son is incomprehensible and so also is the Holy Spirit. Nor do the Father and the Son coalesce; rather there exists eternally a Trinity of the same being. There exists no being other than the divinity nor is there another divinity apart from the being; it is the same divinity, and the Son and the Holy Spirit are of that same divinity.

> Commentary: Epiphanius spoke of the Spirit as the one who teaches all things and guides into truth. Knowledge of the Trinity and faith in the Trinity bring immortality and adopted sonship. The Trinity justifies the person and dwells in that person.

73.[18] The Spirit is the one who glorifies truthfully, teaches all things, gives witness concerning the Son. The Spirit is from the Father and the Son; he alone is the guide to truth. He is the interpreter of the holy laws, the expositor of the spiritual law, the guide of the prophets, the teacher of the apostles, the light-giver of the gospel teachings, the one who gathers

[18]PG 43, 153.

the saints, the true light from true light. This Spirit is with the Son, the Son by nature, the true Son, the genuine Son, the only Son from the only Father; but the Spirit is called 'spirit' and not 'son.' This is the God exalted in the church: eternally Father, eternally Son, and eternally Holy Spirit, the most-exalted, the most-high, the spiritual, the one who has infinite glory and to whom everything created and made, in short, everything finite and limited, is subjected. The one divinity was preached by Moses; the dyad was announced especially in the Prophets; the Trinity was made manifest in the Gospels and so quite fittingly were the just led generation after generation to knowledge and faith. Knowledge of this brings immortality and faith in it brings adopted sonship. At first the divinity proclaimed the justification of the flesh, as if it were building through Moses the outer wall of the temple; secondly the justification of the soul was revealed, as if the divinity were furnishing the sanctuary through the various prophecies; thirdly came the justification of the spirit, as if the divinity were arranging the mercy-seat and the Holy of Holies for its own habitation. This divinity has only the just person as a participant in these things, as a holy tent and a holy sanctuary. Here dwells the one infinite deity, the one incorruptible deity, the one incomprehensible deity.

> Commentary: At the end of the *Ancoratus*, Epiphanius presented two creeds. The second and longer creed was composed by Epiphanius himself and includes an expression of belief in the Spirit and his works that goes far beyond the simple statement of the Nicene creed. It ends with an anathema that extends the condemnation of the Arian doctrine of the Son to those who say the Spirit is a creature or that "there was a time when the Spirit did not exist."

The Creed of Epiphanius[19] ... And we believe in the Holy Spirit who spoke by the Law, who preached through the

[19]TCT 3-4; PG 43, 236.

prophets, and who descended on the Jordan; he speaks in the apostles and dwells in the saints. What we believe about him is this: that he is the Holy Spirit, the Spirit of God, a perfect spirit, a spirit of consolation, uncreated, who proceeds from the Father and receives from the Son; in him we believe.

And the catholic and apostolic Church, your mother and our mother, condemns those who say that "there was a time when the Son did not exist, nor the Holy Spirit"; or that [either] was made out of nothing or out of a pre-existing substance or being; and who say that the Son of God or the Holy Spirit is mutable or subject to change.

Basil of Caesarea (c. 330-379)

Basil was born at Caesarea in Cappadocia about 330 of a noble and wealthy family. He renounced a career as a rhetorician to give his life to God. After retiring into solitude and then founding a number of monasteries, he was ordained a priest in 364 and became bishop of Caesarea in 370. He fought Arianism and worked hard for the unity of the church until his death in 379. He was recognized as an efficient organizer, a defender of Christian doctrine, a liturgical reformer, as well as a founder of Oriental monasticism.

Basil is the first of three Cappadocians. He clearly believed in and affirmed the divinity of the Spirit, but in his works he does not call the Spirit God or explicitly affirm his consubstantiality. He feared that such an explicit affirmation would result in his banishment and the seizure of the church by his enemies. Instead he spoke of "glorifying the Holy Spirit together with the Father and the Son." He contrasted the Spirit with creatures and affirmed the distinction of persons and the unity of nature in God. The distinction of persons is based on their mode of origin. With reference to the work of the Spirit, Basil spoke of the Spirit in creation, the incarnation, the life of Christ, the resurrection from the dead, and the life to come. The Spirit is sanctifier, teacher, and revealer of mysteries. He dwells in Christians and makes them divine.

Basil's contribution to the theology of the Spirit is represented here by selections from several of his letters and from his treatise on the Holy Spirit.

Letter 125

> Commentary: In this letter written in 373, Basil clearly rejected the idea that the Spirit is a creature. The Spirit's place is in the divine nature. Basil related baptism, belief and worship. He also distinguished the three persons by saying that the Father is unbegotten, the Son begotten, and the Spirit proceeds.

3.[20] . . . They must anathematize all who call the Holy Spirit a creature, and all who so think; all who do not confess that he is holy by nature, as the Father is holy by nature and the Son is holy by nature, and refuse him his place in the blessed divine nature. Our not separating him from Father and Son is a proof of our right mind. For we are bound to be baptized in the terms we have received and to profess belief in the terms in which we are baptized, and as we have professed belief in, so to give glory to Father, Son and Holy Spirit. Thus we must hold aloof from the communion of all who call him creature, as from open blasphemers. One point must be regarded as settled; the remark is necessary because of our slanderers. We do not speak of the Holy Spirit as unbegotten, for we recognise one Unbegotten and one Origin of all things, the Father of our Lord Jesus Christ. Nor do we speak of the Holy Spirit as begotten, for by the tradition of the faith we have been taught one Only-begotten. We have been taught that the Spirit of truth proceeds from the Father, and we confess him to be of God without creation.

> Commentary: In Letter 159, also written in the year 373, Basil again made the connection between baptism, the confession of the creed, and worship. Because the Spirit is

[20]NPNF 2.8, 195; PG 32, 549.

not separate from the divine nature, the Spirit is glorified together with the Father and the Son. Basil also contrasted the Spirit and creatures. The Spirit is holy by nature, while creatures receive their sanctification through the Spirit.

Letter 159.2.[21] . . . As we were baptized, so we profess our belief. As we profess our belief, so also we offer praise. As baptism has been given us by the Savior, in the name of the Father and of the Son and of the Holy Spirit, so, in accordance with our baptism, we make the confession of the creed, and our doxology in accordance with our creed. We glorify the Holy Spirit together with the Father and the Son, from the conviction that he is not separated from the divine nature: what is foreign by nature does not share in the same honors. All who call the Holy Spirit a creature we pity, on the ground that, by this utterance, they are falling into the unpardonable sin of blasphemy against him. I need use no argument to prove to those who are even slightly trained in scripture, that the creature is separated from the Godhead. The creature is a slave; but the Spirit sets free. [Rom 8:2] The creature needs life; the Spirit is the Giver of life. [Jn 6:62] The creature requires teaching; the Spirit teaches. [Jn 14:26] The creature is sanctified; the Spirit sanctifies. [Rom 14:16] Whether you name angels, archangels, or all the heavenly powers, they receive their sanctification through the Spirit, but the Spirit himself has his holiness by nature, not as received by grace, but essentially his. From this, he has received the distinctive name of Holy. What then is by nature holy, as the Father is by nature holy, and the Son by nature holy, we do not ourselves allow to be separated and severed from the divine and blessed Trinity, nor accept those who rashly reckon it as part of creation.

On the Holy Spirit

Commentary: The fullest exposition of Basil's doctrine of the Spirit is found in his *On the Holy Spirit* written about

[21]NPNF 2.8, 212; PG 32, 620-621.

375. Objections had been raised against Basil for using in public worship the doxology, "Glory be to the Father with the Son together with the Holy Spirit," instead of, "Glory be to the Father through the Son in the Holy Spirit." In the context of defending the orthodoxy of glorifying the Spirit with the Father and the Son, Basil presented his theology of the Spirit at length. The Spirit is coeternal and inseparable from the Father and the Son and is associated with them in their activity, especially in creation and sanctification. He proceeds from God not by generation, but as "breath of his mouth" in a manner that remains ineffable.

Chapter 18.44.[22] ... There is one God and Father, one only-begotten Son, and one Holy Spirit. We proclaim each of the hypostases singly; and, when we must count, we do not let an ignorant arithmetic carry us away to the idea of a plurality of gods.

45. For we do not count by way of addition, gradually making increase from unity to multitude, and saying one, two, and three, nor even first, second, and third. For "I, God, am the first, and I am the last."[Is 44:6] And up to now we have never heard of a second god. Worshipping as we do God of God, we both confess the distinction of the Persons, and at the same time abide by the monarchy. We do not fritter away the theology in a divided plurality, because one form, so to speak, united in the unchangeability of the Godhead, is beheld in God the Father, and in God the Only-begotten. For the Son is in the Father and the Father in the Son; since such as the Son is, so is the Father, and such as the Father is, so is the Son; therein is the unity. According to the distinction of persons, they are one and other, and according to the community of nature, one and same. How, then, if one and other, are there not two gods? Because we speak of a king and of the king's image, but not of two kings. The majesty is not split in two, nor is the glory divided. The

---

[22]NPNF 2.8, 28-30; PG 32, 150-153.

sovereignty and authority over us is one, and so the doxology ascribed by us is not plural but one; because the honor paid to the image passes on to the prototype. Now what in the example the image is by reason of imitation, in the divine case the Son is by nature. As in works of art the likeness is dependent on the common form, so in the case of the divine and uncompounded nature the union consists in the communion of the Godhead. The Holy Spirit is also one. We speak of him singly, conjoined as he is to the one Father through the one Son, and through himself completing the adorable and blessed Trinity. His intimate relationship to the Father and the Son is sufficiently manifested by his not being ranked in the plurality of the creation, but being spoken of singly. For he is not one of many, but One. As there is one Father and one Son, so is there one Holy Spirit. He is consequently as far removed from created nature as reason requires the singular to be removed from compounded and multiplied bodies. He is united to the Father and to the Son in the way that unit is related to unit.

46. It is not from this source alone that our proofs of the natural communion are derived, but from the fact that he is moreover said to be "of God." [2 Cor 1:12] Not indeed in the sense in which "all things are of God," [1 Cor 11:12] but in the sense of proceeding out of God — not by generation, like the Son, but as Breath of his mouth. But in no way is the "mouth" a bodily member, nor is the Spirit breath that is dissolved. The word "mouth" is used so far as it can be appropriate to God, and the Spirit is a substance having life, endowed with supreme power of sanctification. Thus the close relation is made plain, while the mode of the ineffable existence is safeguarded...

47. And when, by means of the power that enlightens us, we fix our eyes on the beauty of the image of the invisible God, and through the image are led up to the supreme beauty of the spectacle of the archetype, then, I say, the Spirit of knowledge is with us inseparably. In himself he bestows the power of beholding the Image on those who love the vision of the truth. He does not make the exhibition from without, but in himself leads on to the full knowledge. "No one

knows the Father but the Son." [Mt 11:27] And so "no one can say that Jesus is Lord but by the Holy Spirit." [1 Cor 12:3] For it is not said through the Spirit, but by the Spirit. "God is a spirit, and those who worship him must worship him in spirit and in truth," [Jn 4:24] as it is written, "in your light shall we see light," [Ps 36:9] namely by the illumination of the Spirit, "the true light which enlightens every one who comes into the world." [Jn 1:9] Thus in himself he shows the glory of the Only-begotten and in himself he bestows the knowledge of God on true worshippers. Thus the way of the knowledge of God lies from the one Spirit through the one Son to the one Father. Conversely, the natural goodness and the inherent holiness and the royal dignity extend from the Father through the Only-begotten to the Spirit. Thus the *hypostases* are acknowledged and the true dogma of the monarchy is not lost.

> Commentary: Basil showed how the operations of the Spirit in creation, in the incarnation and the work of Christ, in the resurrection of the dead, and in sanctification reveal his dignity and power.

Chapter 19.49.[23] And his operations, what are they? In majesty indescribable, and in number uncountable. How shall we form a conception of what extends beyond the ages? What were his operations before that creation which we can conceive? How great the graces which he conferred on creation? What power he exercised over the ages to come? He existed; he pre-existed; he co-existed with the Father and the Son before the ages. It follows that, even if you can conceive of anything beyond the ages, you will find the Spirit still further above and beyond. If you think of the creation, the powers of the heavens were established by the Spirit; [Ps 33:6] this establishment is understood as an inability to fall away from God. It is from the Spirit that the powers derive their close relationship to God, their inability to change to evil, and their perseverance in blessedness. Is it

[23]NPNF 2.8, 30-31; PG 32, 156-157.

Christ's advent? The Spirit is forerunner. Is there the incarnate presence? The Spirit is inseparable. The working of miracles and gifts of healing are through the Holy Spirit. Demons were driven out by the Spirit of God; the devil was brought to naught by the presence of the Spirit. Remission of sins was by the gift of the Spirit, for, "you were washed, you were sanctified, . . . in the name of the Lord Jesus Christ, and in the Holy Spirit of our God." [1 Cor 6:11] Close relationship with God is through the Spirit, for "God has sent forth the Spirit of his Son into your hearts, crying Abba, Father." [Gal 4:6] The resurrection from the dead is effected by the operation of the Spirit for, "You send forth your Spirit, they are created and you renew the face of the earth." [Ps 104:30] Creation might be taken here to mean the bringing of the departed to life again; how mighty then is the operation of the Spirit, who is for us the dispenser of the life that follows on the resurrection and attunes our souls to the spiritual life beyond? Or here creation might mean the change to a better condition of those who in this life have fallen into sin. It is so understood according to the usage of Scripture, as in the words of Paul, "If anyone be in Christ he is a new creature." [2 Cor 5:17] Then it would indicate the renewal which takes place in this life and the transmutation from our earthly and sensuous life to the heavenly living which takes place in us through the Spirit. In this interpretation, souls are exalted to the highest pitch of admiration. With these thoughts before us, should we be afraid of going beyond due bounds in the extravagance of the honor we pay? Shall we not rather fear lest, even though we seem to give him the highest names which human thoughts can conceive or human tongue utter, we let our thoughts about him fall short?

> Commentary: In these final two paragraphs, Basil exhorted his readers to give glory to the Spirit, to enumerate the wonders of his nature, his operations, and his blessings. He should be glorified with the Father and the Son.

Chapter 23.54.[24] ... Shall we not then highly exalt him who is in his nature divine, in his greatness infinite, in his operations powerful, in the blessings he confers good? Shall we not give him glory? And I understand glory to mean nothing else than the enumeration of the wonders which are his own. It follows then that either we are forbidden by our antagonists even to mention the good things which flow to us from him, or on the other hand that the mere recapitulation of his attributes is the fullest possible attribution of glory. For not even in the case of the God and Father of the only-begotten Son, are we capable of giving them glory otherwise than by recounting, to the extent of our powers, all the wonders that belong to them.

Chapter 24.55. ... Grant, they say, that he is to be glorified, but not with the Father and the Son. But what reason is there in giving up the place appointed by the Lord for the Spirit, and inventing some other? What reason is there for robbing him of his share of glory who is everywhere associated with the Godhead: in the confession of the faith, in the baptism of redemption, in the working of miracles, in the indwelling of the saints, in the graces bestowed on obedience? For not one single gift reaches creation without the Holy Spirit. Not a single word can be spoken in defense of Christ except by those who are aided by the Spirit, as we have learnt in the Gospels from our Lord and Savior. [Mt 10:19,20] I do not think that anyone who has been a partaker of the Holy Spirit will agree that we should overlook all this, forget his fellowship in all things, and tear the Spirit apart from the Father and the Son.

Gregory of Nazianzus (c. 330-389)

Gregory of Nazianzus was a close friend of Basil. He too was of a noble family and received the education of a rhetorician. Attracted by a life of solitude, he was ordained a priest in 362, seemingly against his will. He spent most of

[24]NPNF 2.8, 35; PG 32, 169-172.

his life as a priest either working in Nazianzus or retiring to monastic solitude. The important exception to this was the period from 379 to 381 when he assisted the Christian community in Constantinople which had remained faithful to the Nicene definition in reorganizing after years of Arian domination. In this context, Gregory preached his five *Theological Orations*. The selections given here are from the fifth oration, which deals with the Holy Spirit, and from a sermon Gregory gave on Pentecost.

Gregory did not hesitate to call the Spirit God and affirm his consubstantiality. Like Basil, he distinguished the Persons in terms of mutual relations but clearly affirmed the undivided unity of the Trinity.

The Fifth Theological Oration (XXXI).

> Commentary: Gregory argued that the Spirit is neither an activity nor a creature: he is God. He then dismissed the absurd position that the Spirit must be either a second Son or a grandson by recalling that the Spirit is not begotten but proceeds. He admitted that he could not explain this procession, any more than anyone else can explain the Father's unbegottenness or the Son's begottenness. In the Trinity there are differences of manifestation or mutual relations that distinguish the persons. Unlike Basil, Gregory gave the clearest possible affirmation of the divinity and consubstantiality of the Spirit.

6.[25] ... We will argue thus: The Holy Spirit must certainly be conceived of either in the category of the self-existent or in that of the things which are contemplated in another: those skilled in such matters call the one substance and the other accident. Now if he were an accident, he would be an activity of God. For what else, or of whom else, could he be, since this is what most avoids composition? If he is an activity, he will be effected, but will not effect and will cease to exist as soon as he has been effected, for this is the nature

[25]LCC 3,197-199; SC 250, 286-292.

of an activity. How is it, then, that he acts and says such and such things, and defines, and is grieved, and is angered, [Acts 13:2, Eph 4:30, Is 63:10] and has all the qualities which belong clearly to one that moves, but not to movement itself? If he is, on the other hand, a substance and not an attribute of substance, he will be conceived of either as a creature of God or as God. For anything between these two, whether having nothing in common with either or a compound of both, not even those who invented the goat-stag could imagine. Now, if he is a creature, how do we believe in him, how are we made perfect in him? For it is not the same thing to believe in a thing and to believe about it. The one belongs to deity, the other to any thing. But if he is God, then he is neither a creature, nor a thing made, nor a fellow servant, nor any of these lowly appellations.

7. There — the word is with you. Let the slings be let go; let the syllogisms be woven. Either he is altogether unbegotten or else he is begotten. If he is unbegotten, there are two unoriginates. If he is begotten, you must make a further subdivision. He is begotten either by the Father or by the Son. If by the Father, there are two sons and they are brothers. You may make them twins if you like, or the one older and the other younger, since you are so very fond of the bodily conceptions. But if by the Son, then such a person will say that we get a glimpse of a grandson God: nothing could be more absurd...

8. We do not admit your first distinction, which declares that there is no third option between begotten and unbegotten. As a result, along with your magnificent distinction, away go your brothers and your grandsons; when the first link of this intricate chain is broken they are broken with it, and disappear from your system of theology. Tell me, what position will you assign to that which proceeds, which has originated between the two terms of your distinction, and is introduced by a better theologian than you, our Savior himself? Or perhaps you have taken that word out of your Gospels for the sake of your third testament, "the Holy Spirit, who proceeds from the Father." [Jn 15:26] Because he proceeds from that source, he is no creature; because he is

not begotten, he is no Son; because he is between the unbegotten and the begotten, he is God. Thus escaping the toils of your syllogisms, he has manifested himself as God, stronger than your distinctions. What, then, is procession? Do you tell me what is the unbegottenness of the Father, and I will explain to you the physiology of the generation of the Son and the procession of the Spirit, and we shall both of us be frenzy-stricken for prying into the mystery of God. Who are we to do these things, we who cannot even see what lies at our feet, or count the sand of the sea, or the drops of rain, or the days of eternity, [Sir 1:1] much less enter into the depths of God, and supply an account of that nature which is so indescribable and transcends all words?

9. Then, they say, what is there lacking to the Spirit which prevents his being a Son, for if there were not something lacking he would be a Son? We assert that there is nothing lacking — for God has no deficiency. But the difference of manifestation, if I may so express myself, or rather their mutual relations one to another, causes the difference of their names. For indeed it is not some deficiency in the Son which prevents his being Father (for Sonship is not a deficiency), and yet he is not Father. According to this line of argument there must be some deficiency in the Father, which prevents his being Son. For the Father is not Son, and yet this is not due to either deficiency or subordination of essence. The very fact of being unbegotten or begotten, of proceeding, has given the name of Father to the first, of the Son to the second, and to the third, him of whom we are speaking, of the Holy Spirit, so that the distinction of the three Persons may be preserved in the one nature and dignity of the Godhead. For the Son is not Father, since the Father is one; he is what the Son is. The three are one in Godhead, and the one three in properties. Neither is the unity a Sabellian one, nor does the Trinity countenance the present evil distinction.

10. What, then: Is the Spirit God? Most certainly. Well, then, is he consubstantial? Yes, if he is God.

Commentary: Gregory explained how the Trinity was

only gradually revealed. The Old Testament proclaimed the Father. The New Testament proclaimed the Son. Then the Spirit dwells among Christians and clearly teaches his divinity. This gradual revelation respects the human inability to grasp the full revelation all at once. It also gives some explanation of why the divinity of the Spirit was not openly proclaimed from the beginning.

26.[26] ... The matter stands thus: The Old Testament proclaimed the Father openly, and the Son more obscurely. The New manifested the Son, and suggested the divinity of the Spirit. Now the Spirit himself dwells among us, and supplies us with a clearer demonstration of himself. For it was not safe, when the Godhead of the Father was not yet acknowledged, plainly to proclaim the Son; nor when that of the Son was not yet received, to burden us further (if I may use so bold an expression) with the Holy Spirit. People might, like children loaded with food beyond their strength and looking into the sun's light with eyes as yet too weak to bear it, risk the loss of even that which was within the reach of their powers. Thus, by gradual additions, and as David says, goings up and advances and progress from glory to glory, [Ps 84:7; 2 Cor 3:18] the light of the Trinity would shine upon the more illuminated. For this reason, I think, he gradually came to dwell in the disciples, measuring himself out to them according to their capacity to receive him, at the beginning of the gospel, after the passion, after the ascension, making perfect their powers, being breathed upon them, and appearing in fiery tongues. And indeed it is little by little that he is declared by Jesus, as you will learn for yourself if you will read more carefully. "I will ask the Father," he says, "and he will send you another Comforter, even the Spirit of truth." [Jn 14:16-17] This he said that he might not seem to be a rival God, or to make his discourses to them by another authority. Again, "He shall send him," but it is "in my name." [Jn 14:26] He leaves out the "I will ask," but keeps the "shall send," then again, "I will send" [Jn

[26]LCC 3,209-210; SC 250, 326-330.

15:26] indicating his own dignity. Then, "shall come" [Jn 16:7] indicating the authority of the Spirit.

27. You see lights breaking upon us, gradually; and the order of theology, which it is better for us to keep, neither proclaiming things too suddenly nor yet keeping them hidden to the end. For the former course would be unscientific, the latter atheistic; and the former would be calculated to startle outsiders, the latter to alienate our own people. I will add another point to what I have said — one which may readily have come into the mind of some others, but which I think a fruit of my own thought. Our Savior had some things which, he said, could not be borne at that time by his disciples (though they were filled with many teachings), perhaps for the reasons I have mentioned; and therefore they were hidden. Again he said that all things would be taught us by the Spirit when he came to dwell among us. [Jn 14:26] Of these things one, I take it, was the divinity of the Spirit himself. It would be made clear later on, when such knowledge would be seasonable and capable of being received after our Savior's restoration, when it would no longer be received with incredulity because of its marvelous character. For what greater thing than this did either he promise, or the Spirit teach — if indeed anything is to be considered great and worthy of the majesty of God, which was either promised or taught?

Sermon on Pentecost (XLI)

> Commentary: This sermon was preached on the feast of Pentecost during Gregory's time in Constantinople between 379 and 381. He described how the Spirit worked in the angels, in patriarchs and prophets, and finally in the apostles. He came most fully at Pentecost. The Spirit now shares with the Son in the work of creation and resurrection. He is also the source of spiritual rebirth that raises up prophets and apostles.

11.[27] He worked first in the heavenly and angelic powers,

27NPNF 2.7, 383; PG 36, 444.

and such as are first after God and around God. From no other source flows their perfection and their brightness, and the difficulty or impossibility of moving them to sin, but from the Holy Spirit. Next, he worked in the patriarchs and prophets. The former saw visions of God or knew him. The latter also foreknew the future; they had their master faculty molded by the Spirit, and were related to events that were yet future as if they were present. Such is the power of the Spirit. I omit to mention Christ himself in whom he dwelt not as energizing but as accompanying his equal. Next he worked in Christ's disciples in three ways, as they were able to receive him, and on three occasions: before Christ was glorified by the passion, after he was glorified by the resurrection, and after his ascension or restoration or whatever we ought to call it, to heaven. Now the first of these manifests him: the healing of the sick and casting out of evil spirits, which could not be apart from the Spirit. So does that breathing upon them after the resurrection, which was clearly a divine inspiration. So too the present distribution of the fiery tongues, which we are now commemorating. The first manifested him indistinctly, the second more expressly, this present one more perfectly. In it, he is no longer present only in energy, but as we may say, substantially, associating with us, and dwelling in us. For it was fitting that as the Son had lived with us in bodily form, so the Spirit too should appear in bodily form; that after Christ had returned to his own place, the Spirit should have come down to us. He came because he is the Lord; he was sent because he is not a rival God. For such words no less manifest the unanimity than they mark the separate individuality.

14.[28] This Spirit shares with the Son in the work of both the creation and the resurrection, as you may be shown by this Scripture, "By the Word of the Lord were the heavens made, and all the power of them by the breath of his mouth," [Ps 33:6] and this, "The Spirit of God made me, and the Breath of the Almighty teaches me," [Job 33:4] and again, "You

---

[28]NPNF 2.7, 384; PG 36, 448.

shall send forth your Spirit and they shall be created, and you shall renew the face of the earth." [Ps 104:30] He is the author of spiritual regeneration. Here is your proof: "None can see or enter into the Kingdom, unless he is born again of the Spirit," [Jn 3:5] and is cleansed from his first birth, which is a mystery of the night, by a remolding of the day and of the Light, by which every one individually is created anew. This Spirit is most wise and most loving. If he takes possession of a shepherd, he makes him a psalmist, subduing evil spirits by his song, and proclaims him king; if he possess a goatherd and scraper of sycamore fruit, he makes him a prophet. Recall David and Amos. If he possess a goodly youth, he makes him a judge of elders, even beyond his years; thus Daniel testifies, who conquered the lions in their den. If he takes possession of fishermen, he makes them catch the whole world in the nets of Christ, taking them up in the meshes of the Word. Look at Peter and Andrew and the Sons of Thunder, thundering the things of the Spirit. If of publicans, he makes gain of them for discipleship, and makes them merchants of souls; witness Matthew, yesterday a publican, today an evangelist. If of zealous persecutors, he changes the current of their zeal, makes them Pauls instead of Sauls, as full of piety as he found them of wickedness. He is the Spirit of meekness and yet is provoked by those who sin. Let us therefore experience him as gentle, not as wrathful, by confessing his dignity. Let us not desire to see him implacably wrathful.

Gregory of Nyssa (c. 335-c. 395)

Gregory of Nyssa, the younger brother of Basil, was the best speculative theologian of the three great Cappadocians. In 371 he was made bishop of Nyssa and in 381 he played a prominent role in the Council of Constantinople. He died about 395.

Gregory's contribution to the theology of the Spirit is seen most clearly in his argument from the identity of operation to the identity of nature and in his fully developed doctrine of the distinction of persons. This is the most sophisticated trinitarian theology of the fourth century.

On the Holy Spirit Against the Followers of Macedonius

> Commentary: In his sermon on the Holy Spirit, Gregory contended that the Spirit is of the divine essence and is to be ranked with the Father and the Son. The Spirit is united with the Father and the Son in nature, honor and glory. He has all the attributes of the divinity.

2.[29] ... We, for instance, confess that the Holy Spirit is of the same rank as the Father and the Son, so that there is no difference between them in anything, either thought or named, that devotion can ascribe to a divine nature. We confess that, except for his being contemplated as having peculiar attributes in regard of person, the Holy Spirit is indeed from God, and of the Christ, according to scripture. While not to be confused with the Father in being never originated, nor with the Son in being the Only-begotten, and while to be regarded separately in certain distinctive properties, he has in all else, as I have just said, an exact identity with them...

6. ... So with regard to the Spirit, if when one calls him divine one speaks the truth, neither does one lie when he defines him as worthy of honor, glorious, good, omnipotent. All such conceptions are at once admitted with the idea of deity. Thus they must accept one of two alternatives: either not to call him divine at all, or to refrain from subtracting from his deity any one of those conceptions which are attributable to deity.

7. Since, then, it has been affirmed, and truly affirmed, that the Spirit is of the divine essence, and since in that one word "divine" every idea of greatness, as we have said, is involved, it follows that he who grants that divinity has potentially granted all the rest: the gloriousness, the omnipotence,

[29]NPNF 2.5, 315-320; PG 45, 1304-1317.

everything indicative of superiority. It is indeed a monstrous thing to refuse to confess this in the case of the Spirit; monstrous, because of the incongruity, as applied to him, of the terms which in the list of opposites correspond to the above terms.

* * *

14. This is the view we take, in our usual unprofessional way. We reject all these elaborate sophistries of our adversaries, believing and confessing as we do, that in every deed and thought, whether in this world, or beyond this world, whether in time or in eternity, the Holy Spirit is to be apprehended as joined to the Father and Son, and is wanting in no wish or energy, or anything else that is implied in a devout conception of Supreme Goodness. Therefore, we believe except for the distinction of order and person, no variation in any point is to be apprehended. We assert that while his place is counted third in mere sequence after the Father and Son, third in the order of the transmission, in all other respects we acknowledge his inseparable union with them: in nature, in honor, in godhead, glory, majesty, almighty power, and in all devout belief.

On the Holy Trinity

> Commentary: The greater part of the treatise *On the Holy Trinity* has been attributed to Basil as Letter 189, but it seems clearly to be a work of Gregory. He inferred the oneness of the nature of the Father, Son and Spirit from the identity of their operation.

6.[30] But they say that this appellation [God] is indicative of nature, and that, as the nature of the Spirit is not common to the Father and the Son, for this reason neither does he partake in the community of this attribute. Let them show,

[30]NPNF 2.5, 328-329; PG 32, 692-696.

then, whereby they discern this diversity of nature. . . .it is absolutely necessary for us to be guided to the investigation of the divine nature by its operations. If, then, we see that the operations which are wrought by the Father and the Son and the Holy Spirit differ one from the other, we shall conjecture from the different character of the operations that the natures which operate are also different. For it cannot be that things which differ in their very nature should agree in the form of their operation. Fire does not chill, nor ice give warmth; their operations are distinguished along with the difference between their natures. If, on the other hand, we understand that the operation of the Father, the Son, and the Holy Spirit is one, differing or varying in nothing, the oneness of their nature must be inferred from the identity of their operation.

7. The Father, the Son, and the Holy Spirit alike give sanctification, and life, and light, and comfort, and all similar graces. Let no one attribute the power of sanctification in a special sense to the Spirit, when he hears the Savior in the Gospel saying to the Father concerning his disciples, "Father, sanctify them in your name." [Jn 17:11,17] So too all the other gifts are worked in those who are worthy by the Father, the Son, and the Holy Spirit: every grace and power, guidance, life, comfort, the change to immortality, the passage to liberty, and every other benefit that exists, which descends to us. . . . Thus the identity of operation in Father, Son, and Holy Spirit shows plainly the indistinguishable character of their substance. So that even if the name of Godhead does indicate nature, the community of substance shows that this appellation is properly applied also to the Holy Spirit.

8. . . . If, then, Godhead is a name derived from operation, as we say that the operation of the Father, and the Son, and the Holy Spirit is one, so we say that the Godhead is one. Or if, according to the view of the majority, Godhead is indicative of nature, since we cannot find any diversity in their nature, we reasonably define the Holy Trinity to be of one Godhead.

That We Should Not Think of Saying There Are Three Gods

> Commentary: *That There Are Not Three Gods* was Greg-
> ory's response to the objection that speaking of the divin-
> ity of the Father, Son, and Spirit results in speaking of
> three gods. Gregory first criticized the ordinary misuse of
> language in speaking of nature in the plural. Then he
> explained that every action of God occurs through the
> three persons, so that no activity is distinguished among
> the three persons. Their activity comes from the Father
> through the Son and reaches completion by the Holy
> Spirit. The unity of operation implies a unity of Godhead.

[31]Why is it, then, that we are accustomed to use the plural
when we make a count of those who are shown to have the
same nature? We say there are "so many men," and we do
not call them all "one." And yet, when we refer to the divine
nature, why does our dogma exclude a multitude of gods,
and while enumerating the persons, not admit their plural
significance? If one were speaking superficially to simple
folk, one might seem to give an answer by this, viz., that our
doctrine refused to enumerate a number of gods in order to
avoid similarity with Greek polytheism. If we were to speak
of the Deity not in the singular, but in the plural, as they are
accustomed to do, there might be thought to be some kinship between their doctrine and ours. Such an answer, given
to rather naive people, might seem satisfactory. To others,
however, who demand that one or other of the alternatives
must stand — either that we should not acknowledge the
divinity of the three persons, or that we should, without
hesitation, count as three those who share the same divinity
— such an answer as we have just given would not suffice to
resolve the problem. We must, therefore, make our reply at
greater length, tracking down the truth as best we can, for
the question is no ordinary one.

Our first point is this: To use in the plural the word for the
nature of those who do not differ in nature, and to speak of

[31]LCC 3,257-262; PG 45, 117-125.

"many humans," is a customary misuse of language. It is like saying that there are many human natures.

* * *

Just as we speak of a people, a mob, an army, and an assembly always in the singular, and yet each of them entails plurality, so even the term "human" should properly and most accurately be used in the singular, even if those we observe to share in the same nature constitute a plurality. Thus it would be much better to correct our misguided habit and no longer use the word for a nature in the plural than by bondage to it to transfer the same error to our teaching about God. Yet it is impracticable to correct the habit.

* * *

We do not learn that the Father does something on his own, in which the Son does not cooperate. Or again that the Son acts on his own without the Spirit. Rather every operation which extends from God to creation and is designated according to our differing conceptions of it has its origin in the Father, proceeds through the Son, and reaches its completion by the Holy Spirit. It is for this reason that the word for the operation is not divided among the persons involved. For the action of each in any matter is not separate and individualized. But whatever occurs, whether in reference to God's providence for us or to the government and constitution of the universe, occurs through the three persons, and is not three separate things.

> Commentary: The unity of nature does not imply a confusion of the persons. Gregory distinguished the persons with respect to causality, the Father being without cause and the Son and Spirit being caused. The Son and the Spirit are further distinguished because the Spirit is from the Son as well as from the Father.

[32]Should anyone cavil at our argument that, by refusing to

[32]LCC 3,266-267; PG 45, 133-136.

acknowledge distinctions in the nature, it makes for an admixture and confusion of the persons, we will give the following answer to the charge. Although we acknowledge the nature as undifferentiated, we do not deny a distinction with respect to causality. That is the only way by which we distinguish one person from the other, by believing, that is, that one is the cause and the other depends on the cause. Again, we recognize another distinction with regard to that which depends on the cause. There is that which depends on the first cause. Thus the attribute of being only-begotten without doubt remains with the Son, and we do not question that the Spirit is derived from the Father. For the mediation of the Son, while it guards his prerogative of being only-begotten, does not exclude the relation which the Spirit has by nature to the Father.

When we speak of a cause and that which depends on it, we do not, by these words, refer to nature. For no one would hold that cause and nature are identical. Rather we indicate a difference in manner of existence. For in saying the one is caused and the other uncaused, we do not divide the nature by the principle of causality, but only explain that the Son does not exist without generation, nor the Father by generation. It is necessary for us first to believe that something exists, and then to examine in what way the object of our belief exists. The question of what exists is one thing; the manner of its existence is another. To say that something exists without generation explains the mode of its existence. But what it is is not made evident by the expression. If you asked a gardener about some tree, whether it was planted or grew wild, and he replied either that it had or had not been planted, would his answer tell you what sort of tree it was? By no means. In telling you how it grew, he would leave the question of its nature obscure and unexplained. In the same way here, when we learn that he is unbegotten, we are taught the mode of his existence and how we must think of it. But we do not learn from the expression what he is.

When, then, we acknowledge such a distinction in the Holy Trinity, that we believe that one is the cause and the other depends on it, we can no longer be charged with dissolving the distinction of the persons in the common nature. The principle of causality distinguishes, then, the persons of the Holy Trinity. It affirms that the one is uncaused, while the other depends on the cause. But the divine nature is in every way understood to be without distinction or difference. For this reason we rightly say there is one Godhead and one God, and express all the other attributes that befit the divine in the singular.

Third Sermon on the Lord's Prayer

> Commentary: In this sermon, Gregory further elaborated the distinction between the divine persons which is based on casual relations. He explained the difference between Son and Spirit.

[33]It is the characteristic of the Father to exist without cause. This does not apply to the Son and the Spirit; for the Son went out from the Father, [Jn 16:27] as says the scripture, and the Spirit proceeds from God and from the Father. [Jn 15:26] As the being without cause, which belongs only to the Father, cannot be adapted to the Son and the Spirit, so also the being caused, which is the property of the Son and of the Spirit, cannot, by its very nature, be considered in the Father. On the other hand, the being not ungenerated is common to the Son and the Spirit. Hence in order to avoid confusion in the subject, one must again search for the pure difference in the properties, so that what is common may be safeguarded, yet what is proper may not be mixed. For he is called the Only-begotten of the Father by the holy scripture; [Jn 1:14] and this term establishes his property for him. But the Holy Spirit is also said to be from the Father and is testified to be the Son's. For it says, "If any man have not the Spirit of Christ, he is none of his." [Rom 8:9] Hence the Spirit that is from God is also Christ's Spirit. But the Son, who is from God, neither is, nor is said to be, from the Spirit. This relative sequence is permanent and inconvertible.

[33]ACW 18, 54-55; see intro. to trans. for text.

Hence the sentence cannot properly be resolved and re-
versed in its meaning so that, as we say the Spirit to be
Christ's, we might also call Christ the Spirit's. This individual property distinguishes one from the other with absolute
clarity, and the identity of action bears witness to the community of nature. Thus the right doctrine about the divinity
is confirmed in both: namely that the Trinity is numbered by
the persons, but that it is not divided into parts of different
nature.

Ambrose of Milan (c. 339-397)

Ambrose was born into a noble Christian family about
339. He was educated for imperial service and had attained
high position when in 374 he was selected to succeed the
Arian bishop of Milan. Ambrose had to complete his
instruction and be baptized before his consecration, since he
was still a catechumen when elected. His civil service experience made him energetic in dealing with the government
and his facility in Greek enabled him to borrow extensively
from Eastern authors in his own writing. Indeed, he served
more as a translator and adapter than an original teacher.
He died in 397 when his greatest convert, Augustine, was
already bishop in Hippo.

Ambrose addressed the five books of *On the Christian
Faith* to the Emperor Gratian in the late 370's. These were
followed, at Gratian's request, by *On the Holy Spirit* in 381.
Hilary of Poitiers had argued that the Father and Son share
a single divine nature and operation. Ambrose extended this
reasoning to include the Holy Spirit by proving that he
shares each of the attributes and actions of the deity. It is
noteworthy that whereas Hilary assigned the work of the
incarnation to the divine nature in Christ, Ambrose proved
that the Holy Spirit is Creator by attributing to him the
formation of Christ's human nature in the Virgin.

On the Holy Spirit

> Commentary: Ambrose proved that the Spirit is the Creator of all things. The Spirit graces the world and renews the earth.

Book 2, Chapter 5.32.[34] But who can doubt that the Holy Spirit gives life to all things. He, as the Father and the Son, is the Creator of all things and the Almighty Father is understood to have done nothing without the Holy Spirit. Furthermore, in the beginning of the creation the Spirit moved upon the water. [Gen 1:2]
33. So when the Spirit was moving upon the water, the creation was without grace; but after this created world underwent the operation of the Spirit, it gained all the beauty of that grace, by which it is illuminated. The grace of the universe cannot abide without the Holy Spirit, as the prophet declared when he said, "Take away their Spirit, and they will fail and be turned again into their dust. Send forth your Spirit, and they shall be made, and you will renew all the face of the earth." [Ps 104:29,30] Not only, then, did he teach that no creature can stand without the Spirit, but also that the Spirit is the Creator of the whole creation.
34. And who can deny that the creation of the earth is the work of the Holy Spirit, by whose work it is renewed? If they desire to deny that it was created by the Spirit, while they cannot deny that it must be renewed by the Spirit, those who desire to divide the persons must maintain that the operation of the Holy Spirit is superior to that of the Father and the Son (which is far from the truth). For there is no doubt that the restored earth is better than it was created. Or if, at first, without the operation of the Holy Spirit, the Father and the Son made the earth, but the operation of the Holy Spirit was joined on afterwards, it will seem that what was first made required his aid, which was then added. But far be it from any one to think this, namely, that the divine work should be believed to have a change in the Creator, an error brought in by Manicheus.

[34]NPNF 2.10, 118-119; CSEL 79, 98-100.

> Commentary: The strongest evidence that the Spirit is
> Creator is that the Lord himself was begotten by the Holy
> Spirit. If the Spirit is Creator, then he is certainly not a
> creature and so must be served and venerated.

37.[35] But why do I delay with matters not to the point? Let
them accept a plain proof that there can be nothing which
the Holy Spirit can be said not to have made; and that it
cannot be doubted that all subsists through his operation,
whether angels, archangels, thrones, or dominions. The
Lord himself, according to the flesh, whom the angels serve,
was begotten by the Holy Spirit coming upon the Virgin.
According to Matthew, the angel said to Joseph, "Joseph,
son of David, fear not to take Mary your wife, for that which
shall be born of her is of the Holy Spirit." [Mt 1:20] And
according to Luke, he said to Mary, "The Holy Spirit shall
come upon you." [Lk 1:35]
38. The birth from the Virgin was, then, the work of the
Spirit. The fruit of the womb is the work of the Spirit,
according to what is written, "Blessed are you among
women, and blessed is the fruit of your womb." [Lk 1:42]
The flower from the root is the work of the Spirit, that
flower, I say, of which it was well prophesied, "A rod shall
go forth from the root of Jesse, and a flower shall rise from
his root." [Is 11:1] The root of Jesse the patriarch is the
family of the Jews, Mary is the rod, Christ the flower of
Mary, who budded forth from a virgin womb to spread the
good odor of faith throughout the whole world. As he
himself said, "I am the flower of the plain, a lily of the
valley." [S. of S. 2:1]
39. The flower, when cut, keeps its odor, and when bruised,
increases it, nor if torn off does it lose it. So, too, the Lord
Jesus, on the gibbet of the cross, neither failed when bruised,
nor fainted when torn. When he was cut by that piercing of
the spear, he became more beautiful by the color of the
outpoured blood. He grew comely again, not able in himself
to die, and breathed forth upon the dead the gift of eternal

[35]NPNF 2.10, 119-120; CSEL 79, 100-104.

life. On this flower of the royal rod the Holy Spirit rested.
40. A good rod, as some think, is the flesh of the Lord.
Raising itself from its earthly root to heaven, it bore around
the whole world the sweet-smelling fruits of religion, the
mysteries of the divine generation, pouring grace on the
altars of heaven.
41. So, then, we cannot doubt that the Spirit is Creator,
whom we know as the author of the Lord's incarnation. For
who can doubt when you find in the commencement of the
Gospel that the generation of Jesus was in this way, "When
Mary was espoused to Joseph, before they came together
she was found with child of [*ex*] the Holy Spirit." [Mt 1:18]
42. For although most authorities read "*de Spiritu*," yet the
Greek from which the Latin is translated has "*ex Spiritu
Sancto.*" For that which is "of" [*ex*] any one is either of his
substance or of his power. Of his substance, as the Son, who
says, "I came forth of the mouth of the Most High;" [Sir
24:3] or as the Spirit, "Who proceeds from the Father." [Jn
15:26] Of him the Son says, "He shall glorify me, for he shall
receive of mine." [Jn 16:14] But of the power, as in the
passage, "One God the Father, of whom are all things." [1
Cor 8:6]
43. How, then, was Mary with child of the Holy Spirit? If as
of his substance, was the Spirit, then, changed into flesh and
bones? Certainly not. But if the Virgin conceived as of his
operation and power, who can deny that the Holy Spirit is
Creator?
44. How is it, too, that Job plainly set forth the Spirit as his
Creator, saying, "The Spirit of God has made me"? [Job
33:4] In one short verse he showed him to be both divine and
a Creator. If, then, the Spirit is Creator, he is certainly not a
creature, for the Apostle has separated the Creator and the
creature, saying, "They served the creature rather than the
Creator." [Rom 1:25]
45. He teaches that the Creator is to be served by condemn-
ing those who serve the creature, whereas we owe our service
to the Creator. And since he knew the Spirit to be the
Creator, he teaches that we ought to serve him, saying,
"Beware of the dogs, beware of the evil workers, beware of

the concision, for we are the circumcision who serve the Spirit of God." [Phil 3:2-3]

46. If any one objects because of the variations of the Latin codices, some of which heretics have falsified, let him look at the Greek codices, and observe that it is there written, "who serve the Spirit of God."

47. So, then, when the Apostle says that we ought to serve the Spirit, and also asserts that we must not serve the creature, but the Creator, without doubt he plainly shows that the Holy Spirit is Creator, and is to be venerated with the honor due to the eternal Godhead. It is written, "You shall worship the Lord your God, and him only shall you serve." [Mt 4:10]

> Commentary: Ambrose recalled the image of the Son as the Hand of God and the Spirit as the Finger of God. This does not imply that they are merely a small portion of God. The Son is also called the power of God, but this must be understood in the context of the Son's coeternity with the Father. All of this points to the unity of the Godhead and a unity of operation.

Book 3, Chapter 4.17.[36] But if any one is still entangled in carnal doubts, and hesitates because of bodily figures, let him consider that whoever can think wrongly of the Spirit cannot think rightly of the Son. For if some think that the Spirit is a certain small portion of God, because he is called the Finger of God, [Mt 12:28, Lk 11:20] the same persons must certainly maintain that a small portion only is in the Son of God, because he is called the Right Hand of God. [Mt 26:64] 18. But the Son is called both the Right Hand and the Power of God. [1 Cor 1:24] If then, we consider our words, there can be no perfection without power. Let them therefore take care lest they think what it is impious to say: that the Father was only half perfect in his own substance and received perfection through the Son. Let them cease to deny that the Son is coeternal with the Father. For when did the Power of

[36]NPNF 2.10, 138-139; CSEL 79, 158-159.

God not exist? But if they think that at any time the Power of God did not exist, they will say that at some time perfection existed not in God the Father, to whom they think that power was at some time lacking.

19. As I said, these things are written that we may refer them to the unity of the Godhead, and believe what the Apostle said, that the fulness of the Godhead dwells bodily in Christ, [Col 2:9] and dwells also in the Father, and dwells in the Holy Spirit; and that, as there is a unity of the Godhead, so also is there a unity of operation.

> Commentary: Ambrose noted the role of the Spirit in the Exodus and saw this as a figure of the work of the Spirit in baptism. The Father sanctifies, the Son sanctifies, the Spirit sanctifies, but there is one sanctification because there is one baptism.

20. This may also be gathered from the Song of Moses. After leading the people of the Jews through the sea, he acknowledged the operation of the Father, the Son, and the Holy Spirit, saying, "Your Right Hand, O Lord, has been glorified in power, your Right Hand has dashed the enemy in pieces." [Ex 15:6] Here you have his confession of the Son and of the Father, whose Right Hand he is. And farther on, not to pass by the Holy Spirit, he added, "You sent your Spirit and the sea covered them, and the water was divided by the Spirit of your anger." [Ex 15:10] By this is signified the unity of the Godhead, not an inequality of the Trinity.

21. You see, then, that the Holy Spirit also cooperated with the Father and the Son. Just as though the waves were congealed in the midst of the sea, a wall of water rose up for the passage of the Jews, and then, poured back again by the Spirit, overwhelmed the people of the Egyptians. [Ex 14:22-29] And many think that, from this same origin, the pillar of cloud went before the people of the Jews by day, and the pillar of fire by night, so that the grace of the Spirit might protect his people. [Ex 13:21]

22. Now this operation of God, which the whole world rightly wonders at, did not take place without the work of

the Holy Spirit. The Apostle declared this when he said that the truth of a spiritual mystery was prefigured in it, for we read as follows, "For our fathers were all under the cloud, and all passed through the sea, and were all baptized in Moses in the cloud and in the sea, and all ate the same spiritual meat, and all drank the same spiritual drink." [1 Cor 10:1-4]

23. Without the operation of the Holy Spirit, how could there be the type of a sacrament whose whole truth is in the Spirit? As the Apostle also set forth, "You were washed, you were sanctified, you were justified in the name of our Lord Jesus Christ, and in the Spirit of our God." [1 Cor 6:11]

24. You see, then, that the Father works in the Son, and that the Son works in the Spirit. And therefore do not doubt that, according to the order of scripture, there was in the figure that which the Truth himself declared to be in the truth. For who can deny his operation in the font, in which we feel his operation and grace?

25. For as the Father sanctifies, so, too, the Son sanctifies, and the Holy Spirit sanctifies. The Father sanctifies according to that which is written, "May the God of peace sanctify you, and may your spirit, soul, and body be preserved entire without blame in the day of our Lord Jesus Christ." [1 Th 5:23] And elsewhere the Son says, "Father, sanctify them in the truth." [Jn 17:17]

26. But of the Son the same Apostle said, "Who was made unto us wisdom from God, and righteousness, and sanctification, and redemption." [1 Cor 1:30] Do you see that he was made sanctification? But he was made so for us, not that he should change what he was, but that he might sanctify us in the flesh.

27. And the Apostle also teaches that the Spirit sanctifies. For he speaks thus, "We are bound to give thanks to God always for you, brethren dearly beloved of the Lord; because God chose us as first fruits unto salvation, in sanctification of the Holy Spirit and belief of the truth." [2 Th 2:13]

28. So, then, the Father sanctifies, the Son also sanctifies, and the Spirit sanctifies; but the sanctification is one, for

baptism is one, and the grace of the sacrament is one. [Eph 4:5]

The Nicene-Constantinopolitan Creed

One of the objects of the Council of Constantinople in 381 was to bring the Church's teaching about the Spirit into line with what it believed about the Son. In its first canon, it anathematized the Pneumatomachians who denied the divinity of the Spirit. It also seems to have endorsed the creed now known as the Niceno-Constantinopolitan Creed or simply the Nicene Creed, though the exact origin of this creed is still disputed.

The Creed uses scriptural language in speaking of the Spirit, referring to him as "Lord," "giver of life," who "proceeds from the Father" and "spoke through the prophets." It also clearly, though guardedly, affirms the divinity of the Spirit by stating that he is "adored and honored together with the Father and the Son." This is the language of Athanasius and especially of Basil. For Basil, speaking of identity of honor and worship was equivalent to affirming the consubstantiality of the Spirit, since identity of honor and worship had to be based on identity of nature.

For several reasons, however, the Creed does not explicitly refer to the divinity or the consubstantiality of the Spirit. In the first place, the Council Fathers were attempting to be conciliatory to the Macedonian bishops who questioned the divinity of the Spirit and who finally walked out of the council over this issue. Secondly, not even all those in the orthodox ranks felt at ease with the description of the Holy Spirit as God and as consubstantial.

The Niceno-Constantinopolitan Creed, 381
[37] We believe in one God, the Father almighty, Creator of heaven and earth, of all things both visible and invisible. And in one Lord Jesus Christ, the only-begotten Son of God, born of the Father before all time; light from light, true

[37]TCT 2-3; DS 150.

God from true God; begotten, not created, consubstantial with the Father; through him all things were made. For the sake of us humans and for our salvation, he came down from heaven, was made flesh by the Holy Spirit from the Virgin Mary, and became human; and he was crucified for our sake under Pontius Pilate, suffered, and was buried. And on the third day he arose according to the scriptures; he ascended into heaven, sits at the right hand of the Father, and is going to come again in glory to judge the living and the dead. His reign will have no end. We believe in the Holy Spirit, the Lord, the giver of life; he proceeds from the Father, is adored and honored together with the Father and the Son; he spoke through the prophets. We believe in one, holy, catholic, and apostolic church. We profess one baptism for the forgiveness of sins. We expect the resurrection of the dead and the life of the world to come.   Amen.

Synodical Letter of the Council of Constantinople, 382

In 382 a second council was held at Constantinople. The Eastern bishops sent a letter to Damasus of Rome, Ambrose of Milan, and other Western bishops explaining why they could not attend a General Council at Rome in 382. The letter also affirmed quite explicitly their belief in the consubstantiality of the Spirit. The letter seems to summarize a lost doctrinal tome from the Council of 381.

The Letter
...[38] This [faith] should satisfy you and us, and all who do not pervert the word of truth — for it is the most ancient, it accords with the [creed of our] baptism, and teaches us to believe in the name of the Father and of the Son and of the Holy Spirit — believing, that is to say, in one Godhead and power and substance of the Father and of the Son and of the Holy Spirit, of equal dignity and coeternal majesty, in three perfect hypostases, that is, three perfect persons. Thus no place is found for the error of Sabellius in which the hypos-

[38]LCC 3,344; GCS 19, 292-293.

tases are confused and their individualities taken away, nor does the blasphemy of the Eunomians and Arians and Pneumatomachi prevail, in which the substance or nature of the Godhead is cut up and some kind of later nature, created and of a different substance, is added to the uncreated and consubstantial and coeternal Trinity.

The Council of Rome, 382

The Western Emperor Gratian called the General Council in Rome in 382 because the Western bishops had not been represented at the Council of Constantinople in 381. This Roman council confirmed the *Tome* of Pope Damasus (304-384) which consisted of a creed to which were appended twenty-four anathemas against various heretics. These anathemas leave no doubt that the Western Church affirmed that the Spirit is God and that he is consubstantial with the Father and the Son.

The Tome of Damasus
1.[39] We pronounce anathema against those who do not proclaim with complete freedom that he [the Holy Spirit] is of one power and substance with the Father and the Son.
3. We pronounce anathema against Arius and Eunomius, who with the same ungodliness, though in different words, assert that the Son and the Holy Spirit are creatures.
10. If anyone denies that the Father is eternal, that the Son is eternal, and that the Holy Spirit is eternal; he is a heretic.
16. If anyone denies that the Holy Spirit is truly and properly from the Father, and, Like the Son, is of the divine substance and is true God: he is a heretic.
17. If anyone denies that the Holy Spirit has all power and knows all things, and is everywhere, just as the Father and the Son; he is a heretic.
18. If anyone says that the Holy Spirit is a creature, or was created by the Son; he is a heretic.
19. If anyone denies that the Father made all things through

[39]TCT 125-127; PL 13, 358-361.

the Son and through his Holy Spirit, that is, all things visible and invisible: he is a heretic.

20. If anyone denies that the Father, Son, and Holy Spirit have one divinity, authority, majesty, power, one glory, dominion, one kingdom, and one will and truth: he is a heretic.

21. If anyone denies that the three persons, the Father, the Son, and the Holy Spirit, are true persons, equal, eternal, containing all things visible and invisible, that they are omnipotent, judge all things, give life to all things, make all things, and conserve all things: he is a heretic.

22. If anyone denies that the Holy Spirit must be adored by every creature, just as the Son and the Father: he is a heretic.

24. But if anyone, while saying that the Father is God and the Son is God and the Holy Spirit is God, makes a division [in the Trinity] and says that they [the divine persons] are gods, and does not say that they are one God, precisely on account of the one divinity and power which we believe and know is possessed by the Father and the Son and the Holy Spirit; and if he slights the Son or the Holy Spirit in such a way so as to think that only the Father is called God and in this way believes in one God: he is a heretic on all counts and is even a Jew. For the name of gods was given by God to all the angels and the saints; but, for the Father, Son and Holy Spirit, because of the one same divinity, the name of God and not of gods is indicated and manifested to us in order that we may believe that we are baptized in the Father, Son, and Holy Spirit only, and not in names of the archangels or angels, as heretics or Jews or even foolish pagans believe.

Therefore this is the salvation of Christians: that believing in the Trinity, that is in the Father, Son, and Holy Spirit, and being baptized in the Trinity, we may unhesitatingly believe that in the Trinity there is only one true divinity and power, majesty and substance.

Concluding Reflections

At first reading, the fourth century writings on the Holy Spirit seem to suffer from a great deal of repetition. The arguments for the divinity of the Spirit and the attempts to speak of the unity and diversity in the Trinity progress almost imperceptibly from one author to the next. From Cyril of Jerusalem to the Council of Constantinople, the development of the theology of the Spirit seems far from dramatic. Still, a careful reading of the texts uncovers more than the drama of the struggle in the fourth-century church. It uncovers as well a clear growth in understanding of who the Spirit is and how he relates to the Father and the Son.

Cyril of Jerusalem is the first representative of the century. He displayed reluctance to say more about the Spirit than is given in the scripture. He stressed the work of the Spirit in the Christian, sanctifying and deifying and sealing the soul.

Athanasius, writing perhaps ten years after Cyril, composed the first formal treatise on the Spirit and developed at some length the arguments for the divinity of the Spirit, tying the Spirit's divinity to his work of deification.

The Cappadocians, Basil and the two Gregorys, made the other significant contribution to the development of the doctrine of the Spirit by attempting to establish an accurate terminology for speaking of the unity and the diversity in God. They affirmed the distinction of persons in the unity of nature. Gregory of Nazianzus explicitly called the Spirit God and consubstantial. Gregory of Nyssa argued from the identity of operation to the identity of nature in the Trinity. All three of them grappled with the question of how to distinguish the Spirit from the Son. Their answer was to distinguish them in terms of their mode of origin. The Son is begotten; the Spirit proceeds.

Certainly Athanasius and the Cappadocians were the high points of the development of the doctrine of the Spirit in the fourth century, but we cannot dismiss the contributions of two other Eastern theologians. Epiphanius, writing about the time of Basil, professed that the Spirit is God and is of the divine substance. The Spirit is teacher and sanctifier and the bond of the Trinity. Epiphanius also seemed to equate the Spirit with grace. Didymus the Blind, on the other hand, wrote about the time of the two Gregorys. He stressed the role of the Spirit in sanctification and echoed the argument of Gregory of Nazianzus from the identity of operation to the identity of substance.

In the West, Hilary and Ambrose are the two important representatives from this century. Writing at the same time as Athanasius, Hilary professed his belief in the existence and distinctness of the Spirit and characterized the Spirit as the Gift of God working in the faithful. Ambrose, writing at the same time as the Cappadocians, stressed the unity of the Godhead and the unity of operation in the Trinity. He spoke of the Spirit as the Creator of all things and recognized him as the author of the Lord's incarnation.

Though this chapter presents the major theologians of the Spirit in the fourth century, the writings given actually span less than thirty-five years. In that time, there is a clear continuity and development from Cyril to Athanasius to the Cappadocians. The Councils of Constantinople and Rome do little more than make official the belief in the divinity of the Spirit. The more subtle theological work of Athanasius and the Cappadocians would be carried on in the next century, especially by Augustine.

Chapter Four

LORD AND GIVER OF LIFE: THE FIFTH CENTURY

Introduction

The doctrinal developments of the fourth century which culminated in the Council of Constantinople's assertion of the divinity and equality of the Spirit continued in the fifth century, but centered on the constitution of Christ. Writing and preaching on the Holy Spirit focused on his role in the economy of salvation, both in the individual Christian and in the church community. The struggle in the Eastern Church between the theologians associated with the See of Antioch and those committed to an Alexandrian viewpoint are only dimly reflected in their explanations of the function of the Spirit in preserving a person in goodness and conferring the gifts of eternal life. Selections from the preaching of John Chrysostom and Theodore of Mopsuestia represent the thought of the Syrian Church. Cyril of Alexandria serves as the representative of his partisans.

A long struggle over church discipline in the Western Church finally bore fruit in the preaching and writing of Augustine. He also continued the development of Trinitarian theory along the lines opened by the Cappadocian theologians. The influence of Augustine is evident in both the work of Leo the Great and in the Western Creed which was attributed to Athanasius.

The Writings

John Chrysostom (d. 407)

John was born in Antioch of a noble Christian family sometime between 344 and 354. He was ordained a priest in 386 and until 397 preached in the principal church in Antioch. In 398 he became patriarch of Constantinople. His zeal for reform and his outspoken criticism of abuses in church and society led to numerous confrontations with other bishops and with the empress. He was finally exiled and died in Comana in 407.

John was not involved in any of the great dogmatic controversies of the fourth century. He was not a speculative theologian and contributed little to the development of doctrine. He was a pastor, a reformer, and above all, a preacher. His extensive writings, however, are rich in doctrine and communicate the traditional faith with eloquence and force. The selections here are taken from his homilies, most of which are from the period of 386 to 397 when John was preaching in Antioch. John referred frequently to the Spirit in his homilies on the New Testament, but there are few extended discussions of the Spirit's nature and operation.

First Homily on the Acts of the Apostles

> Commentary: In his opening homily on the Acts of the Apostles, Chyrsostom contrasted the role of the Spirit in the Gospels and in Acts. He spoke of the role of the Spirit in baptism.

5.[1] ... The Gospels, then, are a history of what Christ did

[1]NPNF 1.11, 7; PG 60, 21.

and said; but the Acts, of what that "other Comforter" said and did. The Spirit did many things in the Gospels also; even as Christ here in the Acts still works in people as he did in the Gospels: only then the Spirit worked through the Temple, now through the apostles: then, he came into the Virgin's womb, and fashioned the Temple; now, into apostolic souls: then, in the likeness of a dove; now, in the likeness of fire. And why? Showing there the gentleness of the Lord, but here his taking vengeance also, he now warns them of the judgment as well. For, when the need was to forgive, there was need of much gentleness; but now that we have obtained the gift, it is henceforth a time for judgment and examination.

But why does Christ say, "You shall be baptized," when in fact there was no water in the upper room? Because the more essential part of baptism is the Spirit, through whom indeed the water has its effect. In the same manner, our Lord is also said to be anointed, not that he had ever been anointed with oil, but because he had received the Spirit. In fact, we do find them receiving a baptism with water and a baptism with the Spirit, but at different moments. In our case both take place in one act, but then they were divided. For in the beginning they were baptized by John; since, if harlots and publicans went to that baptism, much rather would they who were subsequently to be baptized by the Holy Spirit.

Thirteenth Homily on Romans

> Commentary: Chrysostom affirmed the undividedness of the Trinity. He enumerated the evils that come of not having the Spirit and the blessings that come of having the Spirit. He referred to the Spirit's role in immortality and the resurrection.

8.[2] ... For it must be that where the Spirit is, there Christ is also. For wherever one person of the Trinity is, there the

[2]NPNF 1.11, 436; PG 60, 519.

whole Trinity is present. For it is undivided in itself, and has a most complete unity. What then, it may be said, will happen, if Christ is in us? "The body is dead because of sin; but the Spirit is life because of righteousness." [Rom 8:10] These are the great evils that come of not having the Holy Spirit: death, enmity against God, inability to satisfy his laws, not being Christ's as we should be, the lack of his indwelling. Consider now also what great blessings come of having the Spirit: being Christ's, having Christ himself, competing with the angels (for this is what mortifying flesh is), and living an immortal life, holding the pledges of the resurrection, easily running the race of virtue. For he does not say simply that the body is no longer active for sin, but even that it is dead, so increasing the ease of the race. For such a person gains the crown without troubles and labors. Then afterward for this reason he adds also, "[dead] to sin," so that you may see that it is the viciousness, not the essence of the body, that he has abolished at once. For if the latter were done, many things which are beneficial to the soul would have been abolished also. This however is not what he says: while it is still alive and abiding, he contends, it is dead. This is the sign of our having the Son and of the Spirit being in us, that with respect to the working of sin our bodies are no different from those that lie on the bier. Do not be frightened at hearing of mortifying. For in this you have true life, with no death to succeed it, the life of the Spirit. It does not yield to death any more, but wears out death and consumes it. What it receives, it keeps immortal. Thus after saying, "the body is dead," he says not, "but the Spirit lives," but instead, "is life," in order to point out that the Spirit had the power of giving this to others also. Then again to strengthen his hearer, he tells him the cause and proof of the life. Now this is righteousness; for where there is no sin, death is not to be found either; but where death is not to be found, life is indissoluble.

"But if the Spirit of him that raised up Jesus from the dead dwells in you, he that raised up our Lord shall also give life to your mortal bodies by his Spirit that dwells in you." [Rom 8:11]

Again, he mentions the resurrection, since this was the most encouraging hope to the hearer, and gave him a security from what had happened to Christ. Now be not afraid because you are surrounded with a dead body. If it has the Spirit, it shall surely rise again.

Theodore of Mopsuestia (d. 428)

Theodore was a contemporary and fellow student of John Chrysostom at Antioch. He became bishop of Mopsuestia in 392 and was a leading proponent of the Antiochene Christology which emphasized the man assumed by the Word of God to be Christ. Although his Christology was attacked shortly after his death and he was finally condemned at the Second Council of Constantinople in 553, the orthodoxy of his doctrine of the Holy Spirit was never disputed.

In his catechetical homilies, Theodore went through each article of the Creed of Nicea, explaining Catholic teaching. He explained the Spirit's procession from the Father as an affirmation of his being of the same nature, eternally in and with the Father. Thence he moved to the expression, "giver of life," showing that the Spirit is the source of immortality.

On the Nicene Creed
10.[3] After this they added in their teaching concerning the Spirit, "giver of life," an expression which aptly demonstrates that the Holy Spirit is God like the expressions discussed above. Our Lord said, "The water that I shall give shall be in him a well of water springing up into life." [Jn 4:14] He refers by his words to the gift of the Holy Spirit which gives everlasting life to those who are worthy of it. And again in another passage, "He that believes in me, as the Scripture has said, out of his belly shall flow rivers of living water." [Jn 7:38] He calls living water the gift of the Holy Spirit because it can grant everlasting life. And the

[3]Woodbrooke Studies 5, 110-111.

Apostle also said, "The letter kills but the Spirit gives life," [2 Cor 3:6] and showed us that he will make us immortal. And again in another passage, "The first Adam was made a living soul and the second Adam a quickening Spirit." [1 Cor 15:45] He shows by his words that Christ our Lord was changed in his body, at the resurrection from the dead, to immortality by the power of the Holy Spirit. He likewise said in another passage, "He was declared to be the Son of God with power and by the Spirit of holiness, and rose up from the dead, Jesus Christ our Lord." [Rom 1:4] And, "If the Spirit of him that raised up Jesus Christ from the dead dwells in you, he that raised up our Lord Jesus Christ from the dead shall also give life to your dead bodies because of his Spirit that dwells in you." [Rom 8:11]

Our Lord also said, when teaching us concerning his body, "It is the Spirit that gives life, the flesh profits nothing," [Jn 6:63] in order to show that he also had immortality from the Holy Spirit and to demonstrate this point to others. Such an act belongs indeed to the nature that is eternal and cause of everything, because to him who is able to create something from nothing belongs the act of giving life, that is to say, to make us immortal so that we should always live. Even among created beings those who have an immortal nature are considered higher in rank, and it is, therefore, clear and evident that he who is able to perform this act is also able to perform other acts. God himself shows that it is the prerogative of the divine nature to do this in saying, "Know now that I am he and there is no God beside me: I kill, and I make alive; I wound, and I heal." [Dt 32:39] He shows that it is his exclusive prerogative to raise from the dead and to free from their pain those who are wounded.

Cyril of Alexandria (d. 444)

Cyril was elected patriarch of Alexandria in 412. He is most famous for the bitter struggle which led to Nestorius' condemnation at the Council of Ephesus in 431. The selections here are from Cyril's commentary on the Gospel of St. John. The commentary has a clear dogmatic flavor and is concerned with the refutation of heretical doctrines. It was written sometime before the beginning of the Nestorian controversy in 429.

In the commentary, Cyril affirmed that the Spirit is God and consubstantial with the Father and the Son. Cyril's greatest contribution, however, was his teaching on the work of the Spirit in divinizing humans, a teaching that is a full expression of the whole Greek theology of divinization. For Cyril, the Spirit is the source of incorruption. Sent by the Father and the Son, he dwells in Christians and makes them partakers of the divine nature. He makes them children of God and conforms them to the image of the Father and the Son. Cyril also affirmed that the Spirit inspired the prophets and was given to the apostles in connection with priesthood and apostleship.

Commentary on the Gospel According to St. John

> Commentary: Cyril referred to humanity's original state of incorruption which was lost by sin. Since the Spirit was the cause of incorruption, God promised the Spirit so that the original state might be restored. The Spirit was first given to Christ to transform human nature for all. The Spirit inspired the prophets, but the Spirit actually dwells in those who believe in Christ.

Book 5, Chapter 2[4] (Jn 7:39) . . . This earthly animal capable of reason, humanity, was in the beginning formed free of all corruption. The Holy Spirit which God had made to dwell in him was the cause of this incorruptibility and of his perseverance in all virtue. As it is written, "God breathed into him the breath of life." [Gen 2:7] But he fell into sin through that old deceit of the devil; within a short time he gradually progressed in this sin. He lost all the good things he had, including the Spirit, so that finally he was not only subject to corruption but prone to every sin. The Maker of all things formed a most excellent plan and decided to

[4]Trans. J.P. Burns; PG 73, 752-756

"gather up all things in Christ," [Eph 1:10] and to restore human nature to its original condition. Along with other goods, he promises to give the Holy Spirit once again since without him humanity could not be restored to a firm and stable possession of the other goods. He sets the coming of Christ as the time for the Holy Spirit to descend upon us. He promises this, "In those days (of the Savior) I will pour out my Spirit manifestly and clearly on all flesh." [Jl 2:28] The time for this generosity and liberality brought the Only-begotten to earth in flesh, as a man born of woman according to the Holy Scripture. [Gal 4:4] God the Father again gave the Holy Spirit; Christ himself received the Spirit first, as the first-fruits of the renewed nature. John the Baptist witnessed this, "I saw the Spirit descend from heaven and rest upon him." [Jn 1:32] How was it that he received? We must explain what we have said. Did he receive what he did not have? In no way! The Spirit belongs to the Son. He is not sent into him from outside, as God bestows him on us. The Spirit is naturally in him just as he is in the Father. The Spirit proceeds through him to the saints as the Father bestows him on each one in the appropriate way. We say that the Son received the Spirit insofar as he had become human, and it was appropriate for him to receive him as human. . . . The Only-begotten did not receive the Holy Spirit for himself; the Spirit is his, is in him and is given through him, as we have already said. As human, he had the whole of human nature in himself, in order to renew all of humanity and restore it to its original state. . . . The Only-begotten became human like us so that the good things which were returned and the grace of the Spirit might first be grounded in him and thereby firmly preserved for the whole nature. It was as though the only-begotten Word of God extended the stability which is proper to his own nature to us, to the human nature which had in Adam been condemned to be changeable and prone to both error and perversion. In the same way, therefore, that the fall of the first human resulted in a loss for all humanity, so the whole race has acquired the benefit of the divine gifts in him who knows no change. If anyone considers that what we are thinking and saying is not right, let him explain why Christ is called the Second Adam in the divine scriptures. In that First Adam, the human race, which did not exist before, came forth into the world and was then corrupted because it broke the divine law. In the Second Adam, Christ, it returned to a new beginning and was restored to a newness of life and returned to incorruption. As Paul says, "If anyone is in Christ, he is a new creature." [2 Cor 5:17] We have been given a renewing Spirit, the Holy Spirit, the source of eternal life, after Christ was glorified in his resurrection, when he burst the bonds of death and showed himself superior to all corruption. He returned to life with the whole nature in himself, as human and one of us.

> Commentary: Cyril stated that the Spirit is the Spirit of Christ and of the Father. Because humans share in the divine nature through the Spirit, the Spirit must be of a different nature. He is God and not a creature.

Book 10[5] (Jn 14:23) . . . When Christ our Savior dwells in us through the Holy Spirit, his Father will most certainly be with us as well. The Spirit of Christ is the same as the Spirit of the Father. Thus the inspired Paul sometimes refers to the Spirit as belonging to the Father and at other times as belonging to Christ. Because this is the nature of the case, he speaks truly in each expression and does not contradict himself. He writes to some, "The one who raised Jesus Christ from the dead will give life to your mortal bodies through his Spirit dwelling in you." [Rom 8:11] Further, "Because you are his children, God sent the Spirit of his Son into your hearts crying, Abba, Father." [Gal 4:6] Do you see that the same Spirit belongs to the Father and the Son? When, therefore, the Only-begotten dwells in your hearts, the Father is never absent. The Son has the Father in himself and is himself by nature in the Father, since he is of one substance with him.

[5]PG 74, 289-292.

This, then, is the definition and incontestable doctrine of the faith. I would like to question those who, through their ignorance of many things, have chosen to adopt other views and have armed their tongues to attack the glory of the Holy Spirit. What would they reply when we say, "If the Spirit is created and foreign to the divine substance, as you say, then how could God dwell in us through him? Or how does a person share in the divine by receiving the Holy Spirit? If we could share in that divine and ineffable nature through some created substance, then what would prevent God from setting aside the Spirit and dwelling in us, sanctifying us through any other creature he might choose? This, however, is impossible. A person can share in the divine nature only through the Spirit. The Spirit is therefore God and of God; he is not one of the creatures, as some suppose.

Something further must be considered. If a being participates in the superior substance and distinct class of another being, then it must itself be different in nature from the being in which it participates. If the Spirit is himself created or made, then what would remain in which the creation could participate? Certainly not part of itself. Being created would be common to both. Since we are both created and made, the Spirit in whom we participate is of a nature different from ours. The Spirit, therefore, is not created. If this is true, and it certainly is, then the Spirit is God and of God, as we have said. Nothing can ever be considered uncreated except he who is by nature God, from whom the Holy Spirit ineffably proceeds so that the one from whom he comes may dwell in us. He belongs to his substance, like a property of his holiness.

> Commentary: Cyril commented on the passage in which Jesus breathes his Spirit upon the apostles on Easter evening. The gift of the Spirit is necessary for those ordained by Christ to be apostles. The Spirit transforms them and gives them power to proclaim the Lordship of Jesus, Christ consecrates and sanctifies them through participation in the Spirit.

Book 12, Chapter 1[6] (Jn 20:22-23). After he honored them with the great dignity of being apostles and made them priests and ministers of the divine altar, as I just said, he immediately sanctified them. By a visible breathing, he endowed them with his own Holy Spirit. He did this so that we too might firmly believe that the Spirit is not a stranger to the Son, but consubstantial with him and proceeding from the Father through him. He showed that those he chooses for the apostolic office must be given the Spirit. Why so? Unless they had been clothed with power from on high and transformed from what they were, they could neither have pleased God nor would they exalt above the snares of sin. . . . We also say that they would never have understood the mystery of Christ or been able to teach it perfectly unless the Spirit had enlightened them and revealed what exceeds human reason and prayer. By this illumination they were raised up to teach what is necessary. Thus Paul says, "No one can say Jesus is Lord except in the Holy Spirit." [1 Cor 12:3] Because they were to proclaim Jesus Lord, that is, to preach him as Lord and God, they received the Spirit's grace which was a necessary adjunct to the apostolic office. Christ sent him from himself, not as the agent of someone else. The Spirit could not come to us from the Father unless he came through the Son.

Augustine of Hippo (354-430)

Augustine was born at Thagaste in the Province of Numidia in Roman Africa in 354, the son of a devout Christian mother and a pagan father. He was educated in Carthage for public speaking and embarked on a career of teaching and civil service. After nine years as an adherent to the Manichean sect, he was converted to Christianity through the ministry of Ambrose of Milan and baptized by him in 387. He returned to his home town intending to follow a life of reflection and writing but was pressed into the clergy of

[6]PG 74, 709-712.

Hippo Regius when he visited there. Even before he succeeded Bishop Valerius about 395, Augustine had emerged
as a brilliant controversialist; he soon became the leading
figure in the Catholic Church of Roman Africa. He played a
major role in winning an imperial condemnation of the
Donatists at the hearing in Carthage in 411 and secured the
rejection of Pelagius and his teaching by the bishops of
Africa and Italy. He died at Hippo on 28 August 430.

Many streams of thought flow together in Augustine's
writing on the Holy Spirit. He was heir to a neo-Platonic
form of Christianity which flourished in Italy, to the Trinitarian theology of Hilary of Poitiers and the Cappadocians.
Yet he fully involved himself in the questions of ecclesiology
which had vexed the African Church since the early third
century. His interpretation of the writings of St. Paul was
innovative even in an age preoccupied with these texts.
Augustine strove to synthesize tendencies which had been
developing in prior centuries. He elaborated a view of the
Holy Spirit which integrated the mission to the church with
the sanctification of the individual. Out of this he drew new
insights into the Trinity itself. His work is at once the
capstone of earlier thought and the foundation of the subsequent Latin theology.

The selections from Augustine's writings are divided into
three categories. Sections from his writings against the Donatists precede the ones from the Pelagian controversy. Selections from his later dogmatic and speculative theology of
the Trinity are then taken together.

i. Writings against the Donatists

Augustine's writings and debate with the Donatists
focused a controversy which had continued since the conflict between Cyprian and Stephen in the third century. The
schismatic followers of Donatus claimed to be a pure communion, free of the pollution of a sinful clergy. Using Cyprian's understanding of the relation of the church and the
Holy Spirit, they insisted that no one could be saved
through baptism given in the Catholic communion.
Catholic baptism was without effect and had to be repeated

when a person converted to the one true Donatist Church which possessed the Holy Spirit. Yet the Catholics recognized the Donatist baptism as valid and refused to repeat the sacrament when a schismatic entered the Catholic Church.

Augustine provided a theology which explained the Catholic position. He identified the Holy Spirit present in the church with the charity by which the saints within the visible communion are bound together in love of God and neighbor. This charity is also the basis of the sanctifying power which is exercised in the prayer of the saints for the forgiveness of sins. Anyone who separates himself from this unity by the sin of schism loses the Spirit and violates the foundational commandment of love of neighbor. He may have baptism, but in the absence of the Spirit's gift of love, neither the sacrament nor his obedience to the other commandments is salvific. Here the Holy Spirit is understood as the source of both unity and sanctification in the church.

On Baptism

> Commentary: In his response to Donatist writings, Augustine had to explain the proper interpretation of some of Cyprian's statements which favored the Donatist position. The quotations come from Cyprian through the Donatist writings. Those who separate themselves off from the Spirit's unity of love in the church, physically or only intentionally, may receive the sacraments but do not receive the sanctifying effects of the Holy Spirit.

Book 3, Chapter 16.21.[7] But when it is said that "the Holy Spirit is given only in the Catholic Church," I suppose that our ancestors meant that we should understand what the Apostle says, "Because the love of God is spread abroad in our hearts by the Holy Spirit who is given to us." [Rom 5:5] For this is that same love which is wanting in all who are cut off from the communion of the Catholic Church; and for lack of this, "though they speak with the tongues of humans

[7]NPNF 1.4, 442-443; CSEL 51, 212-213.

and of angels, though they understand all mysteries and all knowledge, and though they have the gift of prophecy, and all faith, so that they could remove mountains, and though they bestow all their goods to feed the poor, and though they give their bodies to be burned, it profits them nothing." [1 Cor 13:1-3] But those who do not care for the unity of the church do not have God's love. Consequently we are right in understanding that the Holy Spirit may not be received except in the Catholic Church. For the Holy Spirit is not only given by the laying on of hands amid the testimony of temporal sensible miracles, as he was given in earlier days as the credentials of a rudimentary faith and for the expansion of the first beginnings of the church. Who expects now that those on whom hands are laid so that they may receive the Holy Spirit will immediately begin to speak with tongues? But it is understood that invisibly and imperceptibly, for the sake of the bond of peace, divine love is breathed into their hearts, so that they may be able to say, "Because the love of God is spread abroad in our hearts by the Holy Spirit who is given to us." [Rom 5:5] There are many operations of the Holy Spirit, which the same Apostle speaks about in a certain passage at a length he thinks sufficient, and then concludes, "But one and the same Spirit works all of these, dividing to every one individually as he wills." [1 Cor 12:11] The sacrament is one thing, which even Simon Magus could have. [Acts 8:13] The one operation of the Spirit is another thing, which is often found even in wicked people, as Saul had the gift of prophecy. [1 Sam 10:6,10] That other operation of the same Spirit is a third thing, which only the good can have, as "the end of the commandment is charity out of a pure heart, and of a good conscience, and of sincere faith." [1 Tim 1:5] Whatever it is that may be received by heretics and schismatics, the charity which covers the multitude of sins is the special gift of Catholic unity and peace. Nor is it found in all those who are within that bond, since not all that are inside it belong to it, as we shall see in the proper place. Outside this bond that love cannot exist; without it all the other requirements cannot profit or release from sin, even if they can be recognised and approved. But the laying on of hands in reconciliation to the church is not, like baptism, incapable of repetition; for what more is it than a prayer offered over a person?

> Commentary: The peace of the church which is established by charity effects the forgiveness of sins. The saints who constitute the true spiritual church within the visible communion received the command and the power to forgive sins by joining others to themselves in unity. Although the evil who are outside the spiritual unity may give and receive the sacrament, only the saints forgive sins and sanctify.

Book 3, Chapter 18.23.[8] "As my Father has sent me," says our Lord, "even so I send you." And when he had said this, he breathed on them, and said to them, "Receive the Holy Spirit. Whoever's sins you remit, they are remitted; and whoever's sins you retain, they are retained." [Jn 20:21-23] Therefore, if they [the apostles] represented the church, and this was said to them as to the church herself, it follows that the peace of the church looses sins, and separation from the church retains them, not according to the will of humans, but according to the will of God and the prayers of the saints who are spiritual, who "judge all things, but themselves are judged by no one." [1 Cor 2:15] For the rock retains, the rock remits; the dove retains, the dove remits; unity retains, unity remits. But the peace of this unity exists only in the good, in those who either are already spiritual or are advancing by the obedience of concord to spiritual things. It does not exist in the evil who baptize and are baptized whether they cause disturbances outside or are tolerated within the church with lamentations. Those who are tolerated with groanings within the church do not belong to the same unity of the dove and to that "glorious church which has neither spot nor wrinkle, nor any such thing."[Eph 5:27] Still, if they are corrected and confess that they came to baptism most unworthily, they are not baptized again. They

---

[8]NPNF 1.4, 443-444; CSEL 51, 214-216.

begin to belong to the dove, through whose groans those sins are now remitted which were once retained in them when they were estranged from her peace. The same holds for those who are more openly outside the church: if they have already received the same sacraments when they are corrected and come to the unity of the church, they are freed from their sins not by a repetition of baptism, but by the same law of charity and bond of unity. For if "only those who are set over the church, and established by the law of the gospel and ordination as appointed by the Lord may baptize," [Cyprian] were any of these the ones who seized on estates by treacherous frauds and increased their gains by compound interest? I trust not, since the ones established by ordination as appointed by the Lord are those whom the Apostle, in giving them a standard, describes as, "Not greedy, not given to filthy lucre." [Tit 1:7] Yet this kind of persons used to baptize in the time of Cyprian himself; and he confesses with many lamentations that they were his fellow-bishops, and endures them with the great reward of tolerance. Yet they did not confer the remission of sins. This is granted through the prayers of the saints, through the groans of the dove, no matter who baptizes, as long as those who were baptized belong to her peace. For the Lord would not say to robbers and usurers, "Whoever's sins you remit, they shall be remitted to him; and whoever's sins you retain, they shall be retained." [Jn 20:25] "Outside the church, indeed, nothing can be either bound or loosed, since there is no one who can either bind or loose." [Cyprian] But he is loosed who has made peace with the dove, and he is bound who is not at peace with the dove, whether he is openly outside or appears to be inside.

> Commentary: Augustine summarized this disagreement with Cyprian and his own understanding of the operation of the Holy Spirit in the church and the sacraments.

Book 6, Chapter 3.5.[9] But I think that we have sufficiently

9NPNF 1.4, 480-481; CSEL 51, 301-302.

shown, both from the canon of Scripture, and from the letters of Cyprian himself, that evil persons, while by no means converted to a better mind, can have, confer, and receive baptism. Yet it is most clear that they do not belong to the holy church of God, though they seem to be within it. They are covetous, robbers, usurers, envious, evil thinkers, and the like. She is one dove, [Cant 6:8] modest and chaste, a bride without spot or wrinkle, [Eph 5:21] a garden enclosed, a fountain sealed, an orchard of pomegranates with pleasant fruits, [Cant 4:12-13] with all the similar properties which are attributed to her. All these qualities can be understood to be only in the good, the holy and just. They occur where there are not only those operations of the gifts of God which are common to good and bad alike, but where there is also the inner bond of charity conspicuous in those who have the Holy Spirit. To these the Lord says, "Whoever's sins you remit, they are remitted unto them; and whoever's sins you retain, they are retained." [Jn 20:23]

Chapter 4.6. And so it is clear that no good reason has been shown why the bad person, who has baptism, may not also confer it. As he has it to destruction, he may also confer it to destruction. The destruction follows not because of the character of the thing conferred, nor of the person conferring, but because of the character of the person on whom it is conferred. For when a bad person confers it on a good person, that is, on one within the bond of unity who is converted with a true conversion, then the wickedness of him who confers it causes no separation between the good sacrament which is conferred and the good member of the church on whom it is conferred. And when his sins are forgiven him on occasion of his true conversion to God, they are forgiven by those to whom he is united by his true conversion. The sins are forgiven by the same Spirit which is given to all the saints who cling to one another in love, whether they know one another in the body or not. Similarly when a person's sins are retained, they are certainly retained by those from whom the one in whom they are retained separates himself by dissimilarity of life and by the turning away of a corrupt heart, whether they know him in the body or not.

Letter 98, to Boniface

> Commentary: Augustine responded to a Bishop Boniface who asked whether consecrating an infant to a demon harms him and makes him guilty of idolatry. Augustine explained how the Holy Spirit unites distinct individuals to make baptism effective while an evil spirit cannot bind them together in sin.

2.[10] It is one Spirit that makes it possible for a person to be reborn through the agency of another's will when he is offered for baptism, and through him the one offered is reborn. For it is not written, "Unless a person is born again through the will of his parents" or "through the faith of his godparents or the ministers"; but, "Unless a person is born again of water and the Holy Spirit." [Jn 3:5] The water, therefore, manifests the sacrament of grace exteriorly; the Spirit effects the benefit of grace interiorly, looses the bond of guilt, and restores good to his nature. Both regenerate in one Christ the person who was begotten of one Adam. The regenerating Spirit is, then, equally present in the elders offering and in the child offered and reborn. Through this sharing of one and the same Spirit, therefore, the will of those who offer is beneficial to the child who is offered for baptism. When the elders sin by offering the child and trying to subject him to the accursed bonds of devils, however, the same mind is not in both. Thus they cannot share the guilt. Guilt is not communicated by the will of another, as grace is communicated by the unity of the Holy Spirit. The same Holy Spirit can be in this person and in that one, even if they do not know each other, because through him each one has the same grace. The human spirit cannot be in this person and in that, so as to make both share the guilt if one sins and the other does not. It follows from this that a child born of

[10]FC 18, 130-131; CSEL 34, 521-523.

his parents' flesh can be born again of the Spirit of God, so that the stain contracted from them is washed away. One born again of the Spirit of God, however, cannot be reborn of the flesh of his parents so as to contract again the stain that has been washed away. Therefore, the child does not lose the grace of Christ once conferred, except by his own sinful act, if he turns out badly as he grows older. Then, indeed, he will begin to have his own personal sins which are not taken away by baptism, but may be healed by another remedy.

> Commentary: As Augustine indicated above in the selections from *On Baptism*, the Holy Spirit unites the infant to all the faithful in the church who share the gift of charity.

5.[11] Do not be troubled because some bring their children to receive baptism, not through faith so that they may be reborn to eternal life by spiritual grace, but because they think it is a medicine for retaining or regaining bodily health. The children are none the less regenerated even if they are not presented for that reason, because the required actions and words of the sacrament are performed, without which the child cannot be consecrated. The Holy Spirit, who dwells in the saints, out of whom that peerless dove covered with silver [Ps 68:13] is molded by the fire of charity, does his work sometimes through the agency not only of the merely ignorant, but even of the utterly unworthy. Surely, the little ones are offered for the reception of the spiritual grace, not so much by those in whose arms they are carried — although they are offered by them if they are good and faithful — as by the whole company of the saints and believers. We rightly understand that they are offered by all who consent to the offering, and by whose holy and indivisible charity they are helped to share in the outpouring of the Holy Spirit. Mother Church who is in the saints does this wholly, because she wholly brings forth all and each.

[11]FC 18, 133-134; CSEL 34, 526.

Sixth Homily on the First Epistle of John

> Commentary: These expositions seem to be part of Augustine's struggle against the Donatists, though their dating is disputed. In them, he expanded his analysis of the role of the Spirit by concentrating on love of neighbor. He found a manifestation of the Holy Spirit in the love by which Christians who do not even know one another are joined.

10.[12] In the earliest times, "The Holy Spirit came upon the believers and they spoke in tongues," which they had never learned, "as the Spirit gave them to speak." [Acts 2:4] These were signs adapted to the times. It was appropriate that the Holy Spirit should be manifest by all these tongues since God's gospel was to run through the languages of the whole earth. This was done as a sign and it passed away. When we impose hands on people now for the reception of the Holy Spirit, do we look to see whether they speak in tongues? When we laid our hand on these newly reborn, did each of you look to see whether they would speak with tongues? When he saw that they did not, was anyone so perverse as to claim that they had not received the Holy Spirit, since, if they had, they would have spoken in tongues as people did in those days? If, then, the presence of the Holy Spirit is not now manifest through these miracles, what sign is given? How does a person come to know that he has received the Holy Spirit?

Let him ask his own heart. If he loves his brother, then the Spirit of God dwells in him. Let him look into himself and examine himself before the eyes of God. Let him see whether he finds in himself the love of peace and unity, the love of the church spread throughout the world. Let him not be satisfied to love the neighbor whom he can see, for we have many whom we do not see, to whom we are joined in the unity of the Spirit. Is it strange that they are not here with us? We are in one Body and have one Head, who is in heaven. My

---

[12]NPNF 1.7, 497-498; SC 75, 298-300.

friends, our two eyes do not see each other and one could claim that they do not know each other. Could we say, however, that they do not know each other in the charity which joins them together. When both eyes are open, the right cannot focus on some object without the left also centering on it. See if you can gaze on some object with one and not the other. Together they meet in one object; together they are directed to one object. Their positions are separate but they have a single direction. If, then, all who love God with you have a single direction with you, do not attend to the bodily separation. You have together set the vision of your hearts on the light of truth. If, then, you want to know whether you have received the Spirit, ask your heart. Perhaps you have the sacrament without the power of the sacrament. Examine your heart. If you find the love of neighbor there, let your mind be at rest. There can be no love without the Spirit of God, as Paul proclaims, "The love of God is shed abroad in our hearts through the Holy Spirit who is given to us." [Rom 5:5]

> Commentary: John gives another criterion of determining the presence of the Spirit — the confession that Jesus Christ is come in the flesh. Augustine showed that this must be translated into a love of neighbor. The Donatist schismatics violated such love and had only an empty faith.

13[13] ... Now my friends we must attend to what people do and not just to what they say. Let us ask why Christ came in the flesh. Then we will really get at the people who deny that he came in this way. If you are satisfied with words, you will hear many a heresy confessing that Christ came in the flesh. The truth convicts these people. Why did Christ come in the flesh? Was he not God? Is it not written of him, "In the beginning was the Word, and the Word was with God, and the Word was God?" [Jn 1:1] Was he not then, as he is even now, the bread of angels? Did he not come into this world

---

[13]NPNF 1.7, 499-500; SC 75, 306-308.

without leaving heaven? Did he not ascend to heaven without leaving us alone on earth? Why then did he come in the flesh? Because we had to be shown the hope of the resurrection. He was God and he came in the flesh. God could not die but the flesh could die. He came in flesh so that he could die for us. How, then, did he die for us? "No one has greater love than this, that he lay down his life for his friends." [Jn 15:13] It was charity that brought him into the flesh. Anyone, therefore, who does not have charity denies that Christ came in the flesh.

Now put the question to the heretics: Did Christ come in the flesh? "He did come; I believe and confess it." No, you deny it. "How do I deny it? You heard what I said." No, I convict you of denying it. You say it with your mouth but deny it with your heart; you say it in word but deny it in deed. "How do I deny it in deed?" Because Christ came in the flesh in order to die for us and he died for us because in this he taught the depth of charity, "No one has greater love than this, that he lay down his life for his friends." You do not have charity because you destroy unity to honor yourself. This is the way to recognize the Spirit who comes from God. Tap the earthen vessels, check and see whether they are cracked and give off a dull sound. See whether they ring clear and true, whether charity is there. You separate yourself from the whole world's unity; you divide the church by schisms; you tear the Body of Christ. He came in the flesh to gather people together; you raise a shout to scatter them apart. This, then, is the Spirit of God which confesses that Jesus came in the flesh, which maintains it not in words but in deeds, not by loud noises but by love. That spirit is not from God which denies that Jesus Christ came in the flesh, not in words but in deeds, not by talking but by living.

ii. Writings against the Pelagians

Just as the struggle with the Donatists was coming to a climax, a debate opened in which Augustine was primarily concerned with the role of the Holy Spirit in the salvation of the individual. In insisting that human beings require the transforming power of charity which is the gift of the Holy

Spirit in order to love God and to accomplish the good works which lead to eternal life, Augustine drew heavily on themes he had developed in his early writings on Paul and in the controversy with the Donatists. He argued that God demands not only just performance according to his commands but a right intention which the Spirit alone gives. This specified the thesis that no one can be saved outside the Spirit-inspired unity of the church. His reflection on the work of the Spirit within the community and its sacramental action also moved him to reflect upon the efficacy of the Spirit's operation within the individual. Thus during the Pelagian controversy he asserted that the interior action of the Holy Spirit makes the call to faith effective, actually moving a person to believe. Similarly, in his later works Augustine insisted that the Holy Spirit maintains the elect in good willing and performance so that they actually attain eternal life.

Letter 145, to Anastasius

> Commentary: Augustine amplified Paul's doctrine of the relation between the death-dealing law and the life-giving Spirit. The law convicts a person of sin, thereby preparing him for a response of faith to the preaching of the gospel and a prayer for the Spirit's gift of charity.

3.[14] Therefore, the law, by teaching and commanding what cannot be performed without grace, makes a person recognize his own weakness, so that this recognized weakness may seek its Savior, through whom the will made whole can do what in its weakness it cannot do. The law, therefore, leads to faith; faith obtains the outpouring of the Spirit; the Spirit spreads charity abroad; charity fulfills the law. For this reason, the law is called a "pedagogue," under whose severe threats "whoever shall call upon the name of the Lord shall be saved; how then shall they call upon him in whom they have not believed?"[Rom 10:13,14] Consequently, that

[14]FC 20,164-168; CSEL 44,268-272.

the letter without the spirit may not kill, [2 Cor 3:6] the life-giving Spirit is given to those who believe and who call upon him. The charity of God is poured forth in our hearts by the Holy Spirit who is given to us, [Rom 5:5] in order to accomplish what the same Apostle says, "Love is the fulfilment of the law." [Rom 13:10] Thus, "the law is good for him who uses it lawfully," [1 Tim 1:8] but it is used lawfully by the person who understands why it was given, and who takes refuge from its threats in the grace which sets him free. If anyone is ungrateful to this grace by which the wicked is justified, if he trusts in his own strength to fulfill the law, "who not knowing the justice of God and seeking to establish his own, has not submitted himself to the justice of God," [Rom 10:3] then for him the law becomes not an aid to forgiveness but a bond of sin. Not because the law is evil, but because sin, as it is written, brings death upon such persons through that which is good. [Rom 7:13] For, he sins more grievously under the commandment who knows the evil of what he does by the commandment.

> Commentary: Augustine next explained that charity is necessary for the love of justice, which the law requires. Performance inspired by fear does not fulfill the divine command. The love of sinful pleasure must be countered by a delight in good and just works.

4. But it is useless for anyone to think that he has triumphed over sin when he refrains from sin through fear of punishment. Even though the impulse of the evil passion has not been carried into action exteriorly, the evil passion is still the enemy within. Could a person be held innocent before God who would willingly do what is unlawful but does not do it because he cannot escape punishment. Insofar as lies in him, he would prefer that there were no justice to forbid and punish sin, and, therefore, he would abolish it if he could. How, then, can such an enemy of justice be just, who would abolish the obligations of justice, if the power were given him, so as not to have to endure the threats and penalties of justice? Therefore, he who refrains from sin

through fear of punishment is an enemy of justice. He will be its friend if he refrains from sin through love of justice. Then he will truly fear sin. For, a person who fears hell does not fear to sin, he fears to burn; but the one who hates sin itself as he hates hell, he is the one who fears to sin. This same "fear of the Lord is holy, enduring forever and ever," [Ps 19:9] for that other fear is of the torment of punishment, and "is not in charity, but perfect charity casts it out."[1 Jn 4:18]

5. Thus, anyone's hatred of sin is in proportion to his love of justice, and this is not the result of the law causing fear by its letter, but of the Spirit healing through grace. Then, what the Apostle urges is accomplished, "I speak a human thing because of the infirmity of your flesh; for as you have yielded your members to serve uncleanness and iniquity for iniquity, so now yield your members to serve justice for sanctification." [Rom 6:19] What is the meaning of "as that, so also this," except that as you were not forced to sin by any fear, but by the desire and pleasure of sin itself, so you should not be driven to live a good life by the fear of punishment, but you should be persuaded to it by the attraction and love of justice? And this is not yet perfect justice —so it seems to me — but it is, so to speak, a full-grown justice. The Apostle made this preliminary statement, "I speak a human thing, because of the infirmity of your flesh," because he had something else to say, which they could not have stood at that time. For, although corporal punishment does not restrain us from the will to sin, it does restrain us from the act. No one would readily commit sin openly and so reveal its unlawful and impure pleasure, if he were sure that the torments of vengeance would follow at once. Justice, however, is to be so loved that not even bodily sufferings should keep us from performing her works, so loved that, even in the hands of cruel enemies, our works may shine before people to whom such works can be pleasing so as "to glorify our Father who is in heaven." [Mt 5:16]

6. Here is the reason why that strong lover of justice cries out, "Who shall separate us from the love of Christ? Shall tribulation, or distress, or persecution, or famine, or nakedness, or danger, or the sword? As it is written, 'For your sake

we are put to death all the day long; we are accounted as sheep for the slaughter.' But in all these things we overcome because of him that has loved us. For I am sure that neither death nor life, nor angels nor principalities, nor things present nor things to come, nor might nor height nor depth, nor any other creature, shall be able to separate us from the love of God which is in Christ Jesus our Lord." [Rom 8:35-39] Note how he does not say, "who shall separate us from Christ?" Instead, he shows the bond of our union to Christ by saying, "Who shall separate us from the love of Christ?" Therefore, our bond of union to Christ is love, not fear of punishment. Then, after enumerating the things which seem to do violence but have not the power of separation, he makes his conclusion so as to name the same love of God which he had declared of Christ. What is the meaning of "from the love of Christ," if not "from the love of justice?" Of him it is said, "Whom God has made for us wisdom and justice and sanctification and redemption, that as it is written, 'He who glories may glory in the Lord.'"[1 Cor 1:30,31] Therefore, as that person is most wicked whom corporal punishment does not hold back from the impure acts of degrading pleasure, so the person is most just whom the fear of corporal pains does not prevent from the deeds of shining charity.

> Commentary: The love by which a person delights in good and is joined to Christ is the charity which the Holy Spirit inspires in him.

7. That love of God, as we should always keep before our mind, is "poured forth in our hearts by the Holy Spirit who is given to us," [Rom 5:5] so that "he who glories may glory in the Lord." [1 Cor 1:31] When, then, we feel ourselves poor and lacking in this love, we are not, out of our lack, to demand his riches. Instead, in our prayer we should ask, seek, and knock, [Lk 11:9] so that he with whom is the fountain of life may grant us to be inebriated with the plenty of his house, and to drink of the torrent of his pleasure. [Ps 36:8,9] We are flooded and enlivened with this so that we

may not be overwhelmed with sadness, but may even "glory in tribulations, knowing that tribulation works patience, and patience trial, and trial hope; but hope does not confound." Not that we are able to do this of ourselves, "but because the charity of God is poured forth in our hearts by the Holy Spirit who is given to us." [Rom 5:3-5]

Letter 194, to Sixtus

> Commentary: In this letter to the Roman presbyter Sixtus, Augustine attacked the Pelagian assertion that human merits precede and earn divine assistance. He showed that the faith and prayer for help which precede charity, with its good willing and action, must also be attributed to the operation of the Holy Spirit.

Chapter 4.16.[15] May we say that prayer produces antecedent merit so that the gift of grace may follow? It is true that prayer, by asking and obtaining whatever it does obtain, shows clearly that it is God's gift when a person does not think that he has grace of himself, because if it were in his own power, he would certainly not ask for it. But should we think that even the merit of prayer is antecedent to grace? In that case the grace would not be a free gift, and then it would not be grace because it would be the reward which was due. Hence, our very prayer itself is counted among the gifts of grace. As the Doctor of the Gentiles says, "We know not what we should pray for as we ought, but the Spirit himself asks for us with unspeakable groanings." [Rom 8:26] And what does "asks for" mean except that he makes us ask? To ask with groaning is a very sure sign of being in need, but it would be monstrous for us to think that the Holy Spirit is in need of anything. So, then, the word "ask" is used because he makes us ask, and inspires us with the sentiment of asking and groaning, according to that passage in the Gospel, "For it is not you that speak, but the Spirit of your Father that speaks in you." [Mt 10:20] However, this is not accom-

[15]FC 30,310-313; CSEL 57, 189-190.

plished in us without any action on our part, and therefore the help of the Holy Spirit is described by saying that he does what he makes us do.

> Commentary: After demonstrating that faith and prayer are the effects of the Spirit's action in a person, Augustine generalized and affirmed that all good effects derive from the Holy Spirit. The only significant distinction is between the effects which prepare for the Spirit's indwelling in charity and those which follow from it.

18. Therefore, no one has true wisdom or true understanding, or is truly eminent in counsel and fortitude, or has either pious knowledge or knowledgeable piety, or fears God with a chaste fear, unless he has received "the Spirit of wisdom and understanding, of counsel and fortitude, of knowledge and piety and fear of God." [Is 11:2,3] No one has true power, sincere love, and religious sobriety, except through "the Spirit of power and love and sobriety." [2 Tim 1:7] In the same way, without the Spirit of faith no one will rightly believe and without the Spirit of prayer no one will profitably pray. There are not so many spirits, "but all these things one and the same Spirit works, dividing to every one according as he will," [1 Cor 12:11] because "the Spirit breathes where he will." [Jn 3:8] But it must be admitted that his help is given differently before and after his indwelling, for before his indwelling he helps people to believe, but after his indwelling he helps them as believers.

On Rebuke and Grace

> Commentary: Augustine argued for the efficacy of the help which the Holy Spirit gives to the elect to help them attain the good he has already moved them to desire and for which God has predestined them. He contrasted this effective assistance with the assistance Adam needed and received, by which he was made capable of willing and working good but had to persevere in performance by his own free choice. The elect are moved to will, to work, and to persevere in goodness.

Chapter 12.38.[16] And thus God willed that even concerning perseverance in goodness, his saints should glory not in their own strength, but in himself. He not only gives them the kind of aid he gave to the first human, without which they cannot persevere if they will, but in them he also causes the will. Since they will not persevere unless they both can and will, both the capability and the will to persevere should be bestowed on them by the liberality of divine grace. By the Holy Spirit their will is so enkindled that they can persevere because they will to do so; thus they so will because God works in them to will. Amidst the many weaknesses of this life (in which weakness, however, for the sake of checking pride, strength should be perfected) their own will might be left to themselves, so that they would, if they willed, continue in that help of God without which they could not persevere, and God would not work in them to will. In the midst of so many and so great weaknesses their will itself would give way in fact, and they would not be able to persevere. Failing because of infirmity they would not will, or in the weakness of will they would not so will that they would be able. Because of this, aid was brought to the infirmity of human will, so that it might be unchangeably and invincibly influenced by divine grace; and thus, although weak, it still would not fail nor be overcome by any adversity.

> Commentary: In asserting that divine grace is both necessary and effective in bringing a chosen person to salvation, Augustine believed that God could save anyone he chose. He did not, however, believe that God wills to save everyone; thus he had to find a different interpretation of the assertion of 1 Tim 2:4.

Chapter 15.47.[17] Since we are ignorant of who shall be saved God commands us to will that all to whom we preach this peace may be saved, and himself works this willing in us by diffusing that love in our hearts by the Holy Spirit who is

[16]NPNF 1.5, 487; PL 44, 939-940.
[17]NPNF 1.5, 491; PL 44, 945.

given to us. This may also be understood in this way: God wills all people to be saved, because he makes us to will this. In the same way, "he sent the Spirit of his Son (into our hearts), crying Abba, Father"; [Gal 4:6] that is, making us cry, Abba, Father. Because, concerning that same Spirit, he says in another place, "We have received the Spirit of adoption of sons, in whom we cry, Abba, Father!" [Rom 8:15] We therefore cry, but he is said to cry who makes us to cry. If, then, Scripture rightly said that the Spirit was crying when he makes us cry, it rightly also says that God wills when he makes us will.

On the Predestination of the Saints

> Commentary: Good effects in both the humanity of Christ and in the Christian are assigned to the work of the Holy Spirit.

Chapter 15.31.[18] In our Head, let us notice the very source of grace whence he flows out to each of his members according to the measure of each. From the beginning of his faith, this grace makes each one a Christian; the same grace made that person the Christ from his beginning. The one is reborn by the same Spirit from whom the other was born. The same Spirit forgives our sins and preserved him free of all sin. God certainly knew that he would do this. The predestination of the saints is most clearly manifest in this Saint of Saints. No one who properly understands the declaration of truth could deny this. We learn that the very Lord of Glory was predestined since as a human being he became Son of God. The Teacher of the Gentiles proclaims at the beginning of his Epistles, "Paul, the servant of Jesus Christ, called to be an apostle, set aside for the gospel of God, which he had earlier promised through his prophets in the holy scriptures concerning his Son, who was made from the seed of David according to the flesh, who was predestined to be Son of God in power, according to the Spirit of holiness from the resurrection of the dead." [Rom 1:1-4] Jesus was predes-

---

[18]Trans. J.P. Burns; PL 44, 982.

tined, then, so that the one who would be Son of David according to the flesh, would in power be Son of God according to the Spirit of holiness, since he was born of the Holy Spirit and the Virgin Mary.

iii. Writings on the Trinity

Grouped together here are selections from Augustine's treatise *On the Trinity*. This treatise presents both the fullest analysis of the scriptural references to the Trinity and Augustine's speculative synthesis of the doctrinal writers who preceded him. In addition, it is strongly influenced by his controversial writing. The treatise was composed gradually, beginning shortly after the *Confessions* and was perhaps finished only shortly before his death. Like most others, Augustine tended to find the Spirit operative in the church and the Christian rather than in the general creation and governance of the world. In his reflections on the inner structure of the Trinity, Augustine developed the Cappadocian understanding of the three Persons as defined by their mutual relations. To this he added the doctrine of the divine nature, its operations and properties which are common to Father, Son, and Holy Spirit. The development of the Augustinian psychological analogy of the Trinity as a single mind living as memory, understanding and will is omitted, but his explanation of the procession of the Spirit from the Father and the Son is the focus of more than one passage.

On the Trinity

> Commentary: Augustine distinguished the names which apply to the three persons equally as one God from those which are applied to each individually to indicate their relationships to the other persons. The eternal relation of the Holy Spirit to the Father and Son must be distinguished from his role in creation and redemption.

Book 5, Chapter 11.12.[19] The things in the same Trinity that are properly predicated of each person are by no means

[19]FC 45, 189-194; CCL 50, 218-223.

predicated of them as they are in themselves, but in their relations either to one another or to the creature; it is obvious that such things are predicated of them relatively, and not in regard to their substance. Therefore, the Trinity can be called the one God, great, good, eternal, omnipotent, and can even be called his own deity, his own greatness, his own goodness, his own eternity, his own omnipotence. But you are never allowed to say that the Trinity is the Father, except in a metaphorical sense, on account of his relationship to a creature whom he has adopted as his child. For the words that were written, "Hear, O Israel, the Lord your God is one Lord," [Dt 6:4] ought certainly not to be understood as though the Son and the Holy Spirit were excluded. We are also correct in giving the name father to this one Lord our God, since he has regenerated us through his grace.

The Trinity cannot be spoken of in any sense as the Son. But it can be called indeed the Holy Spirit in a universal sense, according to that text of Scripture, "For God is spirit," [Jn 4:24] because the Father is a spirit, and the Son is a spirit, and the Father is holy and the Son is holy. Therefore, the Father, the Son, and the Holy Spirit, since they are one God, and certainly since God is holy and God is a spirit, the Trinity can be called the Holy Spirit.

If by that Holy Spirit, however, not the Trinity but a person in the Trinity is understood, that is to say, if by the Holy Spirit is meant the person to whom this properly belongs, then it denotes a relation. For, he is related to both the Father and the Son because the Holy Spirit is the Spirit of the Father and the Son. The relationship is not apparent in this name, but is revealed when he is called the Gift of God. [Acts 8:20] For he is the Gift of the Father and the Son, since he "proceeds from the Father," [Jn 15:26] as the Lord says; and the saying of the Apostle, "He who does not have the Spirit of Christ, does not belong to him," [Rom 8:9] certainly refers to the Holy Spirit. When, therefore, we speak of the gift of a giver and the giver of a gift, we are clearly expressing their mutual relationship. Hence, the Holy Spirit is in a certain sense the ineffable communion of the Father and the Son. It is perhaps on this account that he has been so called, because the name is also appropriate to both the Father and the Son. For he is called properly what they are called in common, because the Father is a spirit and the Son is a spirit, and the Father is holy and the Son is holy. In order that the communion between them might be signified by a name which is appropriate to both, the Holy Spirit is called the Gift of both. And accordingly the Trinity is the one God, alone, good, great, eternal, and omnipotent. It is itself its unity, deity, greatness, goodness, eternity, and omnipotence.

> Commentary: Actually, however, the name of Gift better expresses the relational reality than the name Holy Spirit.

Chapter 12.13. Neither should anyone who hears us say that the Holy Spirit (not the Trinity itself but the person who is in the Trinity), is named relatively be disturbed because the names of the other persons to whom he is related do not seem to be correlative to this designation. We speak of the slave of the lord and the lord of the slave, of the father of the son and the son of the father, since these are correlative terms. This mode of expression cannot also be applied to the matter now under discussion. For we speak of the Holy Spirit of the Father, but on the other hand we do not speak of the Father of the Holy Spirit, lest the Holy Spirit be understood to be his son. We likewise speak of the Holy Spirit of the Son, but we do not speak of the Son of the Holy Spirit lest the Holy Spirit be understood to be his father. Yet this happens in many relationships, that no term can be found to express the mutual way things are related to each other.

Is there, for instance, a word that brings out more clearly the idea of a relationship than the word pledge? For it refers to that of which it is a pledge, and a pledge is always a pledge of something. As we say the Pledge of the Father and the Son, [2 Cor 5:5] can we also say, the Father of the Pledge or the Son of the Pledge? But while we speak of the Gift of the Father and the Son, we cannot, of course, speak of the Father of the Gift and the Son of the Gift. In order to make these terms mutually correspond to each other, we say the Gift of the Giver and the Giver of the Gift, because here we can use a word that indicates this correlation, while there we could not do so.

> Commentary: The name of Principle can be applied to the Father and the Son and the Holy Spirit in reference in creation. The Three are one Principle and Source of all else.

Chapter 13.14. He is, therefore, called Father relatively, and in this same relative sense he is also spoken of as the Principle, and by an other name that is similar to these. He is called the Father in reference to the Son, but the Principle in reference to everything that owes its being to him. Son is also a relative term, and he is called, again in a relative sense, the Word and the Image. All of these terms signify a relation to the Father, but none of them is applicable to the Father. And the Son is likewise called the Principle. When it was said, "Who are you?", he replied, "The beginning (*principium*) who also speaks to you." [Jn 8:25]

But is he perhaps the Principle of the Father? No! For when he called himself the Beginning or the Principle, he wanted to indicate that he was the Creator, just as the Father is also called the Principle of the creature, because all things receive their being from him. Creator, too, signifies a relation to the creature, as lord does to slave. And therefore, when we say that the Father is the Principle, and the Son the Principle, we do not mean that there are two Principles for the creature. For the Father and the Son are together the one Principle of the creature, as they are the one Creator and the one God.

But if whatever remains in itself and either begets something or works, is a principle to that thing which it begets or works, then we cannot deny that the Holy Spirit is rightly called the Principle, because we cannot separate him from the title of Creator. And it was written of him that he works, and remains in himself while he works, for he himself is not changed or converted into any of those things which he effects. Behold the kind of work that he does.

"Now the manifestation of the Spirit is given to everyone for profit. To one through the Spirit is given the utterance of wisdom; and to another the utterance of knowledge according to the same Spirit; to another faith in the same Spirit; to another the gift of healing in the same Spirit; to another the working of miracles; to another prophecy; to another the distinguishing of spirits; to another various kinds of tongues. But all these things are the work of one and the same Spirit, who allots to everyone according as he wills." [1 Cor 12:7-11] And certainly he does so as God. For who except God can work such great miracles? "But the same God, who works all in all." [1 Cor 12:6] For if we are asked point by point concerning the Holy Spirit, we answer most truly that he is God, and the one God together with the Father and the Son. Hence, with reference to the creature, God is spoken of as one Principle, not as two or three Principles.

> Commentary: The name Principle can also be applied relatively within the Trinity; the Father is Principle of both the Son and Spirit, though in different ways, because the Spirit has a relationship to Christians which the Son does not. He is the Gift given to sanctify. As Givers, the Father and Son are one Principle of the Holy Spirit.

Chapter 14.15. However, in their relations to each other in the Trinity, if the begetter is the Principle of the begotten, then the Father is the Principle of the Son since he begot him. But it is not an easy question whether the Father is also the Principle of the Holy Spirit of whom it was said, "He proceeds from him." For if it is so, then he is not only the Principle of the thing which he begets and makes, but also of that which he gives.

This passage also throws some light, as far as it can, upon the question which generally disturbs many people, why the Spirit is not the Son also, since he likewise proceeds from the Father, as we read in the Gospel. [Jn 15:26] For the Holy Spirit came forth, not as one born, but as one given. And for this reason he is not called the Son, because he was neither born as the Only-begotten Son, nor was he made, so that he might be born through the grace of God into the adoption, as we are.

For he who was born of the Father is related only to the Father when he is called the Son. Therefore, he is said to be the Son of the Father and not ours also. But he who was given bears a relation both to him who gave, as well as to those to whom he was given. Therefore, the Holy Spirit is called not only the Spirit of the Father and the Son who gave him, but ours as well, since we received him. He who gives salvation is called "the Salvation of the Lord," [Ps 3:8] and he is likewise our Salvation who received him.

* * *

Wherefore it was also written of John that he was to come in the spirit and power of Elias; [Lk 1:17] that is, the Holy Spirit which Elias had received is here called the spirit of Elias. The same meaning is to be understood in the case of Moses when the Lord said to him, "I will take of your spirit and give to them," [Num 11:17] that is, I will give to them of the Holy Spirit which I have already given to you. If, then, what is also given has the Giver for its Principle, because it did not receive from any other source that which proceeds from him, then we have to confess that the Father and the Son are the Principle of the Holy Spirit. Not two Principles: as the Father and the Son are one God, and in relation to the creature are one Creator and one Lord, so they are one Principle in relation to the Holy Spirit. But in relation to the creature, the Father, the Son, and the Holy Spirit are one Principle, as they are one Creator and one Lord.

> Commentary: Augustine treated systematically the relationship between the Holy Spirit and the gift of charity. First he showed why love, unlike other divine gifts, should be identified with God himself and the Holy Spirit.

Book 15, Chapter 17.27.[20] We have spoken sufficiently

[20]FC 45, 491-492; CCL 50A, 501-502.

about the Father and the Son, insofar as we have been able to see through this mirror and in this enigma. Now we are to speak about the Holy Spirit, insofar as God the Giver shall permit. According to the sacred scriptures, this Holy Spirit is neither the Spirit of the Father alone, nor of the Son alone, but the Spirit of both, and, therefore, he suggests to us the common love by which the Father and the Son mutually love each other. In order to exercise us, however, the divine word has caused us to inquire with greater zeal, not into those things that lie openly at hand, but into those that are to be searched out in the depths, and brought to light from the depths.

The scripture, therefore, has not said that the Holy Spirit is love: had it done so, it would have removed no small part of this problem. It said, "God is love," [Jn 4:16] so that its meaning is uncertain, and, hence, we must inquire whether God the Father is love, or God the Son, or God the Holy Spirit, or God the Trinity itself. For it is our contention that God is called love because love itself is a substance worthy of the name of God, and not merely because it is a gift of God.

> Commentary: After showing that love can be identified with the divine substance because it belongs to all three persons, he argued that one is justified in identifying the Spirit as love.

31.[21] As the only Word of God is specially called by the name of Wisdom, although in the universal sense both the Holy Spirit and the Father himself are wisdom, so the Holy Spirit is specially called by the name of Love, although in the universal sense both the Father and the Son are love. But the Word of God, that is, the only-begotten Son, has been plainly called the Wisdom of God by the mouth of the Apostle where he says, "Christ, the power of God and the wisdom of God." [1 Cor 1:24] But we find that the Holy Spirit has been called Love, if we carefully examine a statement of John the Apostle. For, when he had said, "Beloved,

let us love one another because love is of God," he immediately added, "And everyone who loves is born of God, and
knows God. He who does not love, does not know God, for
God is love." [1 Jn 4:7-8] He here revealed that God is called
that love which he says, "is of God." The God of God,
therefore, is Love.

But because the Son is born of God the Father, and the
Holy Spirit proceeds from God the Father, the question is
rightly asked, of which of them should we rather take it to be
said here, that God is love? For the Father alone is God in
such a way that he is not of God. Therefore, the Love which
is God in such a way that it is of God, is either the Son or the
Holy Spirit. But in the following verses after speaking of the
love of God (not that by which we love him, but that "by which
he first loved us, and sent his Son as a propitiation for our
sins"), [1 Jn 4:10] he exhorts us to love one another, so that
God might abide in us. Then, because he had said in unmis-
takable terms that God is love, he wanted to speak more
plainly on this subject at once. "In this," he said, "we know
that we abide in him and he in us, because he has given us of
his Spirit." [1 Jn 4:13] Therefore, the Holy Spirit, of whom
he has given us, causes us to remain in God, and God in us.
But love does this. He is, therefore, the God who is Love.

Finally, a little later, when he had repeated and used the
identical expression, "God is love," he immediately added,
"He who abides in love abides in God, and God in him." [1
Jn 4:16] From this, he had said above, "In this we know that
we abide in him and he in us, because he has given us of his
Spirit." [1 Jn 4:13] When God the Holy Spirit, therefore,
who proceeds from God, has been given to a person, he
inflames him with the love for God and his neighbor, and he
himself is Love. For a person does not have the power to
love God, except from God. Wherefore a little later he says,
"Let us love him, because he first loved us." [1 Jn 4:19] The
Apostle Paul also says, "The charity of God is poured in our
hearts by the Holy Spirit, who has been given to us." [Rom
5:5]

Commentary: He then showed that the love of God is the

primary gift which makes all others useful. The theories elaborated against the Donatists and Pelagians were here brought to fruition.

Chapter 18.32. Nothing is more excellent than this gift of God. It is this alone which divides the children of the eternal kingdom from the children of eternal perdition. Other gifts are also bestowed by the Holy Spirit, but without charity they profit nothing. Unless the Holy Spirit, therefore, imparts to everyone so much as to make him a lover of God and of his neighbor, then he is not transferred from the left to the right side. The Spirit is specially called the Gift for no other reason except love; and he who does not have it, even if he should speak with the tongues of men and angels, is as sounding brass and a tinkling cymbal. If he should have prophecy and know all mysteries and all knowledge, and if he should have all faith so as to remove mountains, it is nothing. If he should distribute all his goods, and if he should deliver his body to be burned, it profits him nothing. [1 Cor 13:1-3] How great, then, is that good without which such great goods lead no one to eternal life.

On the contrary, if one does not speak with tongues, does not have prophecy, does not know all the mysteries and all knowledge, does not distribute all his goods to the poor, either because he has none to distribute or is prevented by some necessity, and does not deliver his body to be burned, if there is no occasion for such a suffering, and yet does have love or charity (for they are two names of one thing), then it alone leads to the kingdom. Thus nothing except love makes faith itself useful. For there can indeed be faith without love, but it likewise profits nothing. And, therefore, the Apostle Paul also says, "In Christ Jesus neither circumcision is of any avail, nor uncircumcision, but faith which works through charity," [Gal 5:6] thus distinguishing it from the faith by which the devils also believe and tremble. [Jas 2:19] Love, then, which is from God and is God, is properly the Holy Spirit, through whom the charity of God is poured forth in our hearts, through which the whole Trinity dwells in us. For this reason the Holy Spirit, since he is God, is also most rightly called the Gift of God. [Acts 8:20] What else is to be understood by the Gift in the strict sense except charity which leads to God, and without which no other gift, no matter which, leads to God?

> Commentary: Augustine moved through a long scriptural argument for referring to the Holy Spirit as Gift. After warning against making the Spirit less than God, he used his doctrine that all the external operations of God are common to the three persons.

Chapter 19.36.[22] Since they already see that the Holy Spirit has been called the gift of God, consequently, we must warn them that, when they hear, "the gift of the Holy Spirit," they should recognize that same manner of speech, according to which it was also said, "in the despoiling of the body of the flesh." [Col 2:11] For just as the body of the flesh is nothing else than the flesh, so the gift of the Holy Spirit is nothing else than the Holy Spirit. He is, therefore, the Gift of God, inasmuch as he is given to those to whom he is given. But in himself he is God, even though he is given to no one, because he was God, co-eternal with the Father and the Son even before he was given to anyone. Nor because they give and he is given is he, therefore, less than they, for he is so given as the Gift of God that he also gives himself as God. For it is impossible to say of him that he is not the master of his own power, of whom it was said, "The Spirit breathes where he will," [Jn 3:8] and in the writings of the Apostle which I have mentioned above, "And one and the same Spirit works, dividing what is proper to each one according as he will." [1 Cor 12:11] There is here no subordination of the Gift and no domination of the Givers, but concord between the Gift and the Givers.

> Commentary: The conclusion of this long analysis is reached in the twin assertions that the divine substance is love and that the Holy Spirit is identified as the Love of God.

[22]FC 45, 502-503; CCL 50A, 512-514.

37. Wherefore, if the sacred scripture proclaims, "God is love,"[1 Jn 4:16] and also that love is of God, and acts in us that we remain in God and he in us, and we know this because he has given us of his Spirit, then the Spirit himself is the God who is Love. Furthermore, if among the gifts of God none is greater than love, and there is no greater gift of God than the Holy Spirit, what more logical than that he himself should be Love, who is called both God and of God? And if the love whereby the Father loves the Son, and the Son the Father, reveals in an ineffable manner the union between both, what more fitting than that he, who is the Spirit, common to both, should be properly called Love?

For it is sounder to believe, or to understand, that the Holy Spirit alone is not love in that Trinity. Yet not without reason is he specially called Love, on account of those things which have been said. Just as in that Trinity he alone is not spirit, and he alone is not holy, because the Father is spirit and the Son is spirit, and the Father is holy and the Son is holy, which piety does not doubt, and yet not without reason is he specially called the Holy Spirit. For since he is common to both, he is properly called that which both are called in common.

> Commentary: Near the end of the treatise, Augustine returned to his analysis of the procession of the Holy Spirit and argued that he proceeds from the Son because Christ sent him upon the disciples. The temporal mission mirrors the eternal procession.

Chapter 26.45.[23] There are, furthermore, no intervals of time in that highest Trinity, which God is, that would enable us to show, or at least to inquire, whether the Son was first born of the Father, and the Holy Spirit afterwards proceeded from both, since the sacred scripture calls him the Spirit of both. For it is he of whom the Apostle says, "Because you are sons, God has sent the Spirit of his Son into your hearts." [Gal 4:6] And it is he of whom the same

[23]FC 45, 514-516; CCL 50A, 524-527.

Son says, "For it is not you who are speaking, but the Spirit of your Father who speaks in you." [Mt 10:20] And it is proved by many other testimonies of the divine words that he is the Spirit of both the Father and the Son, who is specially called the Holy Spirit in the Trinity. The Son himself likewise says of him, "whom I will send you from the Father," [Jn 15:26] and in another place, "whom the Father will send in my name." [Jn 14:26] But it so taught that he proceeds from both, because the Son himself says, "He proceeds from the Father." [Jn 15:26] And when he had risen from the dead and appeared to his disciples, he breathed upon them and said, "Receive the Holy Spirit," [Jn 20:22] in order to show that he also proceeded from himself. And this is the power, "which went forth from him and healed all," [Lk 6:19] as we read in the Gospel.

> Commentary: He then explained the significance of the double gift of the Spirit and observed that no human being can give the divine Spirit.

46. But as to the reason why he first gave the Holy Spirit on earth after his resurrection, and later sent him from heaven, it is, I think, because charity is poured forth in our hearts through the Lord himself, by which we love both God and our neighbor, according to the two commandments upon which the whole Law and the Prophets depend. [Mt 22:40] To signify this the Lord Jesus twice gave the Holy Spirit, once on earth on account of the love of neighbor, and again from heaven on account of the love of God. And if perhaps another reason may be advanced why the Holy Spirit was given twice, yet we ought not to doubt that the same Holy Spirit was given when Jesus had breathed upon them of whom he later said, "Go, baptize all nations in the name of the Father, and of the Son, and of the Holy Spirit," [Mt 28:19] a passage in which the Trinity is especially commended. And, therefore, it is he who was also given from heaven at Pentecost, that is, ten days after the Lord ascended to heaven.

How, then, is he not God who gives the Holy Spirit? Nay

rather, how great a God is he who gives God? For none of his disciples gave the Holy Spirit. They indeed prayed that he might come into them upon whom they laid hands, but they themselves did not give him. And the church observes this custom even now in regard to its leaders. Finally, even when Simon the magician offered money to the apostles, he did not say, "Give me also this power so that I may give the Holy Spirit," but, "so that anyone," he said, "upon whom I shall lay my hands may receive the Holy Spirit." [Acts 8:19] For the scripture had not previously said that Simon saw the apostles giving the Holy Spirit, but, "Simon seeing that the Holy Spirit was given through the laying on of the apostles' hands." [Acts 8:18]

> Commentary: As human, Christ himself received the Holy Spirit — at the moment of his conception. Augustine offered a new interpretation of the role of the Holy Spirit in the birth of Christ, the sanctification of his humanity. This parallels the assertions in *On the Predestination of the Saints*.

Therefore, our Lord Jesus himself, too, has not only given the Holy Spirit as God, but has also received him as human, and for this reason he was said to be full of grace and the Holy Spirit. [Lk 4:1] As it was written more plainly of him in the Acts of the Apostles, "since God anointed him with the Holy Spirit." [Acts 10:38] Certainly this was not done with any visible oil, but with the gift of grace which is signified by the visible anointing whereby the church anoints the baptized. Nor indeed was Christ then anointed at his baptism, when the Holy Spirit descended upon him as a dove [Mt 3:16] for he then deigned to foreshadow his Body, namely, his church, in which those who are baptized receive the Holy Spirit in a special manner. We are to understand that he was then anointed by that mystical and invisible anointing when the Word of God was made flesh, that is, when the human nature, without any preceding merits of good works, was joined together to God the Word in the womb of the Virgin, so as to become one person with him. For this reason we confess that he was born of the Holy Spirit and of the Virgin Mary.

For it is very foolish of us to believe that he received the Holy Spirit when he was already thirty years old, the age at which he was baptized by John the Baptist. [Lk 3:23] We believe that as he came to the baptism without any sin at all, so he was not without the Holy Spirit. It was written of his relative and precursor, John himself, "He shall be filled with the Holy Spirit even from his mother's womb," [Lk 1:15] because he, although begotten through the semination of a father, yet received the Holy Spirit when he was formed in the womb. What then are we to understand or to believe of the man Christ, whose conception in the flesh itself was not carnal but spiritual? And in what was also written of him that he received the promise of the Holy Spirit from the Father and that he poured forth this Spirit, [Acts 2:33] his two-fold nature was revealed, that is, human and divine, for he received as human, but he pours forth as God. We, on the contrary, can indeed receive this gift in proportion to our own small measure, yet we are utterly unable to pour it forth upon others; but that this may take place, we call down God upon them, by whom alone this is brought about.

Leo the Great (c. 400-461)

Leo was born around 400, probably in Tuscany. From 427, he was archdeacon of Rome under Bishop Celestine and Bishop Sixtus. At the death of Sixtus in 440, Leo was elected bishop. He was a great administrator who did much to establish the ecclesiastical and political position of the Roman papacy. His famous *Tome to Flavian*, written to the Patriarch of Constantinople in 449, served as a basis for the dogmatic definition on the two natures of Christ at the Council of Chalcedon in 451. Leo was not an original thinker, even in his Christology, but he did give a clear presentation of Christian doctrine in his sermons and letters. A succinct presentation of the doctrine of the Spirit is found in one of his homilies on Pentecost.

Seventy-seventh Homily

1.[24] Today's festival, dearly-beloved, which is held in reverence by the whole world, has been made holy by that advent of the Holy Spirit, who on the fiftieth day after the Lord's Resurrection, descended on the apostles and the multitude of believers, as it had been hoped. There was this hope, because the Lord Jesus had promised that he should come, not then for the first time to dwell in the saints, but to kindle to a greater heat, and to fill with larger abundance the hearts that were dedicated to him. He increased, not began his gifts; he was not new in operation, just richer in bounty. For the majesty of the Holy Spirit is never separate from the omnipotence of the Father and the Son, and whatever the divine government accomplishes in the ordering of all things proceeds from the providence of the whole Trinity. Among them are unity of mercy and loving-kindness, unity of judgment and justice, nor is there any division in action where there is no divergence of will. What, therefore, the Father enlightens, the Son enlightens, and the Holy Spirit enlightens. While there is one person of the Sent, another of the Sender, and still another of the Promiser, both the Unity and the Trinity are at the same time revealed to us. The essence which possesses equality and does not allow aloneness is understood to belong to the same substance but not the same person.

2. The fact, therefore, that with the cooperation of the inseparable Godhead still intact, certain things are performed individually by the Father, certain by the Son, and certain by the Holy Spirit, in particular belongs to the ordering of our redemption and the plan of our salvation. For if humanity, made after the image and likeness of God, had retained the dignity of his own nature, and had not been deceived by the devil's tricks into transgressing through lust the law laid down for him, the Creator of the world would not have become a creature, the eternal would not have entered the sphere of time, nor would God the Son, who is

[24]NPNF 2.12, 191-192; SC 74, 157-158.

equal with God the Father, have assumed the form of a slave and the likeness of sinful flesh. But because "by the devil's malice death entered into the world," [Wis 3:24] and captive humanity could not be set free unless our cause was taken up by him, who without loss of his majesty could both become truly human and alone have no taint of sin, the mercy of the Trinity divided for itself the work of our restoration in such a way that the Father should be propitiated, the Son should propitiate, and the Holy Spirit enkindle. For it was necessary that those who are to be saved should also do something on their part, and by the turning of their hearts to the Redeemer should leave the dominion of the enemy. Thus the Apostle says, "God sent the Spirit of his Son into our hearts, crying Abba, Father;" [Gal 4:6] "And where the Spirit of the Lord is, there is liberty;" [2 Cor 3:17] and, "No one can call Jesus Lord except in the Holy Spirit." [1 Cor 12:3]

3. If, therefore, under the guidance of grace, dearly-beloved, we faithfully and wisely understand what is particular to the Father, to the Son, and to the Holy Spirit, and what is common to the three in our restoration, we shall without doubt so accept what has been wrought for us in humility and in the body as to think nothing unworthy of the one and selfsame glory of the Trinity. For although no mind is competent to think, no tongue to speak, about God, yet whatever the human intellect apprehends about the essence of the Father's Godhead, this selfsame truth must be held concerning his Only-begotten or the Holy Spirit. Otherwise our meditations are impious and beclouded by the intrusions of the flesh. Even what seemed a right conclusion concerning the Father will be lost, because the whole Trinity is forsaken, if its unity is not maintained. What is different by any inequality can in no true sense be one.

The Athanasian Creed

The Athanasian Creed, also called the *Quicunque* from its opening word, probably originated in Southern Gaul sometime between 430 and 500. It was written as a summary of orthodox teaching for the purposes of instruction.

From the seventh to the seventeenth century, the creed was attributed to Athanasius, but since the seventeenth century it has been recognized that the creed was written after the time of Athanasius and originally in Latin. The author, date, and origin of the creed remain a matter of debate.

The creed is stongly Augustinian. The first half of the creed, which is quoted here, offers a precise summary statement of the doctrine of the Trinity in the Western Church in the fifth century. It clearly affirms three distinct persons in one divine substance. It warns against either dividing the substance or blurring the distinction between the persons. It declares the equality of the three persons and traces their distinction to their mode of origin. The Spirit is recognized as a distinct person equal to the Father and the Son and sharing their attributes. The Spirit is one with the Father and the Son, and proceeds from the Father and the Son. The Athanasian Creed, then, provides a fully articulated theology of the Spirit with reference to the Father and the Son. It is a culmination of five centuries of Christian reflection on the Spirit.

The Athanasian Creed[25]

Whoever wishes to be saved must, above all, keep the Catholic Faith; for unless a person keeps this faith whole and entire he will undoubtedly be lost forever.

This is what the Catholic faith teaches. We worship one God in the Trinity and the Trinity in unity; we distinguish among the persons, but we do not divide the substance. For the Father is a distinct person; the Son is a distinct person; and the Holy Spirit is a distinct person. Still, the Father and the Son and the Holy Spirit have one divinity, equal glory, and coeternal majesty. What the Father is, the Son is, and the Holy Spirit is. The Father is uncreated, the Son is uncreated, and the Holy Spirit is uncreated; the Father has immensity, the Son has immensity, and the Holy Spirit has immensity. The Father is eternal, the Son is eternal, and the Holy Spirit is eternal. Nevertheless, there are not three

[25]TCT 6; DS 75.

eternal beings, but one eternal being. Thus there are not three uncreated beings, nor three beings having immensity, but one uncreated being, and one being that has immensity.

Likewise, the Father is omnipotent, the Son is omnipotent and the Holy Spirit is omnipotent. Yet there are not three omnipotent beings, but one omnipotent being. Thus the Father is God, the Son is God, and the Holy Spirit is God. But there are not three gods, but one God. The Father is Lord, the Son is Lord, and the Holy Spirit is Lord. There are not three lords, but one Lord. For according to Christian truth, we must profess that each of the persons individually is God; and according to the Christian religion we are forbidden to say that there are three gods or three lords. The Father is not made by anyone, nor created by anyone, nor generated by anyone. The Son is not made nor created, but he is generated by the Father alone. The Holy Spirit is not made nor created nor generated, but proceeds from the Father and the Son.

There is, then, one Father, not three fathers; one Son, not three sons; one Holy Spirit, not three holy spirits. In this Trinity, there is nothing that precedes, nothing subsequent to anything else. There is nothing greater, nothing less than anything else. But the entire three persons are coeternal and coequal with one another, so that, as we have said, we worship complete unity in the Trinity and the Trinity in unity. This, then, is what he who wishes to be saved must believe about the Trinity.

Concluding Reflections

The role of the Spirit in the resurrection of the flesh was a significant element in the theologies of the fifth century. Perhaps the most significant development of the period, however, was the new emphasis on the operation of the Spirit in the humanity of Jesus. In the fourth century, the Spirit was credited with the formation of the body of Jesus in the womb of the Virgin as a means of demonstrating his creative power. In the fifth century, however, the abiding

presence of the Spirit in the soul of Christ became important. Cyril of Alexandria severely limited this function by
insisting that Christ has the Spirit by his divine nature and
receives him only for others, to serve as the New Adam in
restoring the indwelling of the Spirit to humanity. In the
thought of Theodore of Mopsuestia and Augustine, Christ
became the model of the operation of the Holy Spirit in the
salvation of Christians. Theodore described the Spirit as
transforming the human Christ in the resurrection, making
him a life-giving spirit. Augustine was freer and fuller in his
parallels between the sanctification of Jesus at his conception and his preservation from all sin by the presence of the
Spirit and the conversion, strengthening and preserving of
the Christian in good by the same Spirit.

Cyril and Augustine were closer to one another in other
ways. Cyril taught that the Spirit is the source of human
strength and stability in good, that he unites the Christian to
God in love so that he abides in God and God in him.
Augustine's identification of the Holy Spirit as divine Love,
which lifts a person out of his self-seeking desires for temporal goods, yielded a doctrine of deification or transformation of humanity by the presence of the Spirit. His theology
was rich because it was grounded in individual and especially ecclesial experience through the controversies with
the Donatists and Pelagians.

Augustine developed an understanding of the presence of
the Holy Spirit in the church as its principle of unity and
sanctity. This carried beyond the dilemmas of the third-
century conflict between Carthage and Rome on the efficacy
of the sacraments and the locus of the Spirit in the church.
This doctrine of the Spirit as divine Love established his
thesis of the necessity and gratuity of grace against the
Pelagians. It was, in turn, the ground of his subsequent
distinction between the gifts of nature and of grace.

Augustine's Trinitarian theology was also deeply affected
by his controversial work. He found the inner life of the
Trinity mirrored in the divine operation in the economy of
salvation. Although all external operations belong to all
three persons, certain operations must be attributed to indi-

vidual persons because they demonstrate that person's position or role within the unity. For both Augustine and Cyril of Alexandria, the sending of the Holy Spirit by the Father and the Son indicates his procession from both, but Augustine added the observation of the unifying function of the Spirit because of his work within the church. Thus Cyril followed the Eastern pattern of asserting that the Spirit proceeds from the Father through the Son while Augustine asserted that he proceeds from Father and Son as a single principle. This difference, arising from different ecclesiologies and different understandings of the individual's union to God and the church, affected subsequent Latin theology. It is evident in the work of Leo the Great and in the Athanasian Creed. It continued to be a source of tension between the Latin and Greek parts of the church.

Chapter Five

THE COURSE OF DEVELOPMENT

Introduction

The selections in the preceding chapters have laid out the path of the church's gradual appropriation of the revelation of the Holy Spirit through his works in the economy of salvation. This concluding chapter attempts to sketch the course of this gradual learning process. The early church's reflections on the Spirit are here divided thematically into ten sections which generally follow the sequence of the emergence of the various roles of the Spirit.

Reference is made by page number to the passages which appear in this volume. The themes discussed here often appeared in other passages of the same writer and in the works of other Fathers of the Church. This chapter presents not a comprehensive treatment of the patristic theology of the Holy Spirit but a tracing of its development through this particular set of readings.

1. The Inspiration and Interpretation of Scripture

Christian writers consistently associated the Holy Spirit with witness to Christ and his mission. Attention focused first on the inspiration of Old Testament prophecy which foretold both the coming of Christ and many details of his work.[1] Next it moved to the descent of this same Spirit upon the disciples to endow them with understanding of the life and teaching of Christ. The Spirit bestowed courage to proclaim the gospel and guided the preaching itself; he preserved the apostles in truth.[2] The task of inspiring was extended from prophecy and proclamation to its written record as the New Testament was gradually formed and joined to the Jewish scripture.[3]

Disputes arose over the meaning of Christ and church-men turned to scripture to solve them. The function of the Holy Spirit then expanded from the inspiration to the inter-pretation of the written record. Irenaeus and Tertullian argued for the truth of their explanation of scripture by citing the succession of bishops and communities which linked their own to the apostolic age.[4] More importantly, however, Irenaeus pointed to the Spirit's role in the continu-ing success of the proclamation of the gospel which, he claimed, was actually independent of the written text.[5] Hip-polytus asserted that the apostles received and transmitted the Holy Spirit to the church to maintain it in true teaching.[6] Tertullian proclaimed the Holy Spirit Vicar of Christ, sent to preserve the church in truth, and insisted that he had neither failed nor abandoned his mission.[7] The role of guar-antor of Christian truth tended to settle on officials and approved teachers, but the working of the Spirit extended to the hearer and reader as well. Irenaeus claimed that the barbarians could quickly distinguish true from false doc-trine.[8] Hippolytus implied that the Spirit enables the true

[1] 21, 29, 39-40, 42, 76.
[2] 32, 49-51, 77.
[3] 21-22, 32.
[4] 32-33, 50-51.
[5] 33.
[6] 61.
[7] 50-51, 53.
[8] 33.

Christian to judge the orthodoxy of church officers.[9] Origen rejoiced that the Spirit had bestowed the gift of discerning the figurative or spiritual meaning of the scripture on simple, unlettered Christians.[10]

The prophetic gift of the Holy Spirit, first manifest in Israel, continued to be cultivated by Christians well into the third century. Hermas provided rules for discerning true prophets.[11] Tales were told of martyrs who were suddenly inspired to predict their victories.[12] Tertullian claimed that the Spirit had revealed a new, more rigorous order of discipline through the ecstatic prophecy of the Montanists.[13] Some bishops, such as Ignatius of Antioch and Cyprian, claimed that the Spirit had inspired certain of their admonitions or guided particular decisions through dream revelations.[14] Finally, Origen observed that the Spirit comforts and strengthens the suffering Christian by bringing him to understand the secret reasons for his trials and tribulations.[15]

Revelation and inspiration were perhaps the most significant functions attributed to the Holy Spirit in the second century. Although they continued to be developed, by the fourth century these roles were taken for granted, repeated without elaboration or new application.[16] In the fifth century, in Augustine's dispute with Pelagius, the issue became relevant again. To counter the Pelagian emphasis on the freedom of a person's response to the teaching and example of Christ, Augustine insisted on the primacy of the Spirit's gift of love which makes preaching issue in faith and the teaching of Christ in good willing and working.[17]

[9]62.
[10]71-72.
[11]24-25.
[12]48-49, 79, 80-81.
[13]53-55.
[14]22-23, 82.
[15]72.
[16]48-51, 94.
[17]217.

2. The Unity of the Church.

The Holy Spirit, both as guardian of truth and as sanctifier, was considered the exclusive possession of the Catholic Church and denied to communities which separated themselves in doctrine or discipline.[18] More positively, the Spirit was recognized as the source of the church's unity. Early in the second century, Clement of Rome cited the one Spirit as an opponent of the division within the community at Corinth.[19] Ignatius of Antioch boldly insisted that the Spirit had spoken through him in calling schismatics back to the communion of the church.[20] At the end of the century, Irenaeus spoke of the Holy Spirit as the moisture which softens and unites souls in Christ; heretics and schismatics are deprived of this Spirit.[21] Tertullian boldly asserted that the Spirit gathers Christians into the unity of the one church.[22] Similarly, the eucharistic canon transmitted by Hippolytus contains a prayer that the Spirit be sent upon the offerings and through them transmitted to the saints to join them into one.[23]

At the middle of the third century, the Western Church was convulsed by a schism which pitted the twin roles of the Spirit as sanctifier and unifier against one another. Novatian had repeated the assertion that the Spirit drives away schism.[24] Yet he broke away when his bishop allowed those Roman Christians who had failed to confess the faith during the Decian persecution to return and share the Eucharist. He claimed that the Holy Spirit had forsaken that communion polluted by idolatry. He established a separate church which preserved itself pure of apostasy and thereby retained the sanctifying offices of the Holy Spirit. Cyprian counter-

[18]36-37.
[19]22.
[20]22-23.
[21]34-36.
[22]58.
[23]64.
[24]78-79.

attacked with an argument based on the unifying role of the same Spirit: Novatian's communion had itself lost the Spirit and his sanctifying power through the schism, a sin against the Spirit. He explained that the Holy Spirit was conferred upon the apostles and transmitted to their successors as a group.[25] The universal unity of the church was established by the Spirit in the communion of bishops. Individual bishops could withdraw from this body by schism or apostasy, but no one could destroy its unity, which derives from God. Each bishop's membership in the episcopal college makes the power of the Spirit present and operative in his community. Outside the unity established around the local bishop, then, no one could find salvation.[26] Cyprian conceded, however, that the bishop himself must remain free of apostasy and other sins against the Spirit which would make him an unfit vessel. If the bishop deprived himself of the Holy Spirit communicated to him by his fellow bishops in his consecration, then the sacramental ministry within his local communion lost its efficacy. He must be deposed and a worthy bishop must be consecrated in his place.

The tension between unity and purity as conditions and effects of the presence of the Spirit in the church broke out again in the Donatist controversy early in the fourth century. The schismatics asserted that some bishops had apostatized during the Diocletian persecution and had thereby lost the sanctifying power of the Spirit. Thus, according to Cyprian's ecclesiology they concluded that they could no longer function as bishops. These supposed apostates had, however, been accepted in the universal communion of bishops which had thereby collaborated in their sin against the Spirit and had as a whole itself lost the presence of the Holy Spirit. The separate Donatist communion alone preserved the necessary purity, maintained the true spiritual unity in succession from the apostles, and thereby retained the power to sanctify.

[25] 82-83.
[26] 82-84.

Against Novatian's claim that the participation of anyone who had sinned against the Spirit could deprive a communion of his sanctifying power, Cyprian had restricted the necessary purity to the episcopal college which preserved the Spirit transmitted from the apostles. The Donatists then argued from the toleration of unworthy bishops within this college to the corruption of the Catholic episcopal communion as a group. They replaced it with a college of bishops which was free of all sin against the Spirit and thereby the true heir to the power passed from the apostles. Since all parties to the dispute agreed that the power to forgive sins derived from a possession of the Holy Spirit, the problem was to specify the appropriate conditions for receiving and retaining his presence and to identify a group within the church which met these standards.

Augustine found a theological solution by identifying the Holy Spirit's gift of charity as the source of both unity and sanctity within the church. The unity of the church, he argued, rests not upon a spiritual power received and passed down in a college of bishops but upon the gift of charity inspired by the Spirit which binds Christians together in mutual love. In place of Cyprian's college of bishops, he recognized an invisible society of saints as the true and pure church within the visible communion. Though invisible, the good Catholics joined in mutual charity establish and maintain the unity of the visible communion which includes many unconverted members. In their fidelity to the Spirit's gift and command of love for neighbor, they become the dwelling of the Spirit and enjoy his power to sanctify. Added to this society of saints are the sinners who are held passively within the visible communion by the active love of the saints. These are aided and sometimes converted by the prayers of the saints. Schismatics, who desert and actively oppose the visible unity established by the Holy Spirit through the love of the saints, are deprived of all the sanctifying effects of their prayers. The fullest unity established by the Holy Spirit is invisible in itself though it is located entirely within the visible communion of the universal church.[27] This society of saints is, however, visible in its two effects: the unity of the visible communion, and the church's efforts to convert and incorporate sinners and schismatics. For Augustine, union is both the cause and condition of the sanctifying power within the church.

3. The Spirit as Sanctifier: The Forgiveness of Sins.

The New Testament explicitly linked the forgiveness of sins to the gift of the Holy Spirit. As has been seen, the church assumed that only one endowed with the Spirit could exercise this ministry. Disputes over the church's authority to forgive sins committed after baptism eventually led to the controversy over the conditions under which the sacramental ministry of baptism itself was effective, as has been indicated in the previous section.

Although Tertullian specified that the washing of baptism forgives sins in preparation for the conferral of the Holy Spirit by the imposition of the bishop's hands, he also explained that the Spirit mingles with the water of the font and confers spiritual power on it.[28] Hippolytus' account of the ceremony of episcopal consecration includes a prayer for the sending of the Holy Spirit so that the bishop may forgive sins, may bind and loose. When the bishop imposes hands on the newly baptized, he thanks God for the forgiveness of their sins and prays for the gift of the Holy Spirit.[29] *The Teaching of the Apostles* explains that sins are forgiven through the conferral of the Holy Spirit either by baptizing a heathen convert or by imposing hands upon a repentant Christian.[30] The constant in these varying interpretations is the assumption that sins are forgiven by the Holy Spirit through the baptism of the church.

[27]167-170, 174-175.
[28]52.
[29]63, 67.
[30]68.

The church's power to forgive sins committed after baptism was not, however, universally accepted. The Epistle to the Hebrews [6:4-8] seems to reject it on the grounds that such persons cannot truly repent. In his *Shepherd*, Hermas argued for a second repentance which would permit the baptized sinner a single opportunity to rejoin the communion.[31] In his Montanist writings, Tertullian disputed the right of the bishop to readmit sinners. His episcopal opponent seems to have claimed for himself and the church the power of binding and loosing given to Peter. Tertullian responded that this authority belonged to Peter personally and, in fact, was not a power to forgive the sins of believers. Forgiveness, he argued, was a divine prerogative exercised not through bishops but through spiritual persons who obeyed the Paraclete's current injunction against exercising this ministry lest further sin be encouraged.[32]

The issue was later focused by the attempt of Christians who lapsed during the Decian persecution and then sought readmittance to communion. After consultation, the bishops decided to pursue a program of leniency. Perhaps mindful of Tertullian's earlier argument which separated spiritual persons from bishops, Cyprian claimed that a revelation of the Spirit directed him to adopt this policy.[33] Novatian asserted that, by admitting the lapsed, the bishops had polluted the communion with apostasy and had driven away the Holy Spirit. Thus their church had lost the power to forgive sins, even in baptism. Cyprian responded to Novatian's challenge by locating the Spirit's power in the bishop rather than the community as a whole. As long as its bishops remained faithful, the church's sanctifying power was secure. He, in turn, denied Novatian the Holy Spirit: as a schismatic he did not participate in the power held in the episcopal college and had lost all claim to the Spirit through his sin against the unity of the church. Cyprian accepted

[31] 23-24.
[32] 55-58.
[33] 81.

apostate bishops and presbyters back into communion only as lay persons whose sin could not harm the sanctifying power held by the bishops. Further, he refused to recognize the sacramental ministry they had exercised while outside the church; he insisted on baptizing anew all whom Novatian had originally baptized. Successive Roman bishops opposed this policy of rebaptism, being content to confer the Holy Spirit by imposing hands on the repentant schismatics.[34] The *Treatise on Rebaptism* defends this Roman position that baptism itself need not be repeated but it agrees with Cyprian in denying the saving power of the Holy Spirit to those outside the church.[35]

The church's sanctifying power was challenged again at the end of the Diocletian persecution when the Donatist schismatics in North Africa charged that the toleration of apostate bishops entailed the church's loss of the Holy Spirit. To be saved, they claimed, a person must join the Donatist communion, whose bishops were free of all contact with such sin, and be baptized again in their church, which retained the power to forgive sins. The question of the apostasy itself was disputed, but the theological question to which it gave rise proved to be the more difficult issue.

Almost a century later, Augustine proposed a new understanding of the location of sanctifying power in the church. The mission to baptize and the power to forgive sins, he explained, are given to those who have the Spirit's gift of charity. Charity covers the sins of the saints who receive and exercise it in love of God and neighbor; it then makes their prayer for the forgiveness of their repentant brethren effective before God. The Spirit dwells and works in the church by the love he inspires in the saints, rather than through the ordination of bishops into a college which succeeds to the apostles. In forgiving sins through baptism and the imposition of hands, the bishop serves as the agent of Christ and exercises the power held by the saints within the church. The

[34] 83-84.
[35] 84-85.

efficacy of his ministry does not depend upon his personal holiness.[36]

The same Spirit effects both the unity and the sanctity of the church. Thus a person who receives baptism in a schismatic community rejects the unifying charity of the saints and thereby deprives himself of its forgiving power. He is truly baptized but will be sanctified only by repenting of his sin of schism and being joined to the charity of the saints in the Catholic communion. The holiness of the church realized in the charity of its saints wins the forgiveness of sins in both baptism and post-baptismal repentance. Augustine had, in a sense, returned to Tertullian's insight that the spiritual person possesses the power of forgiveness and exercises it at the prompting of the Spirit. He identified the union of charity rather than the rigor of discipline as the sign of this holiness.

4. The Spirit and the Flesh.

The Holy Spirit works not only through the sacramental ministry of the church but directly in the individual Christian as well. His sanctifying operation affects both the spirit and the flesh, bringing each to eternal life. The salvation of the flesh is considered first. The gnostics asserted that the flesh is by nature corrupt, that its radical opposition to the finality and dynamism of the human spirit prevents its entering into the kingdom of God. Orthodox Christians insisted that even in its earthly condition, the flesh is purified and moved to good works through the actions of the Holy Spirit. He prepares the flesh for its salvation, and he will raise the body from death.

The most striking instance of the Spirit's opposition to the power of evil in the material world seems to have been his strengthening of the martyrs to confess the faith even in the face of bodily suffering and death.[37] The Spirit also works within the Christian to overcome the other desires of the

[36]167-173.
[37]41, 48-49, 79, 81.

flesh, to preserve consecrated virginity, to cleanse the body and prepare it to enter eternal life.[38] For the most part, second and third-century Fathers described these as the fruits of the Spirit's dwelling within the Christian. Only Tertullian, and that in his Montanist period, portrayed the Spirit as an external teacher imposing a new and rigorous discipline, a lord who refuses to tolerate weakness.[39]

The role of the Holy Spirit in purifying the flesh was developed in the fifth century. John Chrysostom and Theodore of Mopsuestia spoke of the Spirit as destroying the power of sin in the flesh, suppressing evil desires, and thus beginning the transformation into immortal life.[40] In his analysis of the contrary forces operating in the human will, Augustine characterized the charity which directs the person to good as the fruit of the Spirit's presence. This gift moves a person to so love the good God commands that he chooses and accomplishes it, overpowering the contrary attraction of fleshly concupiscence.[41]

The Spirit completes the salvation of the flesh by raising the body from the dead and directing its appetites to spiritual satisfactions. Novatian affirmed that the Spirit shares his own eternity with the flesh and thereby brings the body into eternal life.[42] In the fourth century, Basil interpreted the resurrection as a creative operation of the Spirit, a continuation of the original creation in which he participates with the Father and the Son.[43] Finally, in commenting on St. Paul, John Chrysostom explained the parallel between the Holy Spirit's raising Christ from the dead and his communicating the same immortal life to the Christian.[44]

These Christian authors perceived that in opposing the

---

[38] 40-41, 79, 126.
[39] 53-55.
[40] 158-160.
[41] 177-181.
[42] 78.
[43] 126.
[44] 158-159.

works of the flesh which lead to death, the Spirit of Christ was actually purifying the flesh and making a pledge of eternal life to the body. They credited the same Spirit, therefore, with the final salvation of the flesh in the resurrection of the body to an immortal and spiritual life.

5. The Sanctification of the Spirit.

The Holy Spirit not only forgives sins and heals the sinful desires of the flesh; he stabilizes the human spirit in virtue and unites the creature to God. In the second century, Hermas seems not to have distinguished clearly between the Holy Spirit and the dispositions of the human spirit.[45] A century later, however, Novatian spoke of the Spirit dwelling in the Christian to sanctify and make him a temple of God.[46] At the same time, Origen opened a way for later development when he described the Spirit as communicating his essential holiness to beings who are not holy by their own natures.[47]

The fourth century brought significant advances in the understanding of the work of the Holy Spirit. The dogmatic controversies on the divine nature forced theologians to reflect on the essential difference between the Holy Spirit and the creatures as well as to prove that the operations attributed to him indicate his deity. Most followed Origen's lead, arguing that the Spirit who sanctifies must himself be substantially or essentially holy; creatures are made holy only by participating in the Spirit's holiness.[48] The natural light of the Holy Spirit was also credited with illuminating the soul, with activating its faculty for apprehending God.[49] To establish the Spirit's share in the divine operation of creating, these theologians extended his sanctifying role to

[45]23-24.
[46]78.
[47]70.
[48]102-104, 122.
[49]95, 112, 124-125.

the original stabilizing or establishing of the created order in goodness. Basil and Gregory of Nazianzus explained that the Holy Spirit confirmed the angels in their union with God, making them unable to fall from their goodness.[50] Similarly, Ambrose of Milan asserted that he perfects the creatures in goodness and restores those who fail.[51]

The stabilizing function of the Holy Spirit was developed in the fifth century by Cyril of Alexandria, and especially Augustine. Cyril observed that when humans were originally created, the Spirit was given to preserve them in virtue. After being lost, he is given again in Christ to confirm them in good. He indwells and shares his own divine nature, making the Christian a child of God. Thus the Spirit joins a person to God and maintains him in that union.[52] Augustine affirmed that the love which draws a person to God is the charity given by the Holy Spirit.[53] This love of God and of the good he commands enables a person to fulfill the law. The love of goodness and justice, he argued, is foundational to any truly good choice or action. Thus, without the Spirit's gift of charity, nothing a person does can advance his salvation. The gift of charity draws a person toward God and makes his willing and working truly good.[54] Moreover, the Spirit effectively moves a person to choose and remain good. Augustine attributed the convert's faith in the preaching of the gospel, his repentance, and his prayer for God's help to the interior operation of the Holy Spirit. Finally, those whom God has chosen for eternal life are preserved in good and brought to salvation by the working of the Spirit.[55] What the Cappadocians had assigned to the Spirit's operation in the angels was extended by Augustine and applied to the saints on earth.

[50] 125-126, 132-133.
[51] 143.
[52] 161-163.
[53] 191-192.
[54] 177-181, 193-194.
[55] 181-185.

In each of the Holy Spirit's three sanctifying operations, Christian theologians gradually came to recognize his sovereignty in assisting and even effecting the virtuous action of the creature. First they explained that the holiness of the Spirit comes to the saints who have prepared themselves for it; later that it stabilizes the angels in their natural goodness; finally, that it converts the sinner and maintains him in grace even in the midst of the trials of a sinful world. They discovered that the forgiveness of sins could not be dependent upon the purity or fidelity of the human minister. They realized that the Spirit not only strengthens the soul in opposition to fleshly appetites, but purifies the body and redirects it to spiritual satisfactions. Thus, by the middle of the fifth century, the church had come to recognize the sanctifying operations of the Spirit in establishing, restoring, and perfecting the creation.

6. The Spirit of Christ.

The gospel account of the descent of the Holy Spirit upon Christ and his own subsequent sending of the Spirit upon his disciples provided the foundation for a series of affirmations about the relation between Christ and the Holy Spirit. Justin Martyr claimed that with the coming of Christ, all the power of the Spirit passed from Israel and was concentrated upon him. The Spirit rested upon Christ and was then transmitted to those who believe in him.[56] Irenaeus added that in Christ the Spirit became accustomed to dwelling in humanity and then remained with his apostles.[57] Origen offered a more complex explanation of the relation between Christ and the Spirit. Because the Spirit had lesser power and worked only in the saints, he could not undertake an unassisted mission into the sinful world. He asked Christ to go ahead and subsequently descended on him as one capa-

[56]27-28.

[57]34-38; see also 76-78.

ble of bearing his glory. The Spirit remained in Christ and passed from him to others within the world.[58]

The fourth-century proponents of the divinity of the Holy Spirit argued from his participation in the works of Christ. Athanasius asserted that the Spirit is the anointing and seal with which the Word forms Christians.[59] Basil and Gregory of Nazianzus demonstrated that the Spirit is inseparable from the incarnate person of Christ, that he collaborates in all his operations.[60] In order to establish the creative power of the Holy Spirit, Ambrose modified the traditional assumption that the Word had formed his own humanity; he attributed the Virgin's conception to the Holy Spirit.[61] John Chrysostom also affirmed that the Spirit formed the temple in the womb of the Virgin.[62] Augustine, however, interpreted the operation of the Holy Spirit as the anointing which made him Christ from his conception.[63] Both Chrysostom and Theodore of Mopsuestia attributed the resurrection and transformation of Christ's body to the work of the Spirit.[64]

Because of his struggle with Nestorius, Cyril of Alexandria was sensitive to the implication that the Spirit might have descended upon a human Christ. He explained that Christ received the Holy Spirit not for himself, but in order to pass him to others. As the Second Adam he restored the Spirit lost by the First Adam. Thus, by giving the Spirit to his apostles, he shared his own priestly nature with them.[65] Augustine dealt with Cyril's concern in a different manner: he explained that as God, Christ gives the Spirit whom he himself receives as human; indeed, only a divine Christ

[58] 69-70, 74-75.
[59] 103.
[60] 126, 133-134.
[61] 145, 33, 63, 66.
[62] 157.
[63] 197-198.
[64] 158-160.
[65] 165.

could give the Spirit.[66] He then proceeded to describe the parallels between the Spirit's effects in the human Christ and his operations in the Christian. The Spirit who forgives sinners preserved Christ from all sins. The Spirit makes people Christian without prior merit; without any prior merits of the one whom God had predestined, the Spirit made him to be Son and Christ. The generation and consecration of Christ by the Holy Spirit set the pattern for the gratuitous and efficacious generation and sealing of Christians in baptism.[67]

Prior to the fourth-century doctrinal developments, Christian theologians assumed that the Word was subordinate to the Father and the Spirit to the Word. Consequently, they were ready to affirm that the Incarnate Word provided a means for the Holy Spirit to enter the world and undertake his sanctifying mission. During the fourth century, when an effort was made to establish the full deity of the Spirit and his equality with the Father and Son, such affirmations were avoided: the Spirit collaborates with the Incarnate Word in all his works. In the fifth century, different Christological positions determined the various descriptions of the Spirit's relation to Christ. The Alexandrian school feared a separation of Christ into distinct persons and preferred to identify the Spirit as naturally united to Christ, as the one who makes his disciples participate in the divine nature. The Antiochenes and Augustine clearly distinguished the human from the divine nature in Christ. They took great liberties, therefore, in drawing parallels between the Spirit's work in the human Christ and in his disciples.

7. The Divine Spirit

The divinity of the Holy Spirit, his belonging to the unchanging realm rather than to the created universe, was generally assumed in the second and third centuries. In

[66] 196-198.
[67] 184-185.

arguing against the Modalist position which described the three divine persons as manifestations of a single individual, Tertullian reasoned that the sending of the Spirit indicated his separate divine identity. Origen distinguished him through his more limited range of operation: the Spirit works not in the whole creation as the Father, nor in every rational creature as the Word, but only in the saints. These and other contemporary authors assumed inequality and subordination among the divine beings: only the Father is God in the full sense and the Spirit is subject to the Son.[68]

The outbreak of the Arian controversy at the beginning of the fourth century forced the development of a more elaborate demonstration of the divinity of the Holy Spirit. The Arians asserted that the Savior was a created being who had attained a position of pre-eminence in the universe, being designated the Father's agent in creation and governance. The Holy Spirit, they explained, was formed and sent by the Son to carry on his own work in the world. In response, the Nicene party argued that the operations attributed to the Holy Spirit required that he be a divine rather than a created being. Many of their proofs used the theory of participation: only a being who possesses a certain quality by his own nature or essence can make another share in it. The Holy Spirit could not himself depend on another for the qualities which the creatures possess by participation in him. This argument was then applied to a number of the Spirit's operations in the Christian. The one who sanctifies must himself be holy by essence and therefore divine.[69] The one who creates and renews the fallen world cannot himself be counted among the creatures.[70] The giver of life through baptism and the resurrection does not himself receive life from another.[71] Since the Spirit bestows immortal life and unchanging gifts, he must himself be eternal.[72] The one with

[68] 59, 69-70, 72-73.
[69] 102, 122.
[70] 104-105.
[71] 102-103, 122.
[72] 160.

whom the Word anoints and seals in baptism cannot himself be among the creatures who receive this effect.[73] The Spirit divinizes, makes the saints partake in God's own unchanging goodness, hence he must himself be divine.[74] Finally, the very notion of participation separates the divine from the created. Only a divine being can be poured out, can share himself; the creatures are receptive.[75]

Once the divinity of the Son was accepted, the scriptural descriptions of the Spirit's relation to him could be used as further indicators of his sharing in the divinity. Because his union with the Son parallels that of the Son with the Father, he must be the same kind of being as the Father and Son. In mission and operation, he is related to the Son in the same way that the Son is to the Father.[76] As the Son is called Wisdom, Truth, Power, and Glory, so is the Spirit named Spirit of Sonship, Wisdom and all the rest. He is the image of the Son.[77]

Finally, the stance of the Christian toward the Holy Spirit seemed to betray an assumption of divine status. He is glorified with the Father and his works are praised.[78] Christians believe in him, worship and serve him.[79]

Some of the descriptions earlier applied to the Holy Spirit and the limitations used to distinguish him from the Father and the Son had to be corrected or repudiated. His characterization as the Breath of God could not be allowed to imply that he is insubstantial or an occasional divine activity. The power of his action was used to indicate his substantiality and the divine unchangeability to preclude anything accidental or intermittent.[80] Nor is the activity of the Holy

[73] 103.
[74] 104, 163-164.
[75] 115-116.
[76] 101.
[77] 105-106.
[78] 122.
[79] 129, 145-146.
[80] 124, 128-129, 188, 194.

Spirit subject to the limits Origen had suggested: the Spirit fills the whole creation, not just the saints.[81] Finally, although the Spirit has many different operations and gifts, he is himself single and unique. His actions do not divide him; rather he adapts his operations to the stages in the economy of salvation and the needs of individuals.[82]

Most of these arguments were developed during the controversies of the second half of the fourth century. Some of them, of course, simply exploit concessions made in the doctrines presented by the opponents of the deity of the Spirit. Most, however, were built by combing through the scriptures and reflecting on the church's established practices to gather evidence and indications of the fundamental assumptions manifest in invoking the Holy Spirit along with the Father and Son in baptism and worship.

8. Consubstantial with the Father and the Son.

The proof of the divinity of the Holy Spirit actually involved two steps: that he was God and that he was the same God as the Father and the Son. The first was considered in the prior section; the second is discussed here. In the second and third centuries, Christian theologians explained that the Son and Spirit are divine beings distinct from the Father but derived from him, lesser than he, and subject to his will.[83] Thus they protected the *monarchia*, the religious perception of a single divine being who is the source and ruler of all reality. Even when the Council of Nicea affirmed that the Son is like the Father in being unchangeable and therefore divine, the bishops did not assert that they were equal or shared a single nature. Later in the fourth century, as the church approached the definition that the Spirit too was divine and unchangeable, the problem of the implication of equal and therefore independent

[81]70, 107-108, 113-114.
[82]94, 115.
[83]29, 37, 42, 72-73.

divine beings arose. As the argument for the divinity of the Spirit, so too the proof that the divine persons share a single nature rested on a general principle: the operations which flow from a nature manifest their source. If, therefore, the divine persons share a single operation rather than engaging individually in distinct activities, then they must also share a single divine nature. This principle was laid down as the foundation of the orthodox position.[84] Through a close reading of scripture, Christian theologians then proceeded to demonstrate a single divine operation. They proved that the Holy Spirit was active in the work common to the Father and Son, and that they in turn participate in operations traditionally assigned to the Spirit.

The involvement of the Son in the Father's activity of creating the universe and guiding the history of Israel had been generally accepted since the second century. It remained, then, to show the role of the Spirit in these operations. Basil argued that the resurrection of the dead which was attributed to the Spirit should be recognized as a creative act and thus as an indication of his involvement in the original creation from nothing. He assigned to the Spirit the specific role of establishing the creation in goodness.[85] Similarly, Ambrose reasoned that since the Spirit restored beings which had fallen, he must have been involved in their creation. Otherwise, the Spirit would actually demonstrate his superiority to the Creator whose work he completed and perfected. He also found a particular instance of the creative action of the Holy Spirit in the formation of the humanity of Christ in the Virgin's womb.[86] The Spirit who regenerates the Christian in baptism must have been no less involved, he inferred, in the type of this sacrament, the Exodus and crossing of the sea. Thus he concluded that the Spirit shares in these operations traditionally attributed to the Father.[87]

[84] 116, 137, 139.

[85] 125-126.

[86] 144.

[87] 147-148.

The Spirit's participation in the work of the Son was no less evident. He rested upon Christ and collaborated in all his actions: driving out demons, healing, teaching and ruling. The Spirit continues these same works in the church.[88]

Finally, the Spirit's own actions are shared with the Father and the Son. His indwelling makes all three persons present to the Christian.[89] Not he alone, but the three persons together govern the church.[90] Ambrose argued that his particular work of sanctification should be attributed not only to the Spirit but to the Father and Son as well.[91] Gregory of Nyssa extended this to liberation and the giving of life.[92] Ambrose returned to the traditional analogy of the Son and Spirit as the Father's hand and finger. He showed that the image expresses the unity of power among the three in all their actions.[93]

The Council of Constantinople in 381 professed that the Spirit "is adored and honored together with the Father and the Son."[94] Synods held in both Constantinople and Rome during the following year spelled out the meaning of this indirect assertion: the Father, Son and Holy Spirit share equally in a single common divinity, power and authority.[95]

Thus by the end of the fourth century, Christian theologians had established the full divinity of the Holy Spirit and the unity of nature of the three divine persons. In the process they repudiated a division of the economy of salvation into three epochs, each under the direction of one of the divine persons. All three persons are involved, they asserted, in each and every divine operation.

[88] 125-126, 133.
[89] 163.
[90] 116-117.
[91] 148.
[92] 137.
[93] 146-147.
[94] 150.
[95] 150-152.

9. The Procession of the Spirit.

In proving that the Holy Spirit is divine, Christian theologians had demonstrated that he shares fully in the one divine nature. Evidence was advanced to establish the participation of the Father, Son and Holy Spirit in each of the divine operations in the economy of creation and salvation. This implied that no one of the persons had any divine attribute or particular divine activity which was not fully participated in by the other two.[96] This, however, undercut the traditional method of distinguishing the persons.

Earlier theologians had dealt with the three divine persons as subordinate to one another, even assigning lesser power or particular, limited operations to the Son and Spirit. Indeed, they seemed to presume that only the Father is God in the full sense, the sole source and ruler of all reality.[97] After the dogmatic affirmation of their equality in a common divinity and sharing in common operations, new methods of distinguishing them and describing their personal identities had to be developed. This doctrinal or theological problem had two parts: to develop means of distinction within the one Godhead which respected the equality of the three persons, then to describe personal identities in terms of characteristics which could be perceived through divine operations in the economy of salvation.

The Cappadocian theologians developed means of distinguishing three persons who share a single nature. Basil first attempted a distinction between nature and an individual within that nature. The differences between individuals of the same species, he reasoned, do not affect their full possession of the common nature.[98] Gregory of Nazianzus modified this approach by insisting that the divine individuals could not be differentiated by each having or lacking some specific perfection. This would mean that one would be

[96] 136-137.
[97] 59, 69-70, 72-73.
[98] 123-124.

more perfect than another and destroy the equality of the three. Moreover, a composition of common nature and individual distinguishing qualities would violate the divine simplicity and present God as corruptible. He suggested that the persons be distinguished by their relations of origin.[99] Gregory of Nyssa agreed that the distinctions could not be within the common divine nature itself but only in the persons and in the order among them. He then demonstrated that the relationships of origin distinguish three modes of existence in the divine nature.[100] The Father is God without cause; the Son is God caused by the Father; the Spirit is God caused by the Father and the Son.[101] These modes of origin and existence within the divinity differentiate the persons by relationships to one another rather than by positive perfections possessed exclusively by each. Hence they distinguish and identify the three persons without affecting their full participation in the one nature.

The Cappadocians had argued from a single divine operation shared by all three persons to a single divine nature common to them. They then demonstrated that the three modes of origin and participation in the divine nature are paralleled by three modes of sharing in divine operation. As the divine operations in creation and salvation are from the Father, through the Son and in the Holy Spirit, so the divine nature is communicated from the Father to the Son and thence to the Holy Spirit.[102] While their causal schema retained some vestiges of the earlier subordination of one person to another, they argued that the distinct modes of existence and action did not establish degrees of sharing in the one nature which each possesses fully.

Confirmation of this method of distinguishing the divine persons was then found in the economy of salvation. Theologians reasoned that the scriptural language used to

[99] 130.
[100] 139-141.
[101] 141-142.
[102] 125.

describe the missions of the Son and Spirit in the economy
of salvation would reflect the relations of origin within the
Godhead. The Father's distinction from both the Son and
the Spirit by his deriving from neither and being source of
both is reflected in his sending both of them into the world
and his not being himself sent by them. The Son and Spirit
can be distinguished in similar ways. The Son is described as
having been sent from the Father without mention of the
Holy Spirit. The role of the Son, however, is clearly indicated in the mission of the Holy Spirit. Thus, the Son is
shown to be generated by the Father alone while the Spirit
proceeds from the Son as well as the Father.[103] Using the
missions in the economy of salvation, therefore, the Christian theologian could distinguish the three divine persons
through their modes of origin and existence in the divine
nature.

The Greeks generally preferred to retain the earlier
sequential or subordinationist language and spoke of the
Spirit as proceeding from the Father through the Son.[104]
Augustine and most Latins described the Spirit as proceeding from the Father and the Son together as a single principle. Still, Augustine insisted that the Son was not an
independent principle of the procession of the Spirit; he
receives this role from the Father.[105] The Creed of Constantinople had been silent on the role of the Son in the origin of
the Spirit. The Western insertion of its peculiar formulation
of this relationship into the creed in the late sixth century
provided a convenient focus for the tension between the
Greek and Latin Churches.

10. *Naming the Spirit*

Augustine's decision to speak of the Spirit as proceeding
from the Father and the Son rather than from the Father

[103] 165, 195-196.

[104] 113, 125, 140, 141-142, 162, 165.

[105] 189-190.

through the Son actually resulted from his attempt to solve a more complex problem. In defending the divinity and equality of the Holy Spirit, the Cappadocian theologians had demonstrated that a single divine operation is common to all three persons. They then differentiated three modes of causality to distinguish the personal agents: creation and salvation begin from the Father, are carried out through the Son and perfected in the Holy Spirit. In order to avoid the subordination implicit in this language, Augustine stressed the equality of the divine persons in his own construction of the argument. He insisted that the Trinity is a single principle of all divine operations regarding creatures. Not even the sending of one person into the world could be exempted from the general rule of common operation: as God, the Holy Spirit is actually sent by himself, not by an operation of the Father and Son in which he has no active share.[106] In a similar way, Augustine preferred to correct the implication that the Son is the Father's agent in the procession of the Spirit: he affirmed that the Spirit proceeds from the Father and the Son as a single principle.[107]

The rejection of any subordination among the divine persons led Augustine to require that the relations identifying the individual persons, though based upon the order of origin, be described by names which express their mutuality and thus imply their equality. He sought to correct the implication of priority and posteriority in the Cappadocian use of causal distinctions. The names Father and Son were found excellent since the genetic analogy identifies the two persons in relation to one another. The Father eternally exists and shares the divine nature only in his communicating it to his Son. Conversely, the Son is and eternally shares the divine nature in receiving it from the Father. These names describe the two persons in mutual relation and by their order. Thus they exclude an independence or superiority of the Father which would be incompatible with the dogma of the equality of the three persons. The name Holy

[106] 194.
[107] 189-190.

Spirit, however, neither indicates the particular relation of origin which distinguishes this person nor does it express the mutuality which would imply his equality. Augustine sought a more appropriate title for the third divine person.

Augustine's attempt to rename the Holy Spirit was complicated by another factor. Any name applied to a divine person must be based upon some aspect of the economy of creation and salvation which can be associated with that person in particular. The Cappadocians had argued, however, that all operations are common to the three persons. In each divine operation, they allowed only the distinction based on the mode of causality of the individual persons according to the prepositions, "from, through, and in." Augustine, however, had reconstructed this argument to eliminate the subordinationism latent in the Cappadocian formula. He insisted that the whole Trinity should be called Father in relation to creation. The Wisdom evident in the ordering of the universe is common to all three persons, not the peculiar property of the Son. Holiness, love and spirituality are all characteristic of the one divine nature, not properties of a particular person.[108] Thus he seemed to exclude any means of distinguishing and naming the Holy Spirit which could be derived from the economy of salvation.

The more fundamental problem was that the analysis used for the Son could not be extended to the Holy Spirit. As personally united to humanity in Jesus Christ, the Son was the particular subject of a whole set of operations which were not naturally shared with or common to the Father and Spirit. This doctrine had functioned from the second-century beginnings of Trinitarian theology, though it was formally defined only much later. Although the actual sending of the Son by his being joined to humanity to be a particular human agent was a divine operation shared by all three persons, the human action and statements of the Incarnate Son were peculiar to him. They not only manifested him as a distinct person within the deity but revealed

[108] 185-186, 191-192.

his unique personality as the Son and his identity within the Trinity. The genetic relationship used to characterize the Father and Son within the Trinity was therefore clearly revealed in the economy of salvation.

The human activity of the Incarnate Word also revealed the existence of a third divine person who was distinct, derived from, and joined to the Father and Son. The language attributed to Christ in the gospels named this person in a number of ways, particularly as Spirit. Because, however, this third person was not hypostatically united to a created nature, all of his operations were shared with the other divine persons. Unlike the Son, he could not be identified by theologians through actions and effects which were peculiarly his own. Instead, he had to be characterized through some aspect of the operations he shared with the Father and Son.

To solve this theological problem, Augustine needed a name which would characterize the Holy Spirit's relationship of origin to the Father and Son, which would indicate the mutuality of this relationship, and which could be recognized in some particular quality of the divine operations in the economy of salvation. First Augustine attempted to use the name Gift which had been applied by his Latin predecessor, Hilary of Poitiers.[109] This name brought out the relational reality of the person, since he is called the Gift of the Father and the Son. It did not, however, express the mutuality of his relation to the Father and Son: the Spirit is Gift of the Father and Son but neither of them is Father or Son of the Gift. Furthermore the name Gift involves a relation to the creatures, upon whom this person is to be bestowed, a notion which is not intrinsic to the reality of the Father or the Son.[110] Thus the term Gift did not adequately express the equality of the third person to the other two.

A second term, Love, proved much better adapted to the dogmatic and doctrinal specifications of Augustine's prob-

[109] 112.
[110] 186-190.

lem. The scriptural language used for divine love seemed to single out the third person as God from God in a particular way. According to John, Love is both God and from God; according to Paul, God's love to humans is communicated in the Spirit. The term Love does characterize the third divine person by a relationship of origin, as proceeding from the Father and the Son in their union. Although it does not adequately express the mutuality of his relation to the other persons, the term does name the third person by a bond of union which is common to and indeed joins the Father and Son in the one Godhead. He is the Love of the Father for the Son and of the Son for the Father, without which neither could be properly understood. This name also indicates his order, as the third in whom the other two are joined. Finally, as the Love shared by the Father and Son, the third divine person is named without necessary relation to the creatures. Thus the characterization of the divine persons as Father, Son and Love seemed particularly appropriate to Augustine.[111]

Augustine had no difficulty in finding a basis within the economy of salvation for the application of the name Love. Even though the operation of sanctification attributed to the Holy Spirit had to be recognized as common to the three divine persons, still it reveals the distinct personality of the Holy Spirit with an unusual clarity. As has already been noted, Augustine identified charity or divine love as the force which both unifies and sanctifies the church.[112] The divine gift of love which joins many hearts and souls to form the one Christian community reveals the Spirit as the bond of union between the Father and the Son. The power of this same love to join Christians to God by forgiving sins and inspiring good willing and working also manifests the personality of the Spirit within the Trinity.[113] Thus Augustine settled on the term Love as the name appropriate to charac-

[111] 190-195.
[112] 210.
[113] 210-211, 213-214, 217.

terize the divine person who, with the Father and the Son, is one God.

The success of Augustine's venture has been confirmed in Western Christianity. Still, the tension remained between the language of Christian worship, which addresses the divine persons individually, and the theological analysis, which asserts that they relate to the creation as one principle. The affirmation of equal participation by the three persons in all divine operation seems to contradict the practice of attributing particular aspects within a single divine operation to each. Moreover, it provides a tenuous base for identifying the three persons who share the single nature. Subsequent theologians often preferred, therefore, to compromise the theorem of equal participation in a single operation. Leo the Great, for example, distinguished between common operations which indicate the full equality of the three persons in one nature and the particular works which identify each of the three persons.[114] The Athanasian Creed, on the other hand, manifests the Augustinian concern for the full equality of the three persons who share the divine nature.[115] In this, as in most other significant issues, the human language of theology proved inadequate to express the reality grasped by living the mystery of God revealed in Christ.

Conclusion

The Christian community was slow to discern and define the mission and personality of the Holy Spirit. Yet the tradition constantly located his operation particularly in the sanctification and governance of the church. Indeed, controversies about the Spirit tended to take place indirectly, through questions of the accuracy of the church's teaching, the efficacy of its sacramental ministry, and the necessity of

[114]199-200.
[115]201-202.

the grace it supplies. A number of reasons for the late development of the theology of the Holy Spirit, particularly in the Eastern Church, might be advanced. Two from the fourth century seem particularly pertinent. Cyril of Jerusalem remarked that in inspiring the scriptures, the Spirit had revealed as much of himself as he intended.[116] Later, Gregory of Nazianzus explained that the divine persons had to be revealed sequentially lest humans confuse them with one another. Even when the Spirit was sent by Christ, he had to manifest himself gradually in the church, taking account of human weakness.[117]

Whatever the truth of these observations and the reality they were intended to explain, the Spirit never left the church without a sense of his presence. The doctrine of the Holy Spirit began in the New Testament itself and developed without interruption in the early church. The dogma of his full divinity emerged rapidly and fully as soon as it was challenged. The Spirit, at least in the patristic era, hardly deserves the title, "The Forgotten God."

[116]93.
[117]131-132.

TRANSLATIONS

Ambrose of Milan. *On the Holy Spirit.* Translated by H. De Romestin. In *Nicene and Post-Nicene Fathers*, ser. 2, vol. 10, pp. 91-158. Grand Rapids: Eerdmans, 1976.

Athanasian Creed. In *The Church Teaches.* Edited and translated by J. F. Clarkson et al. Reprint ed. Rockford, IL: TAN Books, 1973, pp. 4-6.

Athanasius. *Letters Concerning the Holy Spirit.* Translated by C. R. B. Shapland. London: Epworth Press, 1951.

Athenagoras. *Plea Regarding Christians.* Translated by C. Richardson. In *Library of Christian Classics*, vol. 1: *Early Christian Fathers*, pp. 290-342. New York: Macmillan, 1970.

Augustine. *On Baptism.* Translated by J. R. King. In *Nicene and Post-Nicene Fathers*, ser. 1, vol. 4, pp. 407-514. Grand Rapids: Eerdmans, 1976.

Homilies on the First Epistle of St. John. Translated by H. Browne. In *Nicene and Post-Nicene Fathers*, ser. 1, vol. 7, pp. 459-529. Grand Rapids: Eerdmans, 1976.

Letters. Translated by W. Parsons. In *Fathers of the Church*, vols. 12, 18, 29, 30, 32. Washington: Catholic University of America Press, 1951-1956.

On the Predestination of the Saints. Translated by P. Holmes and R. E. Wallis. In *Nicene and Post-Nicene Fathers*, ser. 1, vol. 5, pp. 493-519. Grand Rapids: Eerdmans, 1976.

On Rebuke and Grace. Translated by P. Holmes and R. E. Wallis. In *Nicene and Post-Nicene Fathers*, ser. 1, vol. 5, pp. 468-591. Grand Rapids: Eerdmans, 1976.

On the Trinity. Translated by S. McKenna. *Fathers of the Church*, vol. 45. Washington: Catholic University of America Press, 1963.

Basil of Caesarea. *On the Holy Spirit.* Translated by B. Jackson. In *Nicene and Post-Nicene Fathers*, ser. 2, vol. 8, pp. 1-50. Grand Rapids: Eerdmans, 1976.

Letters. Translated by B. Jackson. In *Nicene and Post-Nicene Fathers*, ser. 2, vol. 8, pp. 109-327. Grand Rapids: Eerdmans, 1976.

Clement of Rome. *First Clement.* Translated by C. Richardson. In *Library of Christian Classics*, vol. 1: *Early Christian Fathers*, pp. 33-73. New York: Macmillan, 1970.

Council of Constantinople, 381. *Niceno-Constantinopolitan Creed.* In *The Church Teaches.* Edited and translated by J. F. Clarkson et al. Reprinted. Rockford, IL: TAN Books, 1973, pp. 2-3.

Council of Constantinople, 382. *Synodical Letter.* Translated by E. R. Hardy. In *Library of Christian Classics*, vol. 3: *The Christology of the Later Fathers*, pp. 343-345. Philadelphia: Westminster, 1977.

Cyprian. *Letters.* Translated by R. B. Donna. *Fathers of the Church*, vol. 51. Washington: Catholic University of America Press, 1964.

Cyril of Alexandria. *Commentary on the Gospel according to St. John.* Translated by P. E. Pusey and T. Randall. 2 vols. Reprint edition. London: Rivingtons, 1969.

Cyril of Jerusalem. *Catechetical Lectures.* Translated by E. H. Gifford. In *Nicene and Post-Nicene Fathers*, ser. 2, vol. 7, pp. 1-157. Grand Rapids: Eerdmans, 1976.

Damasus. *Tome.* In *The Church Teaches.* Edited and Translated by J. F. Clarkson et al. Reprint ed. Rockford, IL: TAN Books, 1973, pp. 125-127.

Didascalia Apostolorum. [Teaching of the Apostles] Translated by R. H. Connolly. Reprint edition. Oxford: Clarendon Press, 1969.

Epiphanius of Salamis. *Creed.* In *The Church Teaches.* Edited and translated by J. F. Clarkson et al. Reprint ed. Rockford, IL: TAN Books, 1973, pp. 3-4.

Gregory of Nazianzus. *Sermons.* Translated by C. G. Browne and J. E. Swallow. In *Nicene and Post-Nicene Fathers*, ser. 2, vol. 7, pp. 203-445. Grand Rapids: Eerdmans, 1976.

Theological Orations. Translated by C. G. Browne and J. E. Swallow. In *Library of Christian Classics*, vol. 3: *Christology of the Later Fathers*, pp. 128-214. Philadelphia: Westminster, 1977.

Gregory of Nyssa. *On the Holy Spirit.* Translated by W. Moore and H. A. Wilson. In *Nicene and Post-Nicene Fathers*, ser. 2, vol. 5, pp. 315-325. Grand Rapids: Eerdmans, 1976.

On the Holy Trinity. Translated by W. Moore and H. A. Wilson. In *Nicene and Post-Nicene Fathers*, ser. 2, vol. 5, pp. 326-330. Grand Rapids: Eerdmans, 1976.

Sermons on the Lord's Prayer. Translated by H. C. Graef. In *Ancient Christian Writers*, vol. 1, pp. 21-84. Westminster: Newman, 1954.

That There are Not Three Gods. Translated by C. Richardson. In *Library of Christian Classics*, vol. 3, *Christology of the Later Fathers*, pp. 256-267. Philadelphia: Westminster, 1977.

Hermas. *The Shepherd.* Translated by G. F. Snyder. Vol. 6 of *The Apostolic Fathers.* Edited by R. M. Grant. Camden: Thomas Nelson, 1968.

Hilary of Poitiers. *On the Trinity.* Translated by E. W. Watson and L. Pullan. In *Nicene and Post-Nicene Fathers,* ser. 2, vol. 9, pp. 40-233. Grand Rapids: Eerdmans, 1976.

Hippolytus. *The Apostolic Tradition.* Translated by B. S. Easton. Ann Arbor: Archon Books, 1962.

Refutation of All Heresies. Translated by J. H. MacMahon. In *Ante-Nicene Fathers,* vol. 5, pp. 9-153. Grand Rapids: Eerdmans, 1978.

Ignatius of Antioch. *Letters.* Translated by C. Richardson. In *Library of Christian Classics,* vol. 1: *Early Christian Fathers,* pp. 74-120. New York: Macmillan, 1970.

Irenaeus of Lyons. *Demonstration of the Apostolic Preaching.* Translated by J. P. Smith. *Ancient Christian Writers,* vol. 16. Westminster: Newman Press, 1952.

Against the Heresies. Translated by A. Roberts and J. Donaldson. In *Ante Nicene Fathers,* vol. 1, pp. 309-567. Grand Rapids: Eerdmans, 1976.

John Chrysostom. *Homilies on the Acts of the Apostles.* Translated by J. Walker, J. Sheppard and H. Browne. In *Nicene and Post-Nicene Fathers,* ser. 1, vol. 11, pp. 1-328. Grand Rapids: Eerdmans, 1976.

Homilies on the Epistle to the Romans. Translated by J. B. Morris and W. H. Simcox. In *Nicene and Post-Nicene Fathers,* ser. 1, vol. 11, pp. 331-564. Grand Rapids: Eerdmans, 1976.

Justin Martyr. *Dialogue with Trypho.* Translated by T. B. Falls. In *Fathers of the Church,* vol. 6, pp. 139-366. Washington: Catholic University of America Press, 1965.

Leo the Great. *Homilies.* Translated by C. L. Feltoe. In *Nicene and Post-Nicene Fathers,* ser. 2, vol. 12, pp. 115-205. Grand Rapids: Eerdmans, 1976.

Novation. *Treatise on the Trinity*. Translated by R. J. De Simone. In *Fathers of the Church*, vol. 67, pp. 13-111. Washington: Catholic University of America Press, 1974.

Origen. *On First Principles*. Translated by G. W. Butterworth. Gloucester: Peter Smith, 1963.

Commentary on the Gospel according to John. Translated by A. Menzies. In *Ante-Nicene Fathers*, vol. 9, pp. 297-408. New York: Scribner, 1926. (This text was not reprinted in the Eerdmans edition.)

Synod of Alexandria, 362. *Tome to the People of Antioch*. Translated by J. H. Newman. In *Nicene and Post-Nicene Fathers*, ser. 2, vol. 4, pp. 482-486. Grand Rapids: Eerdmans, 1976.

Tertullian. *On Baptism*. Translated by Ernest Evans. London: SPCK, 1964.

To the Martyrs. Translated by R. Arbesmann. In *Fathers of the Church*, vol. 40, pp. 13-29. New York: Fathers of the Church, 1959.

On Modesty. Translated by S. Thelwall. In *Ante-Nicene Fathers*, vol. 4, pp. 74-101. Grand Rapids: Eerdmans, 1976.

On Monogamy. Translated by W. P. LeSaint. In *Ancient Christian Writers*, vol. 13, pp. 67-108. Westminster: Newman Press, 1951.

Against Praxeas. Translated by Ernest Evans. London: SPCK, 1948.

On Prescription against Heretics. Translated by P. Holmes. In *Ante-Nicene Fathers*, vol. 3, pp. 243-265. Grand Rapids: Eerdmans, 1968.

On the Veiling of Virgins. Translated by S. Thelwall. In *Ante-Nicene Fathers*, vol. 4, pp. 27-37. Grand Rapids: Eerdmans, 1979.

Theodore of Mopsuestia. *On the Nicene Creed.* Translated by A. Mingana. *Woodbrooke Studies,* vol. 5. Cambridge: The University Press, 1932.

Theophilus of Antioch. *To Autolycus.* Translated by R. M. Grant. Oxford: Clarendon Press, 1970.

Treatise on Rebaptism. Translated by A. Roberts and J. Donaldson. In *Ante-Nicene Fathers,* vol. 5, pp. 665-678. Grand Rapids: Eerdmans, 1976.

●

Acknowledgments

We wish to acknowledge and thank the following for limited use of quotations from copyrighted works: Wm. B. Eerdmans Publishing Co. for 31 quotations from *Nicene and Post-Nicene Fathers* and 6 quotations from *Ante-Nicene Fathers.* TAN Books for 3 quotations from *The Church Teaches,* edited and translated by J.F. Clarkson, et.al. Epworth Press for 2 quotations from *Letters Concerning the Holy Spirit,* translated and edited by C.R.B. Shapland. The Catholic University of America Press for 16 quotations from *Fathers of the Church,* translated by W. Parsons, S. McKenna, R.B. Donna, T.B. Falls and R.J. De Simone. Westminster Press for 11 quotations from *Library of Christian Classics,* translations by E.R. Hardy, C.G. Browne and J. E. Swallow, and C. Richardson. Clarendon Press for 1 quotation from *Didascalia Apostolorum,* translated by R.H. Connolly and for 1 quotation from *To Autolycus,* translated by R.M. Grant. S.P.C.K. for 1 quotation from *On Baptism,* and for 2 quotations from *Against Praxeas,* translated by Ernest Evans. Peter Smith for 3 quotations from *On First Principles,* translated by G.W. Butterworth. Archon Books for 2 quotations from *The Apostolic Tradition,* translated by B.S. Easton. Newman Press for 3 quotations from *Ancient Christian Writers.* And Fathers of the Church for 1 quotation from *Fathers of the Church,* translated by R. Arbesmann.